Reader Acclaim for I. M. Wright's "Hard Code" Column

Any large organization is prone to fall prey to its own self-made culture. Myths about how things should be or should be done turn into self-fulfilling prophecy. Any such trend is surely terminal for any organization, but it is a rapid killer in a technology company that thrives on perpetual innovation. Eric Brechner does an incredible job at pulling out the scalpel and cutting deep into such organizational fluff. He is also not shy at throwing a full punch—the occasional black eye being an intended outcome. While some of the lingo and examples are somewhat more appealing to the Microsoft insider, there is little in his wit and wisdom that shouldn't become lore across the software industry.
–Clemens Szyperski, *Principal Architect*

Great article on Dev schedules by "I. M. Wright." It applies equally well to infrastructure projects that my group is involved in.
–Ian Puttergill, *Group Manager*

You're not getting any death threats or anything, are you?
–Tracey Meltzer, *Senior Test Lead*

This has got to be a joke—quite frankly, this type of pure absurdity is dangerous.
–Chad Dellinger, *Enterprise Architect*

Eric is a personal hero of mine—largely because he's been the voice of reason in the Dev community for a very long time.
–Chad Dellinger, *Enterprise Architect*

Software engineers can easily get lost in their code, or even worse, in their processes. That's when Eric's practical advice in "Hard Code" is really needed!
–David Greenspoon, *General Manager*

I just read this month's column.... I have to say this is the first time I think you are pushing an idea that is completely wrong and disastrous for the company.
–David Greenspoon, *General Manager*

You kick ass Eric :) I was having just this conversation with my PUM and some dev leads a few months ago. Great thinking piece.
–Scott Cottrille, *Principal Development Manager*

We really like these columns. They are so practical a
refer back to them when I'm trying to help a junior
remember the column since they are usually so ente
–Malia Ansberry, *Senior Software Engineer*

Nice job, Eric. I think you really hit the nail on the head in this column. I think a good message to give to managers is, "Don't be afraid to experiment." How things really work is so different than idealized theories.
—**Bob Fries**, *Partner Development Manager*

I just wanted to let you know how much I love what you write—its intelligent, insightful, and you somehow manage to make serious matter funny (in the good way).
—**Niels Hilmar Madsen**, *Developer Evangelist*

We're going to be doing the feature cuts meetings over the next few weeks, and your death march column was just in time. It's a good reminder of lessons that were hard learned but somehow are still more easily forgotten than they should be.
—**Bruce Morgan**, *Principal Development Manager*

I wanted to let you know that I really appreciated and enjoyed all of your writings posted on the EE site. Until, today, I read ["Stop Writing Specs"]. I have to say that I strongly disagree with your opinion.
—**Cheng Wei**, *Program Manager*

Who are you and what have you done with Eric Brechner?
—**Olof Hellman**, *Software Engineer*

Eric, I just read the "Beyond Comparison" article you wrote and want you to know how much I appreciate that you actually communicated this to thousands of people at this company..... Thank you for your passion in managing and leading teams the right way and then sharing the HOW part of that!
—**Teresa Horgan**, *Business Program Manager*

I. M. Wright's "Hard Code"

Eric Brechner

PUBLISHED BY
Microsoft Press
A Division of Microsoft Corporation
One Microsoft Way
Redmond, Washington 98052-6399

Library of Congress Control Number: 2007931456

Printed and bound in the United States of America.

1 2 3 4 5 6 7 8 9   QWT   2 1 0 9 8 7

Distributed in Canada by H.B. Fenn and Company Ltd.

A CIP catalogue record for this book is available from the British Library.

Microsoft Press books are available through booksellers and distributors worldwide. For further information about international editions, contact your local Microsoft Corporation office or contact Microsoft Press International directly at fax (425) 936-7329. Visit our Web site at www.microsoft.com/mspress. Send comments to mspinput@microsoft.com.

Acquisitions Editor: Ben Ryan
Developmental Editor: Devon Musgrave
Project Editor: Valerie Woolley
Editorial and Production Services: ICC Macmillan Inc.
Cover Illustration: John Hersey

Body Part No. X13-92835

Table of Contents

Foreword. xv

Introduction xvii

1   Project Mismanagement. 1

June 1, 2001: "Dev schedules, flying pigs, and other fantasies" 2

Richter-scale estimating. 2

Risk management. 3

The customer wins 4

October 1, 2001: "Pushing the envelopes: Continued contention
over dev schedules" 4

Software engineering is clearly ambiguous 4

Believe half of what you see and none of what you hear 5

Motivation: It's not just pizza and beer. 6

Sinking on a date 7

May 1, 2002: "Are we having fun yet? The joy of triage." 8

War is hell. 8

It's nothing personal. 8

Five golden rules of triage. 9

The devil is in the details 10

It's hard to let go, isn't it?. 10

Take care of the little things 11

December 1, 2004: "Marching to death" 11

Stabs in the dark. 11

A litany of failure. 13

The turning point 14

The road less traveled 14

October 1, 2005: "To tell the truth" 15

Suffer from delusions. 15

Put a fork in me 16

What do you think of this book? We want to hear from you!

Microsoft is interested in hearing your feedback so we can continually improve our books and learning resources for you. To participate in a brief online survey, please visit:

www.microsoft.com/learning/booksurvey/

Give me a straight answer 17

Lipstick on a pig 17

Look at all these rumors 18

I want the truth 19

2   Process Improvement, Sans Magic **21**

September 2, 2002: "Six Sigma? Oh please!" 22

Egads! What sorcery is this?! 22

Calling in the cavalry 23

Creating order out of chaos 23

October 1, 2004: "Lean: More than good pastrami" 24

All things in moderation 24

Waste not, want not 24

Overproduction 25

Go deep 26

Transportation 27

Motion 27

Waiting 28

Overprocessing 28

Inventory 29

Defects 30

Symbiosis 30

April 1, 2005: "Customer dissatisfaction" 30

Ignorance is bliss 31

Too much, too late 31

Agile delusions 32

Retracing your steps 33

There's more where that came from 33

The right tool for the job 34

Duct tape and baling wire 34

Customer satisfaction 35

March 1, 2006: "The Agile bullet" 35

Enemy of the truth 36

Get the rules straightened out 37

Ready for something different? 38

Let the man speak 39

You complete me 39

A bit extreme 40

Are you ready for some rugby! 40

The more you know 42

3   Inefficiency Eradicated **43**

July 1, 2001: "Late specs: Fact of life or genetic defect?" 44

For every change, churn, churn, churn 44

Hallway meetings 45

Committee meetings 45

Spec change requests 45

Prevention is the best cure 46

June 1, 2002: "Idle hands" 46

Baby did a bad bad thing 47

Tell me what I must do 48

Waste not, want not 50

June 1, 2004: "The day we met" 50

Why are we here? 50

What are we trying to do? 51

Why are they here? 51

Why am I hearing this now? 52

What are the next steps? 52

July 1, 2006: "Stop writing specs, co-located feature crews" 53

Have you lost your mind? 53

Therein lies a dilemma 54

Special needs 54

I don't recall 55

Stick to one thing 55

You ready? 55

February 1, 2007: "Bad specs: Who is to blame?" 56

It's a setup 56

Communication breakdown 57

Keep it simple and easy 57

Make it robust 58

Get feedback 58

Check that quality is built in 59

What's the difference? 60

4   Cross Disciplines **61**

April 1, 2002: "The modern odd couple? Dev and Test" 62

How do I love thee? Let me count the ways 62

Necessary evil or priceless partner? 63

A man's got to know his limitations 64

You complete me 64

July 1, 2004: "Feeling testy—The role of testers" 65

    Advanced protection. 66

    A change will do you good 66

    The twilight zone 66

    Commander Data. 67

    It's quite cool—I assure you 68

May 1, 2005: "Fuzzy logic—The liberal arts" 68

    It takes all kinds 69

    They're not like us 69

    Getting past security 71

    Making things happen 71

    Better together. 72

November 1, 2005: "Undisciplined—What's so special about specialization?" 72

    Days of future past. 73

    Take it to the limit 73

    Football is a science. 74

    The space between 74

    Stuck in the middle with you 75

5   Software Quality—More Than a Dream 77

March 1, 2002: "Are you secure about your security?". 78

    Beware the swinging pendulum 78

    Do the right thing 79

    You're only as secure as your weakest link. 79

    Lead, follow, or get out of the way 80

November 1, 2002: "Where's the beef? Why we need quality" 81

    Things have changed. 81

    Good enough isn't 82

    Hard choices 83

    Time enough at last. 83

    Checking it twice 84

    Physician, heal thyself 85

    Step by step. 86

    Too much to ask? 86

April 1, 2004: "A software odyssey—From craft to engineering" 87

    Craft a desk, engineer a car 87

    It's what you know. 88

    To thine own self be true 88

    What's in a number 88

It's their habits that separate them 89
Think big to get small 90
Good to great 90
July 1, 2005: "Review this—Inspections" 91
A bad combination 91
The perfect storm 91
Who's in charge? 92
So, what do you think? 92
It's just a formality 93
Are you ready, kids? 94
Checking it twice 94
Magical merge meeting 95
Tricks of the trade 95
Getting it right 96
October 1, 2006: "Bold predictions of quality" 96
Enigma? I don't think so 97
Twins of evil 97
The usual suspects 97
You're gonna love it 98
Quit fooling around 98
Quality is no accident 99

6   Software Design If We Have Time 101
September 1, 2001: "A tragedy of error handling" 102
The horror, the horror 102
Taking exception 103
Don't lose it, use it! 103
February 1, 2002: "Too many cooks spoil the broth—Sole authority" 104
A picture is worth a thousand words 104
Does anyone really know what time it is? 104
There can be only one 105
Everything is connected to everything else 105
May 1, 2004: "Resolved by design" 106
What is good enough? 106
Design complete 107
Details, details 108
Show me what you're made of 109
Mind the gap 109
Your recipe for success 110

February 1, 2006: "The other side of quality—Designers and architects" 111

    You'll have to do better than that 111

    A change would do you good 111

    The man just got it wrong 112

    Doing it well 112

    Next time, try sculpturing 113

    Just the right tool 113

    Beyond these walls 114

August 1, 2006: "Blessed isolation—Better design" 114

    Breaking up is hard to do 115

    Doing it well 115

    There is no "I" in team 115

    Step by step 116

    Dogs and cats living together 117

7   **Adventures in Career Development** **119**

December 1, 2001: "When the journey is the destination" 120

    A man's got to know his limitations 120

    Vesting but not resting 120

    I wish they would only take me as I am 121

    We're in this together 121

October 1, 2002: "Life isn't fair—The review curve" 122

    I'm not going to take this anymore 123

    Knowledge is power 123

    Taking care of business 124

    Go ahead, make my day 124

    Reach out and touch someone 124

    Got lemons? Make lemonade 125

    Change your tune 125

    The one behind the wheel 126

November 1, 2006: "Roles on the career stage" 126

    One, in time, plays many parts 126

    Stage right 127

    I aspire, sir 127

    Overqualified 128

    I'm special 128

    There can be only one 128

    What do you want to be? 129

May 1, 2007: "Get yourself connected"...................................129
   It's who you know..130
   I use habit and routine..130
   Aren't you curious?..130
   You have our gratitude 131
   I'll get back to you 132
   Welcome to the world 132

8   **Personal Bug Fixing** **135**
December 1, 2002: "My way or the highway—Negotiation" 136
   An offer you can't refuse 136
   Grow up 137
   A shadow and a threat have been growing in my mind 137
   Don't shoot the messenger 137
   So happy together 138
February 1, 2005: "Better learn life balance" 139
   Balance is key 139
   Words without action..140
   I can't even balance my checkbook.................................140
   Balance good...everything good 142
June 1, 2005: "Time enough" 142
   Give it to me straight 142
   Pardon the interruption...143
   Find your happy place 143
   None of us is as dumb as all of us 144
   A burden we must share 144
   Tell me what I must do..145
   He's just a kid...146
   You deserve a break...146
   Everything's in order here 146
   Keeping it real...147
   Large and in charge 148
August 1, 2005: "Controlling your boss for fun and profit"............148
   I have no hand 148
   Know the enemy and know yourself..................................149
   They succeed in adapting themselves...............................149
   Selling water to fish 150
   Eyes on the prize...151

Engage. 152

Dare to dream. 152

April 1, 2006: "You talking to me? Basic communication" 152

Think about me 153

Tell me what you want 154

You want it when? 154

Got a short little span of attention 154

Are we done? 156

March 1, 2007: "More than open and honest" 156

That's no excuse 156

I'll be honest with you. 157

It's not easy 157

They seem to have an open door policy 158

No place to hide. 158

Not what I had in mind. 159

Getting it right 159

9   Being a Manager, and Yet Not Evil Incarnate 161

February 1, 2003: "More than a number—Productivity". 162

Careful what you wish for. 162

Playing a role 163

The makings of a great dev 163

You be the judge 164

September 1, 2004: "Out of the interview loop". 164

Blaming the help 165

Ninety percent preparation 165

That is the question. 166

The whiteboard compiler 166

Prepping the recruiter. 167

Prepping the interviewers (again). 168

A gentle reminder 168

The last puzzle piece 169

November 1, 2004: "The toughest job—Poor performers". 169

What did you expect? 170

Bite the bullet. 170

Seeking professional help. 171

Failure is not an option 171

The goal is success. 172

Ask and you shall receive. 172
You can't always get what you want 172
September 1, 2005: "Go with the flow—Retention and turnover". 173
I'll just walk the earth. 174
Nice dam, huh?. 174
Flowing like a river 174
Fresh meat 175
Sharing is caring 176
Room to grow 176
I must be traveling 177
Surrender to the flow. 177
December 1, 2005: "I can manage" 177
The gift that keeps on giving 178
Good enough for me. 178
Easy does it 178
I want to work 179
I'm not an object. 180
Good to great 180
I serve 181
May 1, 2006: "Beyond comparison—Dysfunctional teams". 181
Trying to pick a fight 182
This is not a competition. 182
I'll give you a hint 183
One for all 184

10   Microsoft, You Gotta Love It **185**
November 1, 2001: "How I learned to stop worrying and love reorgs". 186
Down the Tower of Babel it goes. 186
Life in hell. 187
The road less traveled 188
Part of the problem or part of the solution? 188
March 1, 2005: "Is your PUM a bum?" 189
The man with a plan. 189
I can't wait to operate 190
The devil is in the details. 190
The rules of the road 191
Back on course 191

September 1, 2006: "It's good to be the King of Windows" 192

    Have you any last request?. 192

    Prepare the ship. 193

    Set a course. 194

    Engage. 194

    Navigation. 195

    Accountability. 196

    Windows, the next generation. 196

December 1, 2006: "Google: Serious threat or poor spelling?" 197

    They falter, we flourish 197

    Failure by design 198

    Smart people, smart clients 198

    Staying vigilant. 199

    Staying out in front 200

April 1, 2007: "Mid-life crisis". 200

    You've changed 201

    Just another tricky day 201

    Leave little to chance. 202

    I don't think the boy can handle it 202

    Not getting any younger 203

    Don't panic 203

    Nobody's perfect 204

Glossary 205

Index. 209

What do you think of this book? We want to hear from you!

Foreword

I was a regular reader of Eric Brechner's columns, penned under the name I. M. Wright, when I met him for the first time. It took me a moment to be sure that I was talking to the same person, since Mr. Wright was notably opinionated, and the modest, polite, and friendly person I was talking to seemed more like Clark Kent.

My favorite columns focused on the relationship between the technical and interpersonal dynamics of people building software in teams at Microsoft. I'm often surprised, given the amount of material that has been written about the company, how much of the story remains untold.

Software engineering managers on large projects have three fundamental problems. First, program code is much too easy to change. Unlike mechanical or civil engineering, where the cost to make a change to an existing system involves actually wrecking something, software programs are changed by typing on a keyboard. The consequences of making an incorrect structural change to the piers of a bridge or the engines of an airplane are obvious even to non-experts. Yet experienced software developers argue at length about the risks of making changes to an existing program, and often get it wrong.

Construction metaphors actually work quite well for software. Lines of program code can be characterized along an axis of "foundation, framing, and trim," based on their layer in the system. Foundation code is highly leveraged but difficult to change without a ripple effect. Trim is easier to change and needs to be changed more often. The problem is that after a few years of changes, complex programs tend to resemble houses that have been through a few too many remodels, with outlets behind cabinets and bathroom fans that vent into the kitchen. It's hard to know the unintended side effect or the ultimate cost of any given change.

The second fundamental problem is that the industry is so young that the right standards for reusable software components really haven't been discovered or established. Not only have we not yet agreed that studs should be placed 16 inches apart to accommodate either a horizontal or vertical 4×8-feet sheet of drywall or plywood, we haven't really decided that studs, plywood, and drywall in combination are preferable to some yet to be invented combination of mud, straw, rocks, steel, and carbon fiber.

The final problem is really a variation of the second problem. The software components that must be reinvented on every project must also be named. It's customary in the software industry to invent new names for existing concepts and to reuse existing names in new ways. The unspoken secret in the industry is that a nontrivial number of discussions about the best way to build software actually consist of groups of people who use different names and haven't the foggiest idea what each other is saying.

On the surface, these are easy problems. Create some standards and enforce them. In the fast-paced world of high-volume, high-value, low-cost software, this is a great way to go out of business. The reality is that software's greatest engineering liability is also its greatest strength. Ubiquitous software, running on low-cost personal computers and the Internet, has enabled innovation at a breathtaking pace.

As Microsoft grew, the company didn't always have the luxury of researching the best engineering practices and thoughtfully selecting the best qualities of each. The success of the personal computer and Windows transformed the company from working on small projects in traditional ways to writing the book on the largest, most complex software ever developed.

Microsoft faces a continuous struggle to create the optimal system that balances risk against efficiency and creativity. Given the enormous complexity of some of our projects, these efforts can be amazingly heroic. Over time, we've created specialists and organizations of specialists, all devoted to the single hardest problem in the industry, "shipping." We have acquired folk-lore, customs, cultures, tools, processes, and rules of thumb that allow us to build and ship the most complex software in the world. Being in the middle of this on a day-to-day basis can be thrilling and frustrating at the same time. Eric's columns are a great way to share and learn with us.

Mike Zintel
Director of Development
Windows Live Core
Microsoft Corporation
August 2007

Introduction

For Bill Bowlus, who said, "Why don't you write it?"

You've picked up a best practices book. It's going to be dull. It might be interesting, informative, and perhaps even influential, but definitely dry and dull, right? Why?

Best practice books are dull because the "best" practice to use depends on the project, the people involved, their goals, and their preferences. Choosing one as "best" is a matter of opinion. The author must present the practices as choices, analyzing which to use when for what reasons. While this approach is realistic and responsible, it's boring and unsatisfying. Case studies that remove ambiguity can spice up the text, but the author must still leave choices to the reader or else seem arrogant, dogmatic, and inflexible.

Yet folks love to watch roundtable discussions with arrogant, dogmatic, and inflexible pundits. People love to read the pundits' opinion pieces and discuss them with friends and coworkers. Why not debate best practices as an opinion column? All you need is someone willing to expose themselves as a close-minded fool.

How This Book Happened

In April of 2001, after 16 years of working as a professional programmer at places such as Bank Leumi, Jet Propulsion Laboratory, GRAFTEK, Silicon Graphics, and Boeing, and after 6 years as a programmer and manager at Microsoft, I transferred to an internal Microsoft team tasked with spreading best practices across the company. One of the group's projects was a monthly webzine called *Interface*. It was interesting and informative, but also dry and dull. I proposed adding an opinion column.

My boss, Bill Bowlus, suggested I write it. I refused. As a middle child, I worked hard at being a mediator, seeing many sides to issues. Being a preachy practice pundit would ruin my reputation and effectiveness. Instead, my idea was to convince an established narrow-minded engineer to write it, perhaps one of the opinionated development managers I had met in my previous six years at the company.

Bill pointed out that I had the development experience (22 years), dev manager experience (4 years), writing skills, and enough attitude to do it—I just needed to release my inner dogma. Besides, other dev managers had regular jobs and would be unable to commit to a monthly opinion piece. Bill and I came up with the idea of using a pseudonym, and I. M. Wright's "Hard Code" column was born.

Since June of 2001, I have written 49 "Hard Code" opinion columns under the name "I. M. Wright, Microsoft development manager at large" for Microsoft developers and their managers.

The tagline for the columns is "Brutally honest, no pulled punches." They are read by thousands of Microsoft engineers and managers each month.

The first 16 columns were published in the *Interface* internal webzine, with many of the topics assigned to me by the editorial staff, Mark Ashley and Liza White. Doctored photos of the author were created by me and Todd Timmcke, an *Interface* artist. When the webzine came to an end, I took a break but missed writing.

I started publishing the columns again 14 months later on internal sites with the help of my group's editing staff: Amy Hamilton (Blair), Dia Reeves, Linda Caputo, Shannon Evans, and Marc Wilson. Last November, I moved all the columns to an internal SharePoint blog.

In the spring of 2007, I was planning to take a sabbatical awarded to me some years before. My current manager, Cedric Coco, gave me permission to work on publishing the "Hard Code" columns as a book during my time off, and Ben Ryan from MS Press got it accepted.

In addition to the people I've already mentioned, I'd like to thank the other members of the *Interface* staff (Susan Fairo, Bruce Fenske, Ann Hoegemeier, John Spilker, and John Swenson), the other people who helped get this published (Suzanne Sowinska, Alex Blanton, Scott Berkun, Devon Musgrave, and Valerie Woolley), my management chain for supporting the effort (Cedric Coco, Scott Charney, and Jon DeVaan), my current and former team members for reviewing all the columns and suggesting many of the topics (William Adams, Alan Auerbach, Adam Barr, Eric Bush, Scott Cheney, Jennifer Hamilton, Corey Ladas, David Norris, Bernie Thompson, James Waletzky, Don Willits, and Mitch Wyle), my transcendent high-school English teacher (Alan Shapiro), my readers who are so generous with their feedback. And most of all, I want to thank my wife, Karen, and sons, Alex and Peter, for making everything I do possible.

Who This Book Is For

The 49 opinion columns that make up this book were originally written for Microsoft software developers and their managers, though they were drawn from my 28 years of experience in the software industry with six different companies. The editors and I have clarified language and defined terms that are particular to Microsoft to make the writing accessible to all software engineers and engineering managers.

The opinions I express in these columns are my own and do not represent those of any of my current or previous employers, including Microsoft. The same is true of my asides and commentary on the columns and this introduction.

How This Book Is Organized

I've grouped the columns by topic into 10 chapters. The first six chapters dissect the software development process, the next three target people issues, and the last chapter critiques how the software business is run. Tools, techniques, and tips for improvement are spread throughout the book, and a glossary and index appear at the end of the book for your reference.

Within each chapter, the columns are ordered by the date they were published internally at Microsoft. The chapters start with a short introduction from me, as me, followed by the columns as originally written by my alter ego, I. M. Wright. Throughout the columns, I've inserted "Eric Asides" to explain Microsoft terms, provide updates, or convey additional context.

The editors and I have kept the columns intact, correcting only grammar and internal references. I did change the title of one column to "The toughest job" because people misinterpreted the previous title, "You're fired."

Each column starts with a rant, followed by a root-cause analysis of the problem, and ending with suggested improvements. I love word play, alliteration, and pop culture references, so the columns are full of them. In particular, most of the column titles and subheadings are either direct references or takeoffs on lyrics, movie quotes, and famous sayings. Yes, I humor myself, but it's part of the fun and outright catharsis of writing these columns. Enjoy!

System Requirements

The tools provided are in Microsoft Office Excel 2003 and Microsoft Office Word 2003 formats. The basic requirement for using the files is to have Word Viewer and Excel Viewer installed on your computer. You can download both viewers from *http://office.microsoft.com/ en-us/downloads/HA010449811033.aspx*.

How Microsoft Is Organized

Because these columns were originally written for an internal Microsoft audience, I thought a short peek inside Microsoft and my role would be helpful.

Currently, product development at Microsoft is divided into three business divisions, around 25 product lines, over 450 product units, and a multitude of feature teams. The divisions are platform products and services, Microsoft business, and entertainment and devices. The product lines within the divisions are organized around related and often integrated product suites, such as Office System and Visual Studio.

Each product line contains roughly 20 independent product units. The product units typically share source control, build, setup, work-item tracking, and project coordination, including value proposition, milestone scheduling, release management, and sustained engineering. Beyond these coordinating services, the product units have broad autonomy to make their own product, process, and people decisions.

A typical product unit has a product unit manager (PUM) and three engineering discipline managers: a group program manager (GPM), a development manager, and a test manager. Other engineering disciplines—such as user experience, content publishing (for content such as online help), and operations—might report into the product unit or be shared by the product line or division.

People reporting into the discipline managers work on individual features by forming virtual teams, called *feature teams*, made up of one or more representatives from each discipline. Some feature teams choose to use Agile methods, some follow a Lean model, some follow traditional software engineering models, and some mix and match.

How does Microsoft keep all this diversity and autonomy working effectively and efficiently toward a shared goal? That's the role of the product line's shared project coordination. For example, the product line value proposition sets and aligns what the key scenarios, quality metrics, and tenets will be for all product units and their feature teams.

To coordinate and facilitate sharing across the divisions and product lines, particularly around quality and efficiency, there is my parent group, Microsoft Trustworthy Computing and Engineering Excellence. In particular, I'm responsible for making the lives of more than 10,000 Microsoft developers around the world more enjoyable and productive as they construct valuable and delightful high-quality customer experiences. Needless to say, it's a continuous work in progress.

My team brings the leadership of development together monthly to talk through issues and direct my team's work. We research engineering methods used across the company and the industry as we look for new opportunities and areas to improve. We share tools, best practices, and career guidance through online portals; hold events and awards; consult with teams; and deliver technical training for all levels and roles within development. It's a great job. I also get to write a monthly opinion column.

Sample Tools and Documents

The sample tools and documents identified in this book as Online Materials can be downloaded from the book's companion content page at the following address:

http://www.microsoft.com/mspress/companion/9780735624351

Table of Online Materials

Tool	Column	Chapter
Sprint backlog: SprintBacklogExample.xls; SprintBacklogTemplate.xlt	The agile bullet	2
Product backlog: ProductBacklogExample.xls; ProductBacklogTemplate.xlt	The agile bullet	2
Spec template: Spec template.doc	Bad specs: Who is to blame?	3
Spec checklist: Spec checklist.doc	Bad specs: Who is to blame?	3
Pugh Concept Selection: PughConceptSelectionExample.xls; PughConceptSelectionTemplate.xlt	Review this	5
Inspection Worksheet: InspectionWorksheetExample.xls; InspectionWorksheetTemplate.xlt	Review this	5
Interview Role Playing, a how-to guide: InterviewRolePlaying.doc	Out of the interview loop	9

Support for This Book

Every effort has been made to ensure the accuracy of this book and the companion content. As corrections or changes are collected, they will be added to a Microsoft Knowledge Base article. Microsoft Press provides support for books and companion content at the following Web site:

http://www.microsoft.com/learning/support/books/

Questions and Comments

If you have comments, questions, or ideas regarding the book or the companion content, or questions that are not answered by visiting the sites above, please send them to Microsoft Press via e-mail to

mspinput@microsoft.com
Or via postal mail to
Microsoft Press
Attn: *I. M. Wright's "Hard Code"* Editor
One Microsoft Way
Redmond, WA 98052-6399

Please note that Microsoft software product support is not offered through the above addresses.

Chapter 1
Project Mismanagement

In this chapter:

June 1, 2001: "Dev schedules, flying pigs, and other fantasies"................2

October 1, 2001: "Pushing the envelopes: Continued contention
   over dev schedules" 4

May 1, 2002: "Are we having fun yet? The joy of triage." 8

December 1, 2004: "Marching to death"....................................11

October 1, 2005: "To tell the truth" 15

My first column was published in the June 2001 issue of the Microsoft internal webzine, "Interface." I wanted a topic that truly irked me, in order to get into the character of I. M. Wright. Work scheduling and tracking was perfect.

The great myths of project management still drive me crazy more than any other topic:

1. *People can hit dates (projects can hit dates, but people can't hit dates any better than they can hit curveballs).*

2. *Experienced people estimate dates better (they estimate work better, not dates).*

3. *People must hit dates for projects to hit dates (people can't hit dates, so if you want your project to hit dates you must manage risk, scope, and communications, which mitigate the frailty of human beings).*

In this chapter, I. M. Wright talks about how to manage risk, scope, and communications so that your projects are completed on time. The first two columns are specifically about scheduling, followed by columns on managing late issues (what we call "bug triage"), a tirade against death marches, and a philosophical column on why people lie.

One last note: a great insight I've gained from my organization and many years at Microsoft is that project management happens differently at different levels of scale and abstraction. There is the team or feature level (around 10 people), the project level (between 50 and 5,000 people working on a specific release), and the product level (multiple releases led by executives). Agile methods work beautifully at the team level; formal methods work beautifully at the project level; and long-term strategic planning methods work beautifully at the product level. However, people rarely work at multiple levels at once; in fact, years typically separate those experiences for individuals. So people think effective methods at one level should be applied to others, which is how tragedies are often born. The moral is: small tight groups work differently than large disjointed organizations. Choose your methods accordingly.

–Eric

June 1, 2001: "Dev schedules, flying pigs, and other fantasies"

A horse walks into a bar and says, "I can code that feature in two days." Dev costing and scheduling is a joke. People who truly believe such nonsense and depend on it are fools, or green PMs. It's not just an inexact science; it's a fabrication. Sure there are people out there who believe that coding can be refined to a reproducible process with predictable schedules and quality, but then my son still believes in the tooth fairy. The truth is that unless you are coding something that's 10 lines long or is copied directly from previous work you have no idea how long it is going to take.

> **Eric Aside**   Program Managers (PMs) are responsible for specifying the end user experience and tracking the overall project schedule, among other duties. They are often seen by developers as a necessary evil and thus are given little respect. That's a shame because being a PM is a difficult job to do well. Nonetheless, PMs are a fun and easy target for Mr. Wright.

Richter-scale estimating

Sure, you can estimate, but estimates come on a log scale. There's stuff that takes months, stuff that takes weeks, stuff that takes days, stuff that takes hours, and stuff that takes minutes. When I work with my GPM to schedule a project, we use the "hard/medium/easy" scale for each feature. *Hard* means a full dev for a full milestone. *Medium* means a full dev for two to three weeks. *Easy* means a full dev for two to three days. There are no in-betweens, no hard schedules. Why? Because we've both been around long enough to know better.

In my mind, there are no dates for features on a dev schedule beyond the project dates—milestones, betas, and release. A good dev schedule works differently. A good dev schedule simply lists the features to be implemented in each milestone. The "must-have" features go in the first milestone and usually fill it. Fill is based on the number of devs and the "hard/medium/easy" scale. The "like-to-have" features go in the second milestone. The "wish" features go in the third milestone. Everything else gets cut. You usually don't cut the "wish" features and half of the "like-to-have" features until the second week of the third milestone when everyone panics.

> **Eric Aside**   Milestones vary from team to team and product to product. Typically, they range from 6 to 12 weeks each. They are considered project dates that organizations (50–5,000 people) use to synchronize their work and review project plans. Individual teams (3–10 people) might use their own methods to track detailed work within milestones, such as simple work item lists or burn-down charts.

Risk management

This brings me to my main point. Dev costing and scheduling is not about dates or time. It is about risk—managing risk. We ship software, whether it's a packaged product or Web service, to deliver the features and functionality that will delight our customers. The risk is that we won't deliver the right features with the right quality at the right time.

A good dev schedule manages this risk by putting the critical features first—the minimum required to delight our customers. The "hard/medium/easy" scale determines what is realistic to include in that minimal set. The rest of the features are added in order of priority and coherency.

Then you code and watch for features that go from harder to easier and from easier to harder. You shuffle resources to reduce your risk of not shipping your "must-have" features with high quality in time. Everything else is gravy and a great source of challenging but nonessential projects for interns.

> **Eric Aside**   The irony is that while almost every engineer and manager agrees with ordering "must-have" features first, few actually follow that advice because "must-have" features are often boring. They are features such as setup, build, backward compatibility, performance, and test suites. Yet you can't ship without them, so products often slip because of issues in these areas.

It is so important to shoot down the "feature dates" myth because devs working to meet feature dates undermine risk management. The only dates that count are project dates, milestones, betas, etc.—not feature dates. Project dates are widely separated, and there are few of them. They are much easier to manage around. If devs believe they must meet a date for a feature, they won't tell you when they are behind. "I'll just work harder or later, eh heh, eh heh."

Meanwhile, you are trying to manage risk. One of your risk factors is an overworked staff. Another is a hurried, poor-quality feature. Another is losing weeks of time when you could have had two or three devs or more senior devs working on a tough issue. You lose that time when your dev staff thinks their reviews revolve around hitting feature dates instead of helping you manage the risk to the product's critical features.

The customer wins

When you make it clear to your dev team that the success of the product depends on your ability to manage the risk to critical features, everything changes. Sure, getting extra features is a nice bonus, but the key is the focus on communicating risk areas and working together to mitigate them.

When everyone understands the goal, everyone works better to achieve it. This also helps to boost morale when the tough cuts are made, and it rewards mature decisions by junior staff. In the end, our customers are the big winners because they get the features they really want with the quality they expect, instead of the features that happened to make it at whatever level of quality sufficed.

BTW, everything I said about dev scheduling applies equally well to test scheduling.

October 1, 2001: "Pushing the envelopes: Continued contention over dev schedules"

Time to reply to comments about my June column: "Dev schedules, flying pigs, and other fantasies." Most comments were quite flattering, but I won't bore you with just how right I am. Instead, allow me to address the ignorant, incessant ramblings of the unenlightened, yet effusive, readers of this column.

> **Eric Aside**   This was my first and only "mail bag" column, with responses to e-mail I received. I continue to get plenty of "feedback" on my column, but once the column became popular the number of new topic requests vastly outweighed the value of answering e-mail on a past topic. However, looking back over this early column makes me wonder if Mr. Wright should empty the mail bag again.

Software engineering is clearly ambiguous

> *I am incredulous at the supposition that development of a feature cannot and should not be scheduled. The statements in the article accurately portray the activity of "coding." Unfortunately, this is what Jr. High schoolers do when they are throwing together a VB app to decode messages to each other. We, on the other hand, are supposed to be software engineers and not hackers.*
>
> *—Incredulous ignoramus*

I hear this kind of thing often, and it just needs to stop. Bank managers don't manage banks and software engineers don't engineer software. They write software, custom software, usually from scratch, with no prior known measures of nominal operating range, tolerances, failure rates, or stress conditions. Sure, we have those for systems, but not for coding itself.

I went to an engineering school. Many of my friends were electrical, civil, aeronautical, or mechanical engineers. Engineers work on projects in which the building blocks and construction process are well defined, refined, and predictable. While there is great creativity in putting the building blocks together in novel ways to achieve an elegant design for a custom configuration, even the most unusual constructions fall within the tolerances and rigor of known qualities and behaviors.

The same cannot be said for software development, although many are trying to reach this goal. The building blocks of software are too low level and varied. Their interactions with each other are too unpredictable. The complexities of large software systems—such as Windows, Office, Visual Studio, and the core MSN properties—are so far beyond the normal scope of engineering that it is beyond hope to make even gross estimates on things like mean-time-to-failure of even small function changes in those systems.

So for better or worse, it's time to get past wishful thinking and high ideals and return to reality. We've got to accept that we are developers, not engineers. We simply cannot expect the predictability that comes with hundreds or even thousands of years of experience in more traditional engineering any more than we can expect a computer to do what we want instead of what we tell it. We just aren't there yet.

> **Eric Aside**   Now, six years after I wrote this column, Microsoft measures mean-time-to-failure of much of our software. In addition, methods are becoming available to treat programming as engineering, which I describe in the later column, "A software odyssey," in Chapter 5. Even so, I stand by this column as an accurate reflection of software development as a field that has grown past its infancy but remains in its teenage years as compared to its fully grown engineering brethren.

Believe half of what you see and none of what you hear

If I'm relying on another team/product group for a feature or piece of code, I sure don't want to hear, "It should be done in this milestone." I want dates. I need specifics.

—In need of a date

I could write several columns on dependencies and component teams, and perhaps I will, but for now I'll just discuss dependency dev schedules. First of all, if your dependency did have a dev schedule, would you believe it? If you said, "Sure, what choice do I have?" start taking Pepcid™ now before your ulcer develops. It's not only the dev schedule either. Don't believe anything dependencies say—ever. If they are in the next room and tell you it's raining, check your window first.

This doesn't mean you can't work with dependencies—you can, and it can be a great experience and a windfall for your team, product, and customers. You just must keep a close eye on what's happening. Get regular drops and conduct automated testing of those drops. Get their read/write RAID RDQs and watch their counts and problem areas. Send your PM to their triage meetings. Get on their e-mail aliases.

> **Eric Aside**   Check the glossary for help with these bug-tracking references.

Basically, watch dependencies like a hawk; they are an extension of your team and your product. The more you stay in touch and current, the better you will be able to account for shortcomings and affect changes. As for when features will be ready, you simply must rely on your influence to up priorities and on your communication channels and private testing to know when features are *really* ready.

Motivation: It's not just pizza and beer

> *Your general sentiments make more sense for early level planning of a project than the final milestone before shipping. You need to address issues such as how schedules are often used as management tools to drive performance of the team, providing deadlines and time constraints to execute against.*
>
> *—Can't find the gas pedal*

First, let me reiterate, if you hold devs to features dates, they will lie and cheat to meet the dates. They will lie about status, and they will cheat on quality and completeness. If you don't want to experience either of these from your dev team, you need to come up with a better motivational mechanism. I've used three different approaches in coordination with each other to great effect.

First, at a basic level, there are the Richter-scale estimates themselves. My devs know that I expect each feature to be done in roughly that amount of time. If a two-week task takes two and a half weeks, that's probably okay. If it's taking much longer, there's usually a good reason and the dev will let me know. The lack of a good reason provides ample motivation. However, because there's no hard date, lying and cheating are rare.

The second motivational tool is finishing the milestone. This can be dangerous in that it can invite shortcuts, but the overall effect is to encourage devs to work hard from the start and to know when they are behind. The key difference between a feature date and a milestone date is that the latter is a team date. The whole team works together to hit it. Therefore, there is less individual pressure to cut corners. However, that still can happen, which leads me to the last and most effective technique.

> **Eric Aside**   This notion of a self-directed team working toward a clearly defined common goal is central to many agile techniques, though back in 2001 I didn't know it.

The last motivational tool that I use is by far the best. I make it clear to the team which features are the must-ship features, the ones we must finish first. I tell them that everything else can and will be cut if necessary. Unfortunately, the must-ship features are often among the most mundane to code and the least interesting to brag about. So I tell my team that if they want to work on the cool features, they must first complete and stabilize the critical features. Then they will be rewarded by working on the less critical and far flashier stuff. This kind of motivation is positive, constructive, and extremely effective. Works every time.

Sinking on a date

> *Continued from the previous quote: [You also need to address] that schedules are an absolute necessity for aligning the work of different functional areas (not just Dev, but PM, QA, UE, Marketing, external partners).*
>
> *–Brain out of alignment*

If you really needed solid feature dates to synchronize disciplines and dependencies, no software would ever ship. Of course, we do ship software all the time–we even shipped a huge effort, Office XP, on the exact date planned two years in advance. Thus, something else must be the key.

What really matters is agreeing on order, cost, and method, and then providing timely status reports. The agreements should be negotiated across the disciplines, and the process for giving status should be well defined and should avoid blocking work.

- **Order**   Negotiating the order of work on features is nothing new, although there are some groups who never agree on priorities.

- **Cost**   Negotiating cost is often done between the dev and PM. (For example, a dev says, "If we use a standard control, it'll save you two weeks.") But sometimes it's left just to the dev. It should also include test and ops.

- **Method**   Negotiating the methods to be used is frequently done for PM specs, but it's done less frequently for dev and test specs–to their detriment.

- **Status reporting**   As for timely reporting of status, you really need check-in mail and/or test release documents (TRDs) to keep PM, test, and ops aware of progress. Test needs to use alerts for blocking bugs. And PM should use something like spec change requests (SCRs) to report spec changes. (To learn more about SCRs, read "Late specs: Fact of life or genetic defect?" in Chapter 3.)

If the different groups can plan the order of their work, know about how long it will take, have confidence in the methods used, and maintain up-to-date status reports, projects hum. Problems are found, risk is mitigated, and surprises are few. More importantly, no one is pressured to do the wrong thing by artificial dates. Instead, everyone works toward the same goal–shipping a delightful experience to our customers.

May 1, 2002: "Are we having fun yet? The joy of triage."

Tell me if I don't have this concept nailed…

Program managers want an infinite number of features in zero time, testers and service operations staff want zero features over infinite time, and developers just want to be left alone to code cool stuff. Now, put the leads of each of these disciplines with their conflicting goals in the same room, shut the door, and give them something to fight over. What happens? Triage!

> **Eric Aside**   As product development issues arise (such as incomplete work items, bugs, and design changes), they are tracked in a work item database. Triage meetings are held to prioritize the issues and decide how each will be addressed. This can be a source of conflict (understatement).

It's amazing that blood doesn't start leaking out from under the triage room door. Of course, that's what solvents are for. But does it have to be a bloodbath? Most triage sessions are certainly set up that way. Some of the most violent arguments I've seen at Microsoft have happened behind the triage door. Is this bad, or is it "by design"?

War is hell

As anyone who's been through a brutal triage can tell you, it's not good. Rough triages leave you battered and exhausted even if you win most of the arguments.

Basically, dysfunctional triages go hand in hand with dysfunctional teams. They generate bad blood between team members and often set a course of reprisals and unconstructive behavior.

Why should this be? We encourage passion around here. We want people to fight for what they believe and to make the right decisions for our customers. What's wrong with a little healthy competition? Well, when it's not little and it's not healthy, it's not good.

It's nothing personal

Bugs shouldn't be considered personal, but they are.

- To the tester who found it, the bug represents the quality of his labor: "What do you mean the bug isn't good enough to fix?"

- To the program manager who wrote the feature, the bug represents a challenge to her design: "It breaks the whole idea of the feature!"

- To the service ops staff, the bug represents real and continuing work: "Yeah, you don't care about the bug; you're not the one who's going to have to come in at 3:00 A.M. to reboot the server!"

> **Eric Aside**   Interesting note here about 3:00 A.M. reboots. Like most software service companies, Microsoft is now moving away from service operations being on call 24/7. Instead, we are designing services to automatically heal themselves (retry, restart, reboot, reimage, replace). Service operations people, working regular business hours, simply swap components on the automatically generated replacement list.

- To the developer, the bug represents a personal value judgment: "It's not that bad."

Triage decisions should be based on doing what is right for our customers and for Microsoft, not on personal feelings. Yet, because of the personal investment that each discipline places on bugs, triage discussions get off track in a heartbeat.

Five golden rules of triage

How can you keep triage on track and constructive? Follow my five golden rules of triage:

1. **Shut the door.** Triage is a negotiation process, and negotiations are best held in private. It is far easier to compromise, to bargain, and to be candid when the decision-making process is confidential. It also allows the triage team members to present their decisions as team decisions.

2. **All decisions are team decisions.** After a consensus is reached, it is no longer the decision of individuals, but of the group. Everyone stands behind the choices as a team—with no qualifications. A triage team member should be able to defend every decision as if it were her own.

3. **Just one representative per discipline.** Triage must be decisive. Unfortunately, the more people involved, the longer the process; the more personal feelings, the more difficult it is to reach a conclusion. A single individual can make a decision the fastest, but you need the viewpoints of each discipline to make an informed choice. So the best compromise between decisiveness and discipline perspective is reached through having one representative per discipline.

4. **One person is designated to have the final say.** If the team can't reach consensus, you need someone to make the call—ideally, this never happens. Personally, I prefer the PM to have the final say because PMs are used to collaboration and realize the consequences dictating decisions. They tend not to abuse the privilege. However, the very threat that someone from another discipline (let alone the PM!) could impose his decision on the team is enough to drive people to consensus.

5. **All decisions are by "Quaker" consensus.** This is the most important rule. Regular consensus implies that everyone agrees, but that bar is too high to meet for something as difficult and personal as triage. "Quaker" consensus means that no one objects—the team must work toward solutions that everyone can live with. This presents a far more achievable and often more optimal outcome. (Note that "Quaker" simply refers to the people who came up with this notion; it has no religious significance.)

Follow these five rules and your triage will become more cordial, constructive, and efficient. However, there are some subtleties that are worth fleshing out.

The devil is in the details

Here are a few more details that can help your triage run more smoothly:

- If your arguments are about people instead of bugs, change the focus to what's best for the customer and the long-term stock price. This perspective takes personal issues out of the discussion and puts the focus where it should be.

> **Eric Aside**   Throughout the columns, I talk about focusing on the customer and the business, instead of on personal issues. You might wonder why you shouldn't just think about the customer and leave the long-term stock price out of it. I'm sympathetic to this point of view, but I also know that we don't get to serve the customer if we are no longer in business. It helps to have a business plan that aligns our work to provide sustainable benefits to our customers.

- If you need extra information about a bug or a fix, it's sometimes necessary to invite someone from outside the triage team to join you, either by phone or in person. Always complete your questioning and bid them farewell before you begin debating your decision. Otherwise, confidentiality is broken and the decision may cease to be a triage decision.

- If you'd like to teach a member of your team about the triage process, invite him to join a triage session, but instruct him to be a fly on the wall during discussions and stress the confidential nature of the negotiating process.

It's hard to let go, isn't it?

If one or more of the triage members can't seem to let go of an issue, give them a small number of "silver bullets." The rule behind silver bullets is that you can use them at any time to get your way, but when they are used, they are gone. When a person won't give in on an issue ask, "Do you want to use one of your silver bullets?" If so, the team is bound to support the decision. Usually the person will say, "Uh, no it's not that important," and the team can move on.

> **Eric Aside**   This triage column has produced a significant amount of controversy over the years, particularly this paragraph about "silver bullets." Some complain about using the term "bullet" instead of "token," but the primary complaint is that a critical team decision could be made by an individual using his "silver bullet." In practice, this never happens. Silver bullets help people prioritize by associating importance with a scarce resource. People who don't need the help don't use their supply. Thus, if someone abused a silver bullet on a critical issue, there's always someone else with spare tokens to counter. That said, I've never heard of this happening.

Finally, when it comes to resolving the triaged bugs in a database:

■ Always use the "Triage" label to indicate that this was a triage decision.

■ Always explain the thinking behind the triage team's decisions.

■ Never resolve a bug (especially external bugs) unless that's the last time you want to see it. Too often, teams resolve ship-blocking bugs as "external" or "postponed" when what they mean is, "We don't want to deal with this bug now, we'll deal with it later." But because the bug is "resolved," it falls off the "active" radar and the issue gets lost.

Take care of the little things

Triage is arguably one of the most important duties that you perform as a team. Triage health almost always directly corresponds to the health of the project and of the group. The real beauty of this relationship is that making triage sessions more positive, productive, and pleasant usually leads to the same change in your work and your team. But fixing triage issues is much easier and involves fewer people than fixing entire team and project issues.

The best thing about improving your team's triage sessions is that when you get it right, it can be the most fun that you have all day. When triage focuses on bugs instead of people and consensus instead of carnage, the stress of the exercise comes out as humor instead of aggression and frustration. Teams working well together often have triages that are filled with wisecracks, inside jokes, twisted ironies, and hilarious misstatements. Make the right adjustments to your triage techniques, and the laughter may be echoing down the halls. Better keep the door shut.

December 1, 2004: "Marching to death"

Ever been in a project death march? Perhaps you are in one now. There are many definitions of such projects. It basically comes down to having far too much to do in far too little time, so you are asked to work long hours for a long time to make up the difference. Death marches get their name from their length, effort, and the toll they take on the participants. (I apologize for how insulting this is to those whose relatives experienced actual death marches in WWII; but unfortunately, software is full of insensitive word usage.)

It's hard to fathom why groups continue to employ death marches, given that they are almost certain to fail, sometimes spectacularly. After all, by definition you are marching to death. The allure escapes me.

Stabs in the dark

Inept management continues to engage in death marches, so I'll take a few stabs at explaining why.

> **Eric Aside** Death marches are hardly unique to Microsoft, nor are they pervasive at Microsoft, a fact I learned much to my surprise when I joined the company. Microsoft's reputation for long hours preceded it when I joined the company in 1995. I was concerned because I had a two-year-old boy and another child in the works, but my boss assured me that death marches were not the rule. His word was true, yet there are isolated instances when management at Microsoft and other companies still resort to this inane and arcane practice.

- **Management is remarkably stupid.**   Managers choose to act without thinking about the consequences. They take a simpleton's approach: Too much work to do? Work harder. At least managers can say they're doing something, even if it is probably wrong.

- **Management is incredibly naive.**   Managers don't know that a death march is doomed to fail. Somehow they were either asleep for the last 25 years or never read a book, article, or Web site. They assume that adding at least four hours a day and two days a week will double productivity. The math works out—unfortunately, humans aren't linear.

- **Management is tragically foolish.**   Managers think that their team will be the one to overcome the insurmountable odds. Rules and records were meant to be broken. They've got the best team in the world, and their team will rise to the challenge. Apparently, they see no difference between outrunning a bull (hard) and outrunning a bullet (impossible).

- **Management is unconscionably irresponsible.**   Managers know that a death march will fail, destroying their team in the process; but they do it anyway in an effort to be worshiped as heroes. Managers reward this behavior with free meals, gold stars, and high ratings, knowing that our customers and partners won't be screwed by the garbage we deliver until after the next review period. I think these managers are the most deserving of a verbal pummeling by Steve's staff.

> **Eric Aside**   *Steve* refers to Steve Ballmer, our beloved Chief Executive Officer, who is a strong advocate for work-life balance and practices it himself. I've met him several times while he was cheering on his son at a basketball game or going out to a movie with his wife.

- **Management is unaccountably spineless.**   Managers know that the death march is doomed, but they lack the courage to say "no." Because they won't be held responsible if they follow the herd, there is little consequence for these cowards. Sure, the project will fail and their employees will hate them and leave, but at least they'll have war stories to share with their gutless, pathetic pals.

Many people have written about the ineffectiveness of software project death marches, but somehow the practice continues. I can't reason with the foolish and irresponsible, but I can enlighten the stupid and naïve and give alternatives to the spineless.

A litany of failure

Some enlightenment for the ignorant: Death marches fail because they...

- **Are set up for failure.**   By definition you have far too much to do in far too little time. Of course you fail.

- **Encourage people to take shortcuts.**   Nothing could be more natural than to find cheap ways to leave out work when you are under pressure. Unfortunately, shortcuts lower quality and add risk. That may be okay for small items and short time periods. But those risks and poor quality bite you when the project drags on.

- **Don't give you time to think.**   Projects need slack time to be effective. People need time to think, read, and discuss. Without that time, only your first guess is applied. First guesses are often wrong, causing poor design, planning, and quality, and leading to dramatic rework or catastrophic defects later.

- **Don't give you time to communicate.**   You could make a good argument that miscommunication and misunderstanding are at the root of all evil. Even good projects commonly fail because of poor communication. When people don't have spare time and work long hours, they communicate less and with less effectiveness. The level of miscommunication becomes an insurmountable obstacle.

- **Create tension, stress, and dysfunction.**   Congeniality is the first to go when the pressure is on. Issues become personal. Accidents get amplified and misconstrued. Voices get raised, or even worse, people stop talking.

- **Demoralize and decimate the workforce.**   All the bitterness, all the tension, and all the long hours away from family and friends take their tolls on the psyche and relationships. When the project inevitably fails to meet its dates and quality goals, people often snap. If you're lucky, it just means switching groups at the end of the project. If you're unlucky, it means leaving the company, divorce, health issues, or even life-threatening addictions.

By the way, managers often confuse the long hours some employees ordinarily put in with death marches. Death marches are an entirely different dynamic. The difference is that a death march forces you to put in those hours. When people voluntarily put in long hours, it's often because they love it. Such hours are full of slack time. There isn't any tension or cause for taking shortcuts.

> **Eric Aside**   This is a critical point people often miss. Voluntary long hours are completely different from death marches.

- **Undermine confidence in the process.**   It doesn't take a genius to realize that death marches are a response to something going wrong. The message this sends to our employees, customers, and partners isn't dedication, it's incompetence. Avoiding the real issues and just working harder only undermine our corporate standing further.

- **Don't solve the problem.**   Working longer hours doesn't solve the underlying problem that caused the project team to have far too much to do in far too little time. Until the underlying problem is solved, no one should expect the project to do anything but get worse.

- **Reduce your options.**   When you've taken shortcuts, introduced poor designs and plans, created dramatic rework and defects, randomized your messaging, encouraged people to slit each other's throats, demoralized the staff, undermined confidence in our ability to deliver, and still failed to hit dates and quality goals—leaving all the original issues unresolved—you have few options left. Usually this leads to dropping the quality bar, slipping the schedule, and continuing the death march. Nice job.

The turning point

So, if you find yourself with far too much to do in far too little time, what should you do? On a practical level, the answer is remarkably easy. Figure out why you've got far too much to do and far too little time to do it.

The answer isn't, "Because those are the dates and requirements from management." Why are those the dates and requirements from management? What would management do if you didn't hit certain dates or certain requirements? Would they slip the schedule? How much? Would they cut? Which features? Are there more fundamental changes you could make in the process or approach that would alter the dynamic? Tell management that your goal is to hit the dates and requirements, but you have to plan for the worst case.

Then plan for the worst case. Build a plan that hits the worst acceptable dates with the least acceptable features. If you are still left with too much to do for the available time, raise the general alarm. Your project is dead in the water. If the worst-case plan is perfectly achievable, focus all your efforts on achieving it. Message to your employees that doing more means a review score of 3.5+, but doing less means a score below a 3.0.

> **Eric Aside**   The numbers refer to the old Microsoft rating system, which ranged from 2.5 to 4.5 (the higher the rating, the better the rewards). While a 3.0 was acceptable, most people pursued and received a 3.5 or higher.

The road less traveled

What you've done is escaped from the death march and created slack time to improve. Your team will likely go far beyond the minimum, but they will do so without taking shortcuts, making poor decisions, or engaging in cannibalism. You will deliver what's needed on time and build confidence with your partners and customers.

As reasonable as this sounds, it is hard to do on an emotional level. Planning for the worst case feels like giving up. It feels weak and cowardly—like you can't handle a challenge. How ironic; in actuality, it is entirely the opposite.

Not facing the crisis is weak and cowardly. Pretending the worst won't happen is deceitful and irresponsible. Show some guts. Face the facts. Be smart and save your partners, customers, and employees from the anguish at the end of the road. Come out on the other side with value delivered and with your team, your life, and your pride intact.

October 1, 2005: "To tell the truth"

I cannot tell a lie—catchy phrase, but a children's tale. Everybody lies from time to time. Sometimes it's strategically leaving out details. Sometimes it's not saying how you truly feel. Sometimes it's an out-and-out fabrication. No matter the reason or circumstance—lying is deception, pure and simple.

Some might rationalize this behavior as "white lies," but it amounts to the same thing: dishonesty. If someone catches me lying, no matter how slight, I fess up immediately, sincerely, and remorsefully. When I was a kid, I would perpetuate and cover up the deception. But I've since learned that covering it up is far more damaging than the original offense. Most people, including me, aren't lying to offend anyone; our motivation is pure expediency.

Therein lies the core truth: deception is basically a quick and dirty way to avoid a problem. How is this relevant to software development? Because by focusing on "when" and "why" you or your team lie, you can pinpoint everything from quality issues to retention troubles to increased productivity.

Suffer from delusions

Lying is one of a handful of valuable process canaries that can warn you of trouble. Why? Because lying, cycle time, work in progress, and irreplaceable people hide problems. Long cycle times and large amounts of work in progress hide workflow difficulties. Irreplaceable people hide tool, training, and repeatability problems. Lying can hide just about anything. Scrutinizing these process canaries exposes the problems and enables improvement.

> **Eric Aside**   I write about each of these process canaries in other columns: "Lean: more than good Pastrami" in Chapter 2, and "Go with the flow," in Chapter 9. As for the five whys, like Lean, that concept comes from Toyota.

The key is getting to the root cause of the lie. One of the best ways to do this is to apply "The five whys"—that is, ask "why" five times:

- Why you are lying? What pain are you hiding from?

- Why hide from that pain? What's the danger?

- Why would that happen? Is there a way to mitigate the danger?

- Why aren't you mitigating the danger already? What actions do you need to take?

- Why are you just sitting there? Act!

To practice applying these ideas, let's go over some common examples of lying at work. We'll apply the five whys to uncover the root cause and discuss how to fix it. Here are our foul foursome of falsehoods:

- Perverting the meaning of the word "Done"

- Weaseling out of a tough review message

- Face-lifting progress reports for your clients and boss

- Denying rumors about a reorganization

Put a fork in me

Say your dev team is supposed to finish up feature development on Monday. On Monday, you go through the team and everyone says, "I'm done." Later, you find that more than half the features are full of bugs and a quarter don't handle error conditions, accessibility, or stress. You could ask, "Why does my team stink?" But the better question is, "Why did my team lie?" Let's ask the five whys:

- **Why did my team lie about being done; what are they hiding from?**　They had a deadline to meet, and not meeting it would drop their standing within the team. The criterion for meeting the deadline was simply saying they were done.

- **Why just say you're done and not mean it—what's the danger?**　No one wants to look bad. Unfortunately, there was no personal danger to saying, "I'm done." So why wouldn't they lie? The danger was to the team. That's the real problem.

- **Why would that happen; can you mitigate it?**　There was no verifiable team definition for "done." This opened the door to deception. To mitigate it, you need a clear definition, accepted by the team, with an objective means of verifying it has been met.

- **Why don't you have a clear definition of "done"? What more do you need?**　When you agree on a definition and means of verification, you need to put the tools in place. Say the definition is 60% unit test coverage with 95% of tests passing, along with a three-peer code inspection that finds 80% of the bugs. Now you need to add code coverage and a test harness to your build for the unit tests, as well as an inspection process with the appropriate time scheduled for the inspectors and inspections.

- **Why are you sitting there?**　Most of what you need is in Toolbox—aside from the nerve to challenge the meaning of "done" in the first place. The key is to focus on the cause of the deception, and then rectify the root of the problem.

> **Eric Aside**   Toolbox is a Microsoft internal repository for shared tools and code. It holds tools that measure code coverage, run unit tests, and even calculate bug yields for code inspections. Many of these internal tools make their way into Visual Studio, Office Online Templates, and other shipping products.

Give me a straight answer

You manage a 4.0 performer you really value, and you've told her so. Your division runs a calibration meeting, and your 4.0 performer drops to a 3.5 relative to her peers in the division. It's easy to say to your employee, "Well, I thought you deserved a 4.0, but as you know, the review system is relative and I can't always give you the rating you deserve."

You're lying, not because what you are saying isn't true, but because you're leaving out your role in the process. Again, let's cover the five whys:

- **Why leave out your responsibility; what are you hiding from?**   You like the employee and don't want to be blamed.

- **Why hide from blame; what's the danger?**   Your employee might not like you and may leave the team.

- **Why would that happen; can you mitigate it?**   You are the messenger, your employee feels helpless, and you are no help. You can mitigate the impact by telling your employee how to get the review score she wants.

- **Why aren't you already telling her; what more do you need?**   You need to know why she got the 3.5 instead of the people who were awarded 4.0.

> **Eric Aside**   The process around differentiated pay based on performance is a common source of complaints across the high technology industry. Like the numerical rating system, we've changed the process many times at Microsoft, but it's always been about comparing your work to the work of others doing the same job at the same level of responsibility. What managers should always do is understand and clearly articulate how their employees can improve to compare more favorably.

- **Why are you sitting there?**   Find out what differentiated the 4.0 from the 3.5 performers, and then tell your employee. She'll have clear guidance on how to improve and be in control of that improvement. Sure, she'll still be unhappy, but at least you helped her and she can do something about it.

Lipstick on a pig

Your team is falling behind on the schedule. You've got a ton of bugs and can't keep up. Your clients and boss demand to know the status. Instead of a fair representation, you paint a rosy picture in the hope that your team will be left alone long enough to catch up. Aside from feeling bad about being a gutless slimeball, what should you do? Here are the five whys:

- **Why the desperate move; what are you hiding from?**   You don't want to look bad or have others interfere.

- **Why hide from blame; what's the danger?**   You're afraid your project will get cut or transferred to someone else because of your perceived incompetence.

- **Why would that happen; can you mitigate it?**   If your clients and boss get blind-sided by your team slipping, they won't trust you to take care of it. You can mitigate the problem by being transparent so that no one gets surprised, and by having a solid plan to get on track, which earns you the confidence of your clients and boss.

- **Why aren't you already transparent; what more do you need?**   It's a ton of work to constantly collect status from your team and post it or send e-mail. Instead, post your schedule and bug data directly on your SharePoint site, warts and all. Have your team update it directly, right there for the world to see. Use charts to make progress (or lack thereof) obvious. When it's posted, point your team to it. Everyone will get the picture, and you'll be able to drive a plan to get on track.

- **Why are you sitting there?**   None of this is hard. Transparency drives the right behavior. It also drives trust, which really is the key asset to being successful.

Look at all these rumors

Rumors are flying around about another reorg. Your PUM has told you to keep it quiet; but meanwhile, your team is getting randomized. Naturally, when the topic comes up at your team meeting, you deny any knowledge of the reorg; instead, you remind folks of the evil of rumors and that the team needs to focus on their deliverables. However, you are overcome with guilt, dreading the day when your whole team realizes that you lied to their faces.

> **Eric Aside**   A Product Unit Manager (PUM) is the first level of multidisciplinary management at Microsoft. PUMs are typically responsible for individual products, such as Excel, that are part of larger product lines, such as Office. PUMs might also be responsible for significant components of larger products, such as DirectX for Windows. Reorganizations, also known as *reorgs*, typically start at the top levels of management and slowly work their way down over the following 9 to 18 months. I wrote more about reorgs in my column "How I learned to stop worrying and love reorgs," which appears in Chapter 10.

- **Why deny the rumors; what are you hiding from?**   Basically, your boss told you to deny them. You don't want your team randomized any more than your boss does.

- **Why worry about randomization; what's the danger?**   You're concerned your team will get so caught up in the rumors that they'll fail to meet their commitments. In addition, some team members might even leave the group for fear of unwanted changes.

- **Why would that happen; can you mitigate it?**   Most team members, particularly the senior ones, know how bad reorgs can sometimes get. However, no one (including you) knows if the reorg will really happen or how a reorg will actually turn out. So your team's concerns are without a strong base in fact.

- **Why is your team still taking the rumors seriously; what more can you do?**   In this case, the problem lies squarely with you. You are taking the rumors too seriously, hiding what you know from your team. You should know by now that only roughly one in three planned reorgs actually happens.

- **Why are you sitting there?**   The solution is simple and obvious here: tell the truth. "Yeah, I've heard lots of rumors too. We talk about them in our staff meetings. However, the bottom line is that no one knows whether or not there really will be a reorg until it actually happens. Most planned reorgs don't happen, and we're going to look pretty foolish missing our commitments because we were daydreaming."

I want the truth

I make no judgments about whether or not people should always tell the truth. To do so would be hypocritical and lead to awkward situations when my mother-in-law asks what I think about her decorating.

However, we all work for the same company. You shouldn't have to lie to your coworkers about business issues. Lying hides problems that need exposure. If you're feeling the need to lie, ask yourself why. Then ask again until you resolve what the real problem is. People wonder about how they can deliver on the fourth pillar of Trustworthy Computing, "Business Integrity." Well, now you know.

Chapter 2
Process Improvement, Sans Magic

In this chapter:

September 2, 2002: "Six Sigma? Oh please!"..................................22

October 1, 2004: "Lean: More than good pastrami" 24

April 1, 2005: "Customer dissatisfaction"..................................30

March 1, 2006: "The Agile bullet"...35

I'm wrong, okay? I know nothing. Now calm yourself! Some people raise process dogma to the level of religious fanaticism. My own pet theory about why relates to superstition. B. F. Skinner noted that superstition arises when animals, like pigeons, associate chance behaviors with desired results. People get locked into very particular practices when by a combination of chance and skill they achieve great outcomes.

Not that there's anything wrong with that, I enjoy superstitious behavior as much as anyone. But when people become inflexible in their application of methods, say eXtreme Programming, superstition becomes counterproductive at best, divisive at worst.

In this chapter, I. M. Wright analyzes a wide collection of process improvements and techniques, minus the superstition. The first column was part of an Interface issue focused on Six Sigma at Microsoft (many of the original "Hard Code" column topics were set by the Interface editorial staff). The second column relates classic Lean concepts to software engineering. The third focuses on traceability of requirements, and the last column focuses on practical application of Agile techniques to the Microsoft production software environment.

Excellent books have been written about all these topics in far more depth than I provide here. If I. M.'s presentation of these concepts doesn't match your precise ideals, please forgive him. After all, he's not trying to be perfect, just right.

−Eric

September 2, 2002: "Six Sigma? Oh please!"

I'm sorry. If you talk to me about yet another totally continuous quality management improvement program, I might have a seizure. Now we're experimenting with the Six Sigma problem-solving methodology.

In only five days over eight weeks, you can be trained as a Six Sigma Green Belt. Or go for it all—in just four months become a Six Sigma Black Belt. I think I'm going to hurl.

I just don't understand why we need buzz words and "Karate Kid" references to apply good engineering practices to our problems. It's like senior managers leave their brains, education, and experience at the door and get seduced into thinking that the latest fashionable regurgitated metric analysis fluff will solve all the ills of our unenlightened workforce.

> **Eric Aside**   I'm constantly confronting management in my columns. Along with PMs, managers are one of I. M. Wright's favorite targets for ridicule. To their enormous credit, Microsoft managers have never taken it personally, and many are avid fans. Sure, my manager has occasionally been asked if these columns are sufficiently constructive. But in six years of writing on fairly contentious topics, I've never had a column censored or altered by management.

But I work at Microsoft under these managers, so I had to read the articles in this issue of *Interface* focusing on Six Sigma and the material on the Six Sigma Web site, like it or not. Am I blown off my feet? Please. Is the content filled with new and exciting ideas that will revolutionize the way we produce our products? As if. Is there anything there of merit? Of course.

Egads! What sorcery is this?!

Six Sigma is a structured problem-solving system with a "toolbox" of techniques used to analyze and interpret issues for all kinds of business, development, and manufacturing processes. The actual techniques themselves are nothing new—brainstorming, the five whys, cause and effect diagramming, statistical analysis, and so on. These techniques have been used for years to discover the root cause of issues in engineering and business.

The methodology is based on tried and true problem-solving principles that date way back: define, measure, analyze, improve, control. This basic cyclic approach to quality improvement is used in just about every product group at Microsoft during stabilization. Bugs are defined (spec'd), measured (found and documented), analyzed (triaged), improved (fixed), and controlled (regressed, prioritized, and triaged again).

So why have a Six Sigma group? Why become a Green Belt? What's with having 20 full-time Six Sigma Black Belts at the company?

Calling in the cavalry

Basically, in the heat of the moment we panic and forget all the engineering knowledge and practices we have learned and know so well. That's everything we knew before the pressure crushed us or we became so engulfed in the problem that we no longer could see the dead tree for all the bugs.

So you call your local Green Belt, or bring in the big old Black Belt, and he reminds you of what you should have been doing in the first place. However, because of the highly structured nature of the Six Sigma system, all the passion and personalities get removed.

Instead of placing blame or getting caught up in guesswork and blind alleys, the Six Sigma folks look dispassionately at the real data and derive what's actually wrong and what can be done to improve the problem. Then they leave you with a process to track your improvement and control its effects.

Creating order out of chaos

Yes, anyone with a good engineering background could find the same problems and fix them. Anyone who made it through interviews at Microsoft should have the intellectual horsepower to figure out a solution to a problem. But sometimes when you're in it too deep and tempers are flaring, you need an outside calm influence to help you get centered and focused on doing the right things.

In addition, the Six Sigma folks get exposed to a wide range of techniques and best practices from around the company. They can bring those experiences to your group and come up with interesting solutions that may have escaped your notice.

Does this make me a Six Sigma booster? Nah, I still think the idea of Green Belts and Black Belts is goofy and that the methodology itself is recycled TQM and CQI. However, Six Sigma is the process that Microsoft has chosen to experiment with—if there's a group that can come in and help when problems get out of hand, that's a good thing to me.

> **Eric Aside**   While Six Sigma never quite took hold in product development at Microsoft, the concept of having coaches and groups you can turn to in a pinch did. I'm a manager in just such a group.

October 1, 2004: "Lean: More than good pastrami"

Ever walk through a public space, like an airport terminal or public park, and get accosted by crazies trying to convert you or scare you or assault your supposed ignorance? Get into a conversation with one of these people and logic and reasoning become ludicrous. Everything to them is blind faith and irrefutable truth. Even if you wholly agree with them, there is still no room for questions or analysis. You must believe, you cannot question, even in part.

This makes me sick. I mean truly physically sick. I was given a mind of my own, and I fully intend to use it. Not just at parties and social occasions but on every subject and dealing I have. Questioning why and understanding how are at the center of who I am.

You'd think my sensibilities would be the norm for software developers, who can't debug what they don't understand. But the same zeal that some folks devote to religion, political battles, and environmental concerns also gets directed by some developers toward new development practices like eXtreme Programming (XP), Agile, and the Team Software Process (TSP).

All things in moderation

I love many of the ideas and approaches advocated by these development paradigms. But if I question a true believer why a certain thing is done or suggest a small change in a rule or practice to better adapt it to my work, look out! It's like showing a ring of power to an old hobbit—the fangs come out, the hair raises on end. For some developers, eXtreme Programming and the Agile Manifesto have become a cult. For some developers, TSP is a measure of allegiance—you're either with us or against us.

Well excuse me for being practical. Excuse me for using my head. Excuse me for doing something because it's useful instead of magic. I don't do things because "That's the way you must do it." I do things because there's a darn good reason why they work, and there are also good reasons why working some other way fails.

> **Eric Aside**   There, I feel better. Often these rants that lead columns overstate my own feelings on a subject, but not this time. There's harmless superstition and then there's lunacy. I'm not a big fan of lunatics.

Waste not, want not

Which brings me to Lean. Ah yes, the title of the column. While there are many wonderful things in XP, Agile, and TSP, there is at least one concept that they all have in common: reduce wasted effort. That is the focus of Lean Design and Manufacturing, a concept from Toyota that predates XP, Agile, and TSP by more than 30 years. While XP, Agile, and TSP attack the problem of waste in different ways, we can better understand what each is doing by using the Lean model.

So, at the risk of offending some zealots' sensibilities, let's break it down. Lean focuses on delivering as much value as possible to the customer with a minimum of wasted effort. It accomplishes this by using a pull model and adopting continuous improvement. The pull model means simply, "Don't do work until it's needed." This reduces unused, unnecessary, and undesirable work. The continuous improvement is focused on reducing waste and creating a smooth-flowing stream of customer value.

> **Eric Aside**   Kudos to Corey Ladas who first introduced me to Lean, as well as Axiomatic Design, Scrum, Quality Function Deployment (QFD), Set-Based Design, Kaizen, Pugh Concept Selection, and who knows how many other great ideas. We worked together for two productive years, and he's left my team with a hole that cannot be easily filled. He's got a Lean Software Engineering Web site now with another great former team member, Bernie Thompson.

Lean defines seven types of waste that disrupt the flow of customer value:

- Overproduction
- Transportation
- Motion
- Waiting
- Overprocessing
- Inventory
- Defects

These are obviously manufacturing terms, right? They can't possibly be relevant to software, right? Oh, to be young and foolish. All seven of these sources of waste are directly related to software development. I'll treat them like the seven deadly sins and talk about how XP, Agile, TSP, and plain common sense can help.

Overproduction

The first deadly waste is producing more than you need. Like this never happens. Has a product ever shipped without cutting features that were already spec'd and coded? Has a product ever shipped without keeping features customers never use? Too complex, too general, too extensible, too fancy, too redundant, too convoluted. Overproduction is a killer. It's an unbelievable waste.

XP solves this with short and tight iterations. It insists on constant contact with customers and constant communication between developers. This ensures that everyone knows what others are doing and the customer always thinks it's a good idea. As a result, almost all the work that gets done is of value to the customer. Of course, the Microsoft customer is supersized, so many Microsoft teams have turned to Agile.

Agile is a collection of Lean practices, including XP. Because Agile is more of an alliance than a specific technique, it provides a number of interesting approaches to development. One of these is a project management practice called "Scrum" (named after the rugby term). Teams meet with the customer's representative regularly, usually every 30 days, to demonstrate progress, reprioritize items, and make process improvements. As with XP, team members also meet daily to keep tabs on each other's progress and any blocking issues.

By reprioritizing work monthly and reorganizing work daily, a Scrum team tunes itself to only what's important to the customer. Little work is wasted. By focusing on process improvements at regular intervals, the value stream can be constantly optimized.

Go deep

Of course, you can use Scrum and XP poorly by making the customer wait for value while you work on "infrastructure." There is a fundamental premise behind quick iterations built around regular customer feedback: develop the code depth first, not breadth first.

Breadth first in the extreme means spec every feature, then design every feature, then code every feature, and then test every feature. *Depth first* in the extreme means spec, design, code, and test one feature completely, and then when you are done move on to the next feature. Naturally, neither extreme is good, but depth first is far better. For most teams, you want to do a high-level breadth design and then quickly switch into depth-first, low-level design and implementation.

This is just what Microsoft Office is doing with feature crews. First, teams plan what features they need and how the features go together. Then folks break up into small multidiscipline teams that focus on a single spec at a time, from start to finish. The result is a much faster delivery of fully implemented and stable value to demonstrate for customers.

> **Eric Aside**   Naturally, the idea of feature crews isn't new. However, finding a way to implement Lean software development within a huge live production environment like Office is a major achievement. Keep in mind, Office is now a system of 15 desktop applications, 8 server applications, and 2 major online services.

Depth first reduces overproduction by staying focused on work that can be used, rather than on "infrastructure" that may never be leveraged or a little bit of everything that may never stabilize. Another great method for depth-first development is Test-Driven Development (TDD), but I'll save that for the overprocessing section.

Transportation

The second deadly waste is waiting for stuff to arrive. In manufacturing, this typically means the transportation of parts. For software, it's the transportation of deliverables between teams. There are three nasty sources of transportation issues: builds, branches, and e-mail.

- **Builds**   The longer the build, the bigger the waste of time. Like I need to tell you this. XP and Agile both insist on daily builds, a rule they may well have gotten from Microsoft. For huge teams, a daily build has become a fantasy. Luckily, we have good people working on the issue, but it's a big problem. Enough said.

- **Branches**   I love Source Depot. It's been huge for the company. But the frigging thing has become a pet elephant. Sure they're cute when they're a baby, but in a few years you're constantly either feeding or shoveling, and your mobility suffers. While branching is great, many large teams have taken to branching branches. So if you are on branch A2.B3.C1 and your buddy with a key feature or fix is on branch A3.B1.C2, your buddy needs to reverse integrate C2 into B1 then B1 into A3, and then you have to integrate A3 into A2 then B3 then C1. AHHHHHHHHH!!!!!!!! You might as well watch grass grow. The solution is one level of branching off your current release line, period.

> **Eric Aside**   Source Depot is the large-scale source control system Microsoft uses to manage hundreds of millions of lines of source code and tools, including version control and branching.

- **E-mail**   The last transportation nightmare is e-mail notification: PM telling dev and test that specs are ready; dev telling test that code is ready; test telling dev it's blocked on a bug; dev telling PM it's blocked on a design change; and, my personal favorite, any kind of communication between a client and dependency or vendor, particularly overseas. XP and Agile solve the e-mail notification problem by removing the roles and having the team meet daily. For remote vendors and dependencies, this can't work. For now, we must rely on automated notification where possible, Live Meeting where reasonable, and clear e-mail that answers anticipated responses to reduce roundtrips everywhere else.

Motion

The third deadly waste is spending time just finding stuff. On the manufacturing floor, it's the wasted motions of robots and people. In the software world, it's time spent figuring out what to do, where to go, and how to fix. Poor search technology is a great example of wasted motion. So is untestable, unmaintainable, unmanageable code.

Using asserts and validating input help find bugs faster and reduce wasted motion. So do design reviews, code reviews, code analysis, and unit testing. XP even suggests pair programming, but personally, I think that wastes resources (except for devs learning a new code base). TSP measures all your activities and defects, which allows you to study exactly how your time is spent and significantly cut down on your wasted motion.

> **Eric Aside**   My team has since adopted pairing for creating new content in unfamiliar areas. It works extremely well.

One particularly annoying and avoidable source of wasted motion is duplicating bug fix information for code comments, Source Depot, Product Studio, and check-in mail. And everyone wastes motion managing multiple copies of bugs and project schedule data. Tools that make these things easier by entering the information once and automatically populating it to all other places can go a long way toward reducing deadly motion sickness.

Waiting

The fourth deadly waste is waiting around for work. Transportation issues cover a big part of waiting for builds, branch integrations, and timely communication. But there are plenty more places to wait. The most common dead zone is caused by teams not agreeing on the priority order of features or simply not following the predetermined order. That is, PMs writing specs out of order so devs have to wait. Devs writing features out of order so testers have to wait. Testers writing tests out of order so everyone has to wait.

XP, Agile, and TSP all force teams to decide on a priority order, get buy-off from the customer or their representative, then work in that order until they decide to review the priorities again. TSP is particularly rigorous in this way, but also can be less iterative about plans without a flexible leader.

Another source of waiting is unstable code. As long as the code is unstable, the test team has to wait, as do any other mechanisms you have for customer feedback. XP and Agile put a premium on verifiably stable code, another essential element of the depth-first strategy.

Overprocessing

The fifth deadly waste is over-engineering. You see this all the time in the form of producing overly complex features, fine-tuning performance in areas that already perform adequately or aren't the true bottleneck, and adding generalization or extensibility when it isn't required. This waste is related to overproduction but focused on specific feature implementations.

The cure: Test-Driven Development (TDD). TDD is an XP and Agile technique for implementation design. As a side benefit, it provides unit tests with full code coverage. The process is fairly simple:

1.   Define your API or public class methods.

> **Eric Aside**   This is a point of contention between me and some members of the Agile community: do you define your API or public class methods before writing unit tests or after? Purists will say after; I say before. The difference is the amount of up-front design and the nature of your relationship with outside groups that depend on your code. I tackle up-front design in other columns, which when taken in moderation, I believe is essential to success in projects with more than 100,000 lines of code.

2. Write a unit test for a requirement of the API or class.

3. Compile and build your program, and then run the unit test and ensure that it fails. (If it passes, skip step 4.)

4. Write just enough code to make the unit test pass. (Also ensure that all previous unit tests continue to pass.)

5. Repeat steps 2 through 4 until all API or class requirements are tested.

Naturally, after you get the hang of it, you can write unit tests for more than one requirement at a time; but when you first get started, try doing just one. It builds the right habits.

When you use TDD, you don't write any more code than is absolutely required. You also automatically get easily testable code, which usually correlates to strong cohesion, loose coupling, and less redundancy—all very good things indeed. Oh, and did I mention you also get unit tests with full code coverage? What's not to like?

Inventory

The sixth deadly waste is undelivered work product. This is related to cut features, but it also includes the amount of work in progress. When you develop breadth first, all your work is in progress until the code is complete and stable. All the completed specs, designs, and code that are waiting to pass tests are inventory. Their value is not yet realized.

Unrealized value is wasteful because you can't demonstrate the value to customers and partners. You can't get their feedback. You can't improve and optimize your customer value stream. Of course, if product plans change, this unrealized inventory often becomes a huge wasted effort.

The Lean pull model of working only on things as they are needed drives low inventory, as demonstrated in Scrum and TDD. Scrum pays special attention to work in progress, tracking it and working hard to minimize it. Scrum also leverages regular opportunities to improve and optimize the way you deliver value. TDD has you implement code only as needed to satisfy requirements, and no more.

Defects

The seventh deadly waste is rework. It's the most obvious one and the one I've ranted about incessantly in the past (see Chapter 5, "Software Quality–More Than a Dream"). XP and Agile get at reducing bugs and rework by a variety of techniques, not the least of which is TDD, daily builds, continuous code reviews, and design reviews.

However, XP and Agile also reduce bugs in a more subtle way–by creating a structure where you learn as you go. Using depth-first development, you figure out parts of the project step by step before you've designed and coded the whole product. This prevents serious architectural issues from remaining concealed until it's too late to adjust. Sound familiar?

Reducing defects is a specialty of TSP. Teams using TSP have dropped their bug rates by a factor of a thousand from the industry average. I wrote in detail about the TSP defect prediction, tracking, and removal approach in "A software odyssey," in Chapter 5. While TSP isn't inherently lean, it doesn't preclude depth-first development either.

Symbiosis

This brings me to the point where I get to infuriate the XP, Agile, and TSP true-believers. There's no reason why you can't combine these techniques to be greater than the sum of their parts. Use Scrum to drive a lean, depth-first, flexible, and optimized development schedule. Use TDD to create a lean implementation. And use TSP to analyze your defects and your work, which will result in vastly reduced bugs and wasted effort. While that may be heresy to some, it sounds like common sense to me.

Now if I could just find some good pastrami.

> **Eric Aside**   I grew up in New York. It's tough to find good pastrami in Redmond.

April 1, 2005: "Customer dissatisfaction"

You always hurt the one you love. We must really love our customers. We ship buggy code, though that's not the big problem. We miss our ship dates–not the big problem. We don't have a clear, broad, and prioritized understanding of customer needs, but that's not the big problem. We don't communicate to our customers well and with one voice, but that's not the big problem. We don't listen to our customers well and then transfer that information to the right people; but again, that's not the big problem. No, the big problem is that all too frequently we have no idea when we are tormenting our customers and how badly we're doing it until it's too late.

> **Eric Aside**   I am severely overstating the case here for dramatic effect. In fact, we do a very good job of listening to our customers and integrating that value into our products. It's been a huge competitive edge for Microsoft over the years. Regardless, our customers' expectations have risen as the software market has matured, so to keep our competitive edge we must continue improving. This column discusses the advantages of tracing every code change back to the customers who needed or requested the change.

If we ship bug-free, high-quality code, but it wasn't what the customer wanted, then customers are dissatisfied. The same is true for shipping undesirable code on time. Even if we do have a clear, broad, and prioritized understanding of customer needs, we still have to ship code that meets those needs or the customer will be dissatisfied. Communicating well and listening well aren't enough. Nothing counts if we don't deliver what the customer wanted.

Ignorance is bliss

In fact, good communication and listening actually hurt us. Say we talk to some customers and find out exactly what they want. The customers are pleased that we listened to them, and they know that we know just what they need. Two years later, we deliver a solution that falls short of their expectations. Uh oh. Now the customer is

- Disappointed because the product doesn't perform as desired.
- Insulted because we wasted their time and raised, then dashed, their hopes.
- Incensed because we broke our commitment to serve them. They may never trust us again.

At least if we had ignored the customer, we could have excused the mistake. "We're ignorant ninnies" could be our claim. Unfortunately, we did know, we did acknowledge, and we did commit. Even if the commitment wasn't legal and contractual, it's a commitment nonetheless, and we broke it.

Too much, too late

Think this doesn't happen? You are so wrong. We break our commitments all the time. It's amazing that we still have customers. Our salespeople talk to customers and tell them about our plans. Our consultants visit customers and say they'll work with product teams to enable certain solutions. Our marketing and product planning people run focus groups and tell customers, "We're working on it."

> **Eric Aside**   When I say, "We break our commitments all the time," I mean we fall short of the ideal. We deliver what the customer requested but not what they really wanted or needed. Customers don't know what they want till they see it. That's why many Agile methods focus on iterative customer feedback. I use the word "commitment" because it has strong connotations for Microsoft employees. It is too easy to let "little" problems persist in our products, yet it's those little problems that cause big headaches for customers and I want engineers to feel that.

And we do work on it. Market opportunities drive our product plans and visions. But we don't close the loop with customers until it's too late. Heaven forbid that when a customer clicks a button in a working product, we should have time to rethink what we've done. Heck, most of the time we've already gotten past code complete before customers touch the product.

> **Eric Aside**   Let me promote betas and technical previews here, since I failed to mention them in the original column (a significant oversight). Most Microsoft products use betas, but only one or two and often late in the development cycle. However, a number of products are starting to use technical previews and betas early and often—a practice I adore.

In fact, we're getting really good at closing the loop with customers *after* we ship. Watson and SQM tell us all about the horrible experiences our customers are having with our shipped products. It's a phenomenal step forward. We fix the bugs and ship again three months or three years later, and Watson can show us if the annoying problems are gone.

> **Eric Aside**   *Watson* is the internal name for the functionality behind the Send Error Report dialog box you see when an application running on Microsoft Windows crashes. (Always send it; we truly pay attention.) *SQM* is the internal name for the technology behind customer experience improvement programs for MSN, Office, Windows Vista, and other products, which anonymously aggregate customer usage patterns and experiences. (Please join when you install our software; it lets us know what works and what doesn't.)

But what about the problems that cause us to break our commitments, throttle our business opportunities, and shred what little trust we still have with our customers? How do we detect those before we ship? How do we prevent those from happening?

Agile delusions

By now the Agile fanatics out there are screaming, "Use Agile methods!" Yeah, well try meeting weekly or monthly with 100 million customers. It's not as easy as it looks. I'm not saying it's a bad concept, I'm saying you're hallucinating.

Sure, you can have the PM or product planner stand in for the 100 million customers, but the chances of them representing all those customers accurately are similar to you winning the lottery. It happens, a lot of people play that game, but you don't want to build your business or your retirement on those odds.

You need a direct connection back to the customer that closes the loop, like the connection we have with Watson. Any code you write should map back to a specific customer request, market opportunity, business need (like TwC), or customer issue (like a Watson bucket). That way, if a specific question comes up or you want regular feedback on your progress, you know who of the 100 million customers to call.

> **Eric Aside**   In fact, we don't have a direct connection back to the customer with Watson—the information we get is anonymous and aggregated. What we do have is a direct connection to the customer's problem. Each "Watson bucket" represents and stores a customer issue that thousands, sometimes millions of customers have experienced. So we don't know who to "call" with a Watson issue, but we can figure out what their problem was. Trustworthy Computing (TwC)—the Microsoft initiative on security, privacy, reliability, and sound business practices—has produced tremendous gains for our customers from Watson data.

Retracing your steps

So how can you tie a specific customer request to a line of code? For bugs, we've come close to doing this, but what about feature development? To figure this out, you must retrace your steps:

- Why are you writing that code? What was the requirement or feature?

- Where did that requirement or feature come from? What was the customer scenario?

- Where did that customer scenario come from? What was the market opportunity or customer engagement?

- Who wrote that market opportunity or ran that customer engagement? What is her e-mail alias?

If you can't trace the work back to a customer, then you're hopelessly caught up in guesswork about what the customer really wanted. Traceability is the key to any hope of satisfying our customers.

There's more where that came from

But that's just the beginning. Like all great pivot points, traceability resolves far more than the immediate need of a relevant customer contact:

- Traceability allows our customers to check on the status of their issues and solutions. Customers can do this somewhat today when they check the status of an error or crash because we now have backward traceability, from servicing to product development. Forward traceability, from product definition to product development, is rewarding for us and for customers.

- Traceability helps us prioritize and make tradeoffs, as well as get the features right. Because traceability can connect us with the business impact of our changes, we can intelligently decide the appropriate number of resources to apply to a feature or change.

- Traceability helps us architect solutions, determine dependencies, and organize projects. This is the most unexpected advantage to me. With traceability, you can know what customer scenarios drove what feature development. So you can know how features are related. This determines the right architecture and dependencies, and with them, the appropriate way to organize the project. Amazing.

Of course, without traceability, the customers have no idea if their needs will be met and when; the product group has no idea what the real business impact will be, and therefore can only guess at tradeoffs; and each group has no idea why they need one feature or another and how they depend on each other. So our lives become an intertwined chaotic catastrophe.

> **Eric Aside**   Again, I'm overstating the problem for effect, but I'm not overstating the benefits of traceability. I admit it openly. I'm in love with traceability.

The right tool for the job

So how do you get traceability? Ideally, we'd have a tool that traces scenarios and requirements the same way we track bugs and crashes:

- Salespeople and consultants could use the tool to document customer requirements, scenarios, and commitments.

- Marketing people and product planners could use the tool to submit market opportunities, link them to customer engagements, and define key cross-product scenarios.

- Product planners and PMs could use the tool to consolidate requirements; track duplicates; link related scenarios across products; and draft product-level scenarios, requirements, and feature specs.

- Product groups could use the tool to triage feature requests and track their progress through design and implementation.

- Test teams could relate test cases and bugs to scenarios so that the team could easily see the impact of issues.

- The originators of customer requirements could track progress on their requests, be contacted by product teams to clarify issues or contribute feedback, or contact product teams to update requirements when situations change.

Duct tape and baling wire

Some groups are actually trying to use Product Studio for traceability, but it's not the full solution yet. Until we have the right tools in place, there are still ways to trace customer requirements and scenarios throughout your entire design:

> **Eric Aside**   Product Studio is our internal work item tracking database. We productized it as part of Microsoft Visual Studio Team System.

- When you write a market opportunity document, link to the related customer engagement documents and ensure those documents have contact information. Include your own contact information in the market opportunity document as well.

- When you create a high-level scenario, link to the related market opportunities and customer engagements, and again include your contact information.

- When you write a feature spec, requirements list, or product scenario, link to the related high-level scenarios, requirements, market opportunities, and customer engagements. Be specific about which documents relate to which features—don't just create a laundry list.

- When you create design documents, link to the specs and other supporting documents. Again, don't create one long list of references—link to specific information as much as possible. You may even want to pull out specific contacts.

- When you are making tradeoffs or reviewing work, trace all the way back through the links to the people who know. Contact the true source.

Customer satisfaction

Today, we run our business like a child's game of "telephone." Each person tells the next what he thought the customer said she wanted. Each step along the way twists and distorts the message. By the time we ship, the customer doesn't even recognize what she asked for. (This may remind you of the classic cartoon in which the customer wants a tire swing hung from a tree, but instead gets a tree on stilts with a hole in the middle.)

As the product changes and develops, you need to check back with customers to ensure that you're making the right decisions. Equally important is the ability for customers to check with you whenever their requirements or scenarios change. Without a closed loop, this just isn't possible.

Traceability closes the loop, but you have to be aware of what to do and remain diligent. Any breakdown along the way risks breaking a commitment. But getting it right means getting the customer just what he needed every time. And that is a reward well worth the effort.

March 1, 2006: "The Agile bullet"

I'm having a tough time with a decision; maybe you can help. I can't quite decide who is more nauseating: people who use "Agile" methods and wonder why Microsoft can't adopt Agile across the company, solving every ill we face; or people who think the Agile fad amounts to retreaded foolishness preached by ignorant academics to free developers from any sense of responsibility. It's a toss-up; I get the same squeamish feelings in my gut listening to either of them.

> **Eric Aside**   This is one of my favorite columns because of the overwhelming love-hate reaction it evoked, often from the same person. Though imperfect, it's a fairly balanced overview of the topic.

Let's get two things straight right now:

- If you think Agile methods fix all that is wrong with how we build products, you are, in fact, a fool. Employing thousands of people to build highly complex and deeply integrated software that hundreds of millions of customers depend on is hard. No one in the world, including those clever folks in the Agile Alliance, knows as much about the task as we do. Not everything we are doing is wrong, and not everything Agile professes is right for our needs.

- If you are an anti-Agile curmudgeon who thinks Scrum is an acronym for a System of Clueless Reckless Untested Methods, you are as much a fool and just as ignorant. Dismissing anything thoughtlessly for whatever reason is prejudicial and unprofessional. Grassroots movements, like Agile, are always grounded in some fundamental truths that can be used to benefit our teams and customers. Those notions may not always fit our business directly, but fundamental truths have a way of applying themselves to any situation when you stop to understand them.

> **Eric Aside**   Agile has really been a grassroots effort at Microsoft, led by a wide collection of individuals and small teams throughout the company.

It's time to expel the myths around Agile methods and explain how to use the innovative thinking behind these methods to our advantage.

Enemy of the truth

First, let's break down the Agile myths…

- **Myth #1: Agile = eXtreme Programming (pair programming, Scrum, Test-Driven Development, user stories, or some other Agile method).**   Agile methods are actually a collection of software development practices that share a common set of defining principles but are otherwise unrelated and at times contradictory. You can learn more about what Agile really is from the Agile Alliance.

- **Myth #2: Agile methods can't work for large groups.**   This statement is absurd. Agile is a collection of disparate methods. Some of those methods won't work for large groups, some will, and some can if you get creative. You have to study the specific method in question before jumping to inane conclusions.

- **Myth #3: Agile methods can work for large groups.**   The Agile philosophy values "customer collaboration over contract negotiation" and "responding to change over following a plan." Customer collaboration is tough with over 100 million customers. Contract negotiation is essential to manage cross-team dependencies. (See "My way or the highway" in Chapter 8.) Following a plan is required for business commitments because partners get touchy when millions of dollars are involved. Applying Agile methods to large-scale projects requires you to be flexible and creative to deal with these issues.

■ **Myth #4: Agile means no documentation.**   The Agile philosophy values "working software over comprehensive documentation." Many Agile zealots read this and say, "Yay, no documentation!" If you think the world ends where your hallway ends, you don't deserve a cut of revenue generated beyond your walls. The Agile philosophy states, "While there is value in the items on the right, we value the items on the left more." In other words, working software is valued more than documentation, but essential documentation is still valuable for customers, partners, and cross-group dependencies.

■ **Myth #5: Agile means no up-front design.**   The Agile philosophy values "responding to change over following a plan." Many Agile zealots misinterpret this to mean, "No need to think or plan; the design will just emerge!" Emerge from what—a radioactive sewage dump? The point is to value responding to change over taking your original plans too seriously—it's not to jump off a cliff and see what happens next.

■ **Myth #6: Agile means no individual accountability.**   The Agile philosophy values "individuals and interactions over processes and tools" and "responding to change over following a plan." Many terrified managers think this means zero accountability. In fact, Agile has an interesting twist in this area. Agile makes the individual accountable to the team and the team accountable to management. Accountability is strongly emphasized, but the extra level of indirection allows Agile teams to be more efficient, resilient, and...well,... agile.

■ **Myth #7: Scrum is an acronym.**   This is a silly myth, but it drives me crazy. Scrum is one of the best-known and most widely practiced Agile methods, but it is not an acronym. Scrum is named after the rugby term that describes when the teams get together, arms latched in a circle, trying to obtain possession of the ball. It also is the name of the daily standup meeting used by Scrum teams. At Microsoft, we've been using a form of Scrum for decades—well before the term existed. It is one of the simplest Agile methods and the closest to what many Microsoft teams already practice. More on Scrum later.

Get the rules straightened out

Talking about Agile in the abstract makes for entertaining debate, but applying it is where the action is. Because we've established that Agile is actually a collection of software development practices, the question remains, "Which ones work well in large-scale projects?" Many people have thought and written about this question—but many people don't write this column. Before I give my opinion, some ground rules...

- **No change for change's sake.**   If a team is already working well by all the measures the business cares about, there's no need to change. Change is costly no matter how nice the result might be. You should change only to eventually improve. So if no improvement is needed, no change is needed.

- **Don't get carried away.**   If change is needed, don't change everything at once. Have feature teams pick one or two improvements each and see how that goes. Not every team needs to change simultaneously, and not every team needs to change identically. Of course, if you are changing a central service, like the build system, then all teams will eventually need to adopt it. But even those kinds of changes can be either spread out or made transparent to individual teams. The idea is this: try a little, learn a little, and then try a little more.

- **Differentiate between the project level and the feature level.**   The biggest area where people get confused—particularly with Agile methods—is differentiating between the project level and the feature level. At the project level, you need firm dates and firm agreements between teams. At the feature level, you...well actually,...whatever. That's the bizarre idea many managers fail to understand—your team can hit whatever date you care to set; the question is only what features you end up including. As long as the project-level plan can be tracked and followed, your feature teams should choose whatever method allows them to be the most effective.

> **Eric Aside**   This is a power-packed paragraph. One caveat: groups generally work better when the small teams within them are using similar methods. The methods needn't be identical, but teams will work best together if they have the same pacing. Otherwise, coordination and communication get muddled between teams because they have different expectations around timing.

Ready for something different?

So you're thinking about trying Agile—or perhaps you just want to placate the Agile maniacs in your group with Scrum snacks to go with the hypnotic Kool-Aid the maniacs are drinking. What should you try, and how can you best integrate it into common practices? There are a large number of Agile methods, so I'll address only the most popular ones: Scrum, eXtreme Programming, Test-Driven Development, pair programming, user stories, refactoring, and continuous integration.

First, there are two methods that we've been using for more than a decade at Microsoft: refactoring and continuous integration. Refactoring is simply reorganizing your code without changing what it does. Refactoring is used to break up complex functions (spaghetti code) or to add new functionality to existing code—like changing a class that reads CSV files into an abstract class that could read CSV or XML files. Continuous integration is the philosophy of always integrating new code into regular, ideally daily, full builds so that everyone can test it.

Let the man speak

Next are user stories, which are like a combination of scenarios and one-page specs. The idea of user stories is to provide just enough information to be able to estimate what it would take to implement and test the functionality specified.

The difficulty with user stories is that they are supposed to be written by the user. Many Agile methods assume that the user can regularly hang around with the feature team. Unfortunately, that presents a problem when you've got 100 million users.

Like it or not, we need proxies for users. Groups like marketing, product planning, user experience, sales, and support can play that role. Their findings can be codified in value propositions and vision documents that draw from a broad collection of user research. However, as those broad visions and end-to-end scenarios are broken down, we can still use the concept of user stories at the feature level to provide just enough documentation to estimate the implementation and verification of a feature set.

You complete me

Pair programming involves two people sharing a desk and a keyboard and coding together. The idea is that as one person is typing, the other is seeing the bigger picture and catching suboptimal design or implementation. The pair switches off from time to time. While two heads are better than one, they also cost twice as much. I'd rather see the two heads be put to better use in design and code inspections. However, pair programming is great for getting people up to speed in new code bases by pairing developers familiar and unfamiliar with the code.

> **Eric Aside**   My team has since adopted pairing for creating new content in unfamiliar areas. It works extremely well.

Aside from refactoring and continuous integration, Test-Driven Development (TDD) and Scrum have proved to be the easiest and most effective agile methods applied at Microsoft. As I described in my column on Lean engineering (earlier in this chapter), in TDD you start with a class definition of functions or methods and then write unit tests for the public functions and methods before you write the code. It is an iterative procedure, in which you are writing only a few unit tests and a little code at a time. The technique is popular because it gives developers the unit test code coverage they need while producing a minimal, yet high-quality, implementation design.

It's also more fun to write the tests first. When you write the code first, the unit tests are a pain to retrofit and will only give you bad news—not exactly reinforcing. When you write unit tests first, it's easy to fit the code to the tests and you feel vindicated when tests pass.

> **Eric Aside**   While I agree with many practitioners that TDD's true purpose is exceptional implementation design, the benefits of positive reinforcement for unit testing cannot be overstated.

TDD can be used in conjunction with pair programming by having one developer write a few tests and the other implement enough code to make the tests pass, switching off from time to time. Finally, TDD gives developers a clear sense of when they are done with the implementation: when all requirements have tests and those tests pass.

A bit extreme

eXtreme Programming is a whole development methodology. It combines user stories, pair programming, TDD, refactoring, continuous integration, and a bunch of other practices into a coherent set. It is ideally applied by small teams working closely with their customers.

eXtreme Programming relies a great deal on team knowledge and direct customer interaction, using almost no documentation. This is great if your team is isolated and your customers are down the hall, but that's not exactly common at Microsoft. Our situation would be tragic if not for the billions of dollars we earn every year. However, as I've already mentioned, many of the individual methods used within eXtreme Programming apply nicely to our product development.

Are you ready for some rugby!

The last and perhaps most misunderstood Agile method I'll cover is Scrum. Aside from people confusing Scrum with eXtreme Programming (which doesn't really use Scrum) or thinking that Agile equals Scrum (huh?), the most bewildering part of Scrum is all the strange terms associated with it: Scrum Masters, backlogs, burn-downs, sprints, and even pigs and chickens. It's enough to scare any manager away. Big mistake.

For better or worse, Scrum was invented by a person who enjoys funny names and stories. The practice itself is neither complicated nor contentious. So, aside from refactoring and continuous integration, Scrum is the closest Agile method to what we've been doing internally for years, with a few significant improvements.

Let's start by mapping some of the confusing terms. Scrums are daily stand-up meetings, Scrum Masters are feature team organizers, backlogs are feature or work item lists, burn-downs are graphs of remaining work, sprints are mini milestones, and pigs and chickens are entrepreneurial farm animals (long story, cute joke).

None of these concepts are new, but Scrum does introduce some big improvements:

- The daily stand-up meetings in Scrum are highly organized and collect useful data. The team organizer (Scrum Master) simply asks all the team members what they accomplished since yesterday (and how long it took), what they are working on until tomorrow (and how much is left to do), and what's impeding progress.

> **Eric Aside**   Tracking how long it took is my team's small contribution to Scrum at Microsoft. By adding this information to the burn-down data (how much is left to do), you can produce fantastic cumulative flow diagrams, measure time on task and work in progress, and better estimate team capacity. Typical time on task is around 42% for production teams; 30% for teams focused on communication—like mine—and as much as 60% for co-located feature teams.

- The data collected at Scrums is entered into a spreadsheet or database. From the spreadsheet, you can analyze time on task, completion dates, work in progress, plan changes, and a whole host of project issues. One of the most popular graphs is a burn-down chart that plots time vs. total work remaining.

> **Online materials**   Sprint Backlog (SprintBacklogExample.xls; SprintBacklogTemplate.xlt)

- The Scrum Master is an independent force on the team. It's best if he or she isn't even part of the group, but often that's not realistic. The Scrum Master has permission to keep meetings short and cut through the crud.

- The feature list or schedule is called the *Product Backlog,* and the work item list or schedule is called the *Sprint Backlog.* By keeping these two lists separate, management can focus on the work they want done (the Product Backlog) while the team focuses on the work at hand (the Sprint Backlog). Typically once a week, the Scrum Master meets with management (for example, at the weekly lead's meeting) and updates status, ensuring everything stays on track.

> **Online materials**   Product Backlog (ProductBacklogExample.xls; ProductBacklog-Template.xlt) and Sprint Backlog (SprintBacklogExample.xls; SprintBacklogTemplate.xlt)

- Sprints, the mini milestones, are fixed in length. They are over when the specified number of days is over—typically around 30 days.

- After every sprint, the feature team reviews its work with management (nice change, huh?); discusses what went well and improvements for the next sprint (a wee bit better than waiting a year or decade until the post-ship postmortem); and plans and re-estimates the work items for its next sprint (the plan and estimates changed? No way!).

By using daily, weekly, and monthly feedback mechanisms, Scrum allows teams to work efficiently and resiliently in a changing environment. By collecting a little key data, Scrum allows teams and management to know how teams are operating and to spot issues before they become problems. By separating the feature list owned by management from the work item list owned by the feature team, Scrum allows teams to direct themselves and stay focused. It drives accountability to each member within the team and to management outside the team.

The more you know

Not all Agile methods are for everyone, and many won't work on big Microsoft projects. But Scrum, Test-Driven Development, refactoring, and continuous integration are being used by many Microsoft teams with great effects. Pair programming and user stories are being applied to a lesser degree, but they can be effective in the right situations. As long as you don't get carried away and start forcing Agile down your team's throat, there's a great deal to be gained by applying these methods.

> **Eric Aside**   Managers have forced methodology changes down engineers' throats almost everywhere I've been employed. It never works, even for something popular like Scrum. Managers can suggest, support, and subsidize behavioral change, but they should never coerce it.

To learn more, search for Agile methods on our internal network or on the Web. Also watch for new courses on Agile methods coming in spring 2006. If everything is going great on your team, then don't change a thing. But if you'd like to see a little higher quality or better feature-team project management, you owe it to yourself to take some antacid and give Agile a try.

Chapter 3
Inefficiency Eradicated

In this chapter:

July 1, 2001: "Late specs: Fact of life or genetic defect?" 44

June 1, 2002: "Idle hands" 46

June 1, 2004: "The day we met" 50

July 1, 2006: "Stop writing specs, co-located feature crews" 53

February 1, 2007: "Bad specs: Who is to blame?"...........................56

As I described in "Lean: More than good pastrami" in Chapter 2, waste and evil are close companions in the work environment. Nowhere is that more evident than in group communications, a popular target of these columns, or in the proper use of unstructured time between projects. These areas affect whole teams, not just individuals, so their impact is multiplied.

Specification documents (specs) and meetings hold a special place of honor in my museum of horrors. I guess that's because engineers spend so much time in meetings, often talking about specs. While I'd love to simply banish both from the world as we know it, meetings and specs do serve a purpose. The trick is to focus on that purpose and slice away all the excess.

In this chapter, I. M. Wright describes strategies for eliminating common inefficiencies. The first column deals with last-minute spec changes. The second tackles appropriate use of slack time in between projects. The third focuses on minimizing meeting malaise. The last two columns try to eliminate specs entirely and, if that isn't feasible, at least make them shorter and simpler.

Other columns have plenty more to say about group communications—everything from cross-team negotiation to dealing with nontechnical folks. Still others talk about actions individuals can take to improve their lot. But this set strikes at the core of what groups can do to make the best use of their limited time.

—Eric

July 1, 2001: "Late specs: Fact of life or genetic defect?"

You've hit code complete, you're burning the bugs, when what arrives in your Inbox? Look, oh joy, it's a new spec! Punt it, right? But wait, it's a key feature that you figured was spec-less, or as we often like to say, "The code is the spec."

> **Eric Aside**   A feature is code complete when the developer believes all the code necessary to implement the feature has been checked into source control. Often this is a judgment call, but on better teams it's actually measured based on quality criteria (at which point it's often called "feature complete").

Of course, test is now furious because they didn't get the spec earlier and feel "out of the loop," it's too late, the code doesn't match, and they haven't tested it. Dev is upset because feature work was supposed to be finished, test is now mad at them for coding the "wrong" thing, there's a ton of rework to do, and what's worse, dev has been caught coding an improperly documented feature. It gets even more pleasant as people argue over the new spec, find holes, make changes, and basically churn the code to death at the very time it should be stabilizing.

For every change, churn, churn, churn

An extreme example, perhaps, but it's happened, probably more than once. Even if they aren't that late, specs often are incomplete or aren't reviewed and inspected in time for dev to start work.

So what happens? Churn, and lots of it. Dev starts coding too early. The spec has issues, so the code has issues. Someone points these out, ad hoc meetings are held, someone gets left out, the code is reworked, whoever was left out finds something else wrong, there are more ad hoc meetings, and so it goes.

What can be done about this? Some folks might say, "PMs are scum, persecute them till they produce." Even for me, that seems harsh. Specs come in late; it's a fact of life. The question is how you deal with it. I've seen a few different approaches.

> **Eric Aside**   I know eXtreme Programming buffs out there are yelling, "Get a room!" (a team room). I make the same argument in a later column, "Stop writing specs, co-located feature crews." However, Microsoft is a fairly diverse environment. Not every team can co-locate, and dependencies often make documentation a must, so we need more than one solution.

Hallway meetings

The first approach is the hallway meeting. A dev finds holes in the currently available spec and sees a PM passing by. A hallway meeting commences; some issues are worked out. The dev goes happily back to her desk thinking she now knows the right thing to do. The PM goes back to his office thinking the code will reflect what he wanted. Maybe they are thinking the same thing, maybe not. Maybe test and ops would agree with the solution, maybe not. Maybe they thought of everything, maybe they didn't. Maybe this is the best way to handle changes, maybe monkeys will fly out of my... well, you get the idea.

Committee meetings

A second approach is the committee meeting. It goes by other names on other teams, but it's basically a leads' meeting to discuss spec changes. Often they're held on a regular basis, and the group of leads gets together to talk about holes or problem areas in the specs and work out solutions as a group. The lead PM writes up the results and mails them out to the whole team.

The good news: committee meetings include the right folks, come to final decisions, and then document and communicate those decisions to the team. The bad news: committee meetings are a frigging nightmare. They are long, painful, and exhausting. They use up huge cycles of critical resources. They block progress and form the worst kind of bottleneck—self-inflicted and self-perpetuating.

Spec change requests

The approach I like most is the spec change request (SCR), also known as a design change request (DCR) with a twist. It's a combination of the committee meeting and hallway meeting with a few key differences. You start with an idea of how you'd like to change or add to a spec. Maybe you arrived at the idea on your own, maybe through a hallway conversation, maybe through a leads' meeting.

Regardless of whether you're the PM, dev, test, or ops, you write up the idea in an e-mail with the subject line "SCR: *<affected spec>* - *<short description of change>*." You end the e-mail with these words in bold, "**Unless there are strong objections, this is now considered spec.**" Then you send it to the PM, dev, test, and ops folks who are most directly affected by the change. A few days later, after adding whatever alterations are suggested by peers, you send it to the rest of the team and track it with other SCRs in RAID and/or a public folder.

The key is that the change is documented and reviewed but does not block progress. Objections are almost always the exception, not the rule. The dev can proceed whenever she likes, trading risk of objections against time. Typically, a dev waits till the SCR is sent to the full team after the initial alterations.

Prevention is the best cure

Of course, the best thing is for a spec not to be late in the first place or at least for it not to blindside you. That's where T-I-M-E Charting can help. In T-I-M-E Charting, the first spec lays out the design of the entire project. Not simply a requirements document, not a set of mini-specs, but a high-level spec of the project much like a high-level architecture document a dev lead might write. It should lay out what functions and UI the project will have and how they will act together, leaving details for later specs. All future specs and features should be referred to by the first high-level spec.

Now dev, test, and ops, can make plans that account for all future features. They can make a better integrated product that feels smoother to the user. PMs can also use the first spec to schedule the rest of the specs, hitting the high-priority ones first, without worrying about missing something or surprising someone. It's an idea whose T-I-M-E has come (couldn't resist).

> **Eric Aside**   Totally Inclusive Mutually Exclusive (T-I-M-E) Charting, from Donald Wood, never quite caught on in the form that a peer of mine, Rick Andrews, originally envisioned it. However, value propositions, vision documents, cross-product scenarios, and thoughtfully designed prototypes now serve the same purpose.

June 1, 2002: "Idle hands"

Your dev team hit zero bug bounce (ZBB) two weeks ago, and suddenly you realize—you've hit a lull. Any dev who has hit ZBB on a box product knows about the lull. If your team is on Internet time, feel free to stop reading now. (Wait a minute, where did you find the time to read that first sentence? Get back to work!)

> **Eric Aside**   Zero bug bounce (ZBB) describes the first moment in a project when all features are complete and every work item is resolved. This moment rarely lasts. Often within an hour a new issue arises through extended system testing, and the team goes back to work. Nevertheless, ZBB means the end is predictably within sight.

ZBB marks the team shift from being blocked by dev to being blocked by test. (Being blocked by PM has no transition.) After handling the initial wave of new bugs the first couple of weeks after shipping, most dev teams enter "hurry up and wait" mode, pouncing on new bugs when they arrive and otherwise just wondering what to do.

The crazy, scary part is that the lull can sometimes last from ZBB until the first milestone of the next version. That could be months on big projects! A dev manager's hands are always full, so it's easy to forget that two-thirds of the team members are idle, and you know what they say about idle hands—well, it's not good.

Baby did a bad bad thing

Here are a few very bad things that idle devs often do:

- **Poach bugs.**   After ZBB, your team should be in lockdown, which means that all bugs go through triage before a fix is even considered. Idle devs sometimes sit by their desks hitting F5 on Raid (now Product Studio) waiting for a bug to appear. When they don't see one, they check the active bugs headed for triage, find a juicy one, and start digging. Before you know it, they've got a fix and are looking to sneak it in. That's poaching, and no self-respecting dev should do it.

> **Eric Aside**   In software engineering, bugs have traditionally meant mistakes in the code. However, internally we use the term "bug" to refer to anything we want to add, delete, or change about the product. Externally, people generally call these "work items," some of which may be code mistakes. I prefer the term "work item" so that I know which "bugs" are really bugs.

Who knows if the triage team will accept that bug? Who knows if the dev fixed the right bug, as opposed to a larger or smaller related bug? Investigate potential showstoppers—sure. Poach—never.

- **Fix bugs that are not logged.**   Okay, a bug made it through triage and you are fixing it. You notice other bugs nearby, often related to the original. No one has logged them yet, but what the heck. There you are in the code; the bugs are right in front of you. Why not take care of them now, when the getting is good? Ahhhhhhhhhhh!!!!! Stop right there!

Your team performs code reviews to prevent this evil nonsense. In these days of trust-worthy computing, the team should code review every check-in throughout the project. During lockdown, you should code review every change with three sets of eyes (the dev and two other people). As for the other bugs that you find—log, triage, and track them.

> **Eric Aside**   There's a great Calvin and Hobbes cartoon in which Calvin magnanimously opens the front door to let out a fly, only to allow three more back inside in the process. That's why you study and triage every bug toward the end of a project. Once my team changed the value of a single parameter a month before we released. A week later testers across the company noticed that all applications froze whenever you opened the CD tray. Eventually, we traced it back to the seemingly innocuous parameter, and reverted the change. You just never know.

■ **Fix postponed bugs.**   Naturally, you shouldn't be fixing postponed bugs before RTM, but should you fix them while planning the next version? Uh, no. During the project, the team judges which bugs will have the most impact on our customers and must be fixed—but you have no way of verifying that these were the correct choices until you ship. After release, you no longer have to guess. Product Support Services (PSS), Watson, and Microsoft Consulting Services (MCS) will tell you. Candidly. Use the postponed bugs as a reference to understand why these bugs weren't fixed originally. But don't second-guess your real customers. Go to the source to fix the bugs that are really affecting your users.

■ **Rewrite "yucky" code.**   Devs hate "yucky" code. It's embarrassing, unreadable, and unmaintainable. So when they have some extra time on their hands, devs will often say to themselves, "Gee, I don't have a spec, so I can't write anything new. How about I rewrite that yucky code I hate instead." They know that they could do better given a second chance, and they will. Devs will write much better code the second time, and more clearly, with far fewer bugs than the first time they wrote it.

Unfortunately, the rewrite will actually have more bugs than the current yucky code has today because of all the months, even years, of testing and fixes that the yucky code received after it was first written.

Sometimes a rewrite is necessary to make the code more performant, scalable, reliable, secure, or adaptable to new technology. In that case, make the rewrite a feature, and then spec and schedule it like you would any other feature. Otherwise, don't be a fool and regress a ton of nasty bugs while adding no value to your customers.

> **Eric Aside**   This goes for refactoring too, as much as I hate to say it. Even if the refactoring is computer generated, you just never know. This doesn't mean you shouldn't refactor or rewrite code, regularly. It means you shouldn't do so arbitrarily. Decide and commit to it as a team, be sure sufficient unit tests are in place to minimize the introduction of new bugs, and do it right.

■ **Wage wars over coding style.**   Talk about the ultimate dev team time suck—arguing over white space, braces, and Hungarian have to be in the top five. Keep this in mind: using a consistent coding style has great benefits to the maintainability and quality of your code base, but the specific style your team chooses makes little difference. You are the dev manager; pick one and go with it. Who said this was a democracy?

Tell me what I must do

Enough of the dark side of idle time. What can your dev team focus on that's constructive during quiet times?

Naturally, your test team will insist that devs find bugs during the time before RTM, but most devs are terrible at finding bugs, even in someone else's code. Your PM team will insist that devs spend all their time reading and reviewing specs after RTM, but that won't keep a dev team happy, engaged, and motivated.

So what can a dev do during the lull? Here are a few ideas:

- **Analyze your bugs.**   Look for patterns in the bugs that your team fixed during the past product cycle. What were the common mistakes for individuals and for the team? What can each member of the team focus on next time to produce a better product?

- **Write tools for your group.**   While devs aren't often great at finding bugs, they are pretty terrific at writing tools to help find bugs. They can also write tools to smooth out processes, like check-in, setup, build, and prop. Instrumenting code or writing a good harness can go a long way toward promoting good feelings with the test team. Naturally, you should check the Toolbox Web site first to see if a tool that meets your needs already exists.

- **Make your PM happy by working on prototypes of design ideas.**   Writing prototypes is great; just don't write them in your usual code base. Try a different language or at least a separate build. The big mistake with making prototypes within the normal code base is that PMs and upper managers start thinking that the code is almost ready to ship, when in fact there are often all kinds of issues with localizing, platform dependence, logo issues, roaming, performance, security, and compatibility. Confusing prototypes with shipping code can mess up schedules as well as expectations. In contrast, writing a prototype in another language can be a great learning experience. Speaking of which...

> **Eric Aside**   It's been said before but bears repeating, "Don't ship prototype code." It doesn't save time, it costs time. Just don't do it. Prototypes are for learning—that's all. In addition to writing prototypes in another language, I used to hook the escape key to an abort call. That way, if my boss ever got too excited watching a demo, I'd hit the escape key, watch it crash, and then point out, "Of course, it's not exactly ready to ship."

- **Learn new technologies or skills.**   Folks always complain that they don't have enough time to learn new technologies or skills and that they can't get the training they need to move up. Well, the quiet times are perfect for this. Don't let the opportunity pass you by.

- **Talk to research.**   Right after ZBB is the perfect time to talk to the research team. It's early enough to adopt some new technology and quiet enough to learn about it and figure out what you can use. By the time you ship and begin planning the next release, you could have a prototype ready with all the risks resolved and really wow your team. In addition, you and your research contact can plan new areas of research work that will be ready for future products. This is so valuable and easy to do.

- **Write a patent disclosure or white paper.**   When else do you have the time to reflect and write about what you've done? If a dev on your team has come up with a novel idea that added a nice or significant touch to your product, then have your dev write a patent disclosure. It's easy, short, and a huge morale boost. Go to the Patent Group home page for more details. If you want to document information or share an idea with other teams, write a white paper. It's relatively easy to do and can bring respect and influence to the author and your team.

- **Reflect on your career.**   Last but not least, these quiet dev times are ideal for examining your career status. Are you where you want to be? Is your career moving in the right direction? Are you ready for a new challenge? What do you need to do to stay engaged and motivated? If upon reflection you feel that you need to make a change, the earlier you put the wheels in motion, the better off you'll be.

Waste not, want not

Far too frequently, time spent between versions is wasted needlessly, often on tasks that harm instead of help. With just a little thought and consideration, your dev team can be improving themselves, the product, their outlook, and the entire group without getting into any mischief. Don't pass up this opportunity for you and your team. Plan for your downtime and keep the momentum moving forward.

June 1, 2004: "The day we met"

Quit wasting my time. Would you, could you, PLEASE quit wasting my time? Maybe if I jump across the table and duct tape your mouth shut, I could take action instead of sitting here incredulously while you incinerate 60 minutes of my life. How does calling a meeting give people license to act like you're worthless? If time is money, most meetings are a market collapse. I am so tired of people who could sooner drive a bus off a cliff than run a decent meeting.

Well I'm not going to take it any more. If you force me into a meeting room, be prepared for me to call you on any stunts you try to pull. You waste my time, and I'll ensure yours gets torched with it. Don't like it? Don't test me. What am I going to call you on? Listen up, 'cause here it comes....

Why are we here?

The first question I'll interrupt your self-serving soirée with is, "Why are we here?" What was the point of us getting together? Was there a reason? If you haven't made that reason clear to everyone, we all probably think it's something different and will chase our tails for the allotted time, accomplishing nothing. I don't know—maybe send an agenda and the documents that we're going to discuss in advance? Thanks.

If you did make the point of the meeting clear, I'm probably reminding you to stick to the point! I don't care if there are 50 other meetings with 50 other decisions to make, topics to cover, or bits of information to share. I'm in this meeting now, and I darn well want to at least bury this one. If someone wants to talk about something else, let him put on his own show after we're done.

> **Eric Aside**   How do you politely cut off someone trying to switch topics? My favorite approach is to say, "Let's get closure on this topic first, then we'll focus on your topic." Typically, after you close on the first topic everyone will want to leave. The interrupter will have to schedule a separate meeting with the right people (much better). Should the interrupter insist that closure on his topic is necessary first, discuss why that is the case (which actually focuses on the original topic). If the interrupter is right, your meeting is premature and should be rescheduled. No one will mind leaving.

What are we trying to do?

My next question will be, "What are we trying to do?"

- **Are we trying to reach a decision?**   Great, let's decide and skip the idea generation, status checks, and rumor mill.

- **Are we trying to share information (like a status meeting)?**   Great, then get through the information list and stop trying to make decisions or solve problems.

- **Are we trying to generate ideas?**   Great, then capture everyone's ideas and stop critiquing or judging what's possible. At the end, pick the best idea and be done with it.

The point is that combination meetings are ineffective and wasteful. Know why you are all there and what you are trying to accomplish. If you need to switch contexts, be deliberate about it, and let everyone know that the rules have changed. Otherwise, you'll waste everyone's time, spin endlessly, and eventually have to meet again. When you do, don't bother inviting me; I'm not coming.

> **Eric Aside**   A common special case of this issue is bringing up design issues at Scrum meetings. Scrum meetings are about sharing information, not generating ideas or making decisions. Nothing derails a Scrum meeting like a design discussion. However, because design discussions are worthwhile, we keep a list of discussion topics on the whiteboard during Scrum. When the Scrum meeting is complete, whoever wants to can stay and participate in the design meeting.

Why are they here?

Okay, so we've got a reason for meeting and we know what we're doing. Now why are *they* here? You know—the people who don't belong here. The people who are asking the unnecessary questions, who are repeating other people's points, who have to speak up just to say they agree. Why are those people here?

The length of a meeting is directly proportional to the number attending, and I doubt that the relationship is linear. You should invite only those who NEED to be there.

- **Trying to reach a decision?**   Invite the decision makers. Everyone else can find out later via e-mail. All the necessary decision makers can't attend? Cancel the meeting. NOW! Otherwise, you'll have to recap the whole meeting again when everyone can attend.

- **Status meeting?**   Invite the people who will share their status. Everyone else can find out later via e-mail. Some status people can't make it? I guess they're slackers.

- **Brainstorming meeting?**   Invite a few creative, open-minded people who'll make the meeting successful. Everyone else can find out later via e-mail.

Sometimes you must invite a few others who are key to the meeting's success: facilitators, mediators, cheerleaders. But that's it. If too many others are signed up to attend, cancel the meeting. (You can tell how many people plan to attend because when folks accept a forwarded meeting, you receive the confirmation.)

Try booking a small room; it dissuades uninvited guests. Try scheduling the meeting for just 30 minutes—it makes folks show up on time and keeps the meeting moving. You can say it's a "working meeting" and even use information rights management (IRM) to prevent forwarding the appointment if necessary.

Why am I hearing this now?

For important topics, you don't want to surprise key players. No one likes to be rushed in making critical decisions, and no one wants to be uninformed about critical areas. If you need the meeting to go smoothly, talk to the key players beforehand. You can discover the issues, negotiate a compromise, and get everyone on the same page in advance. Then the meeting becomes a mere formality. This is a good practice for every decision meeting, but it is time-consuming. For critical decisions, it is a critical step.

What are the next steps?

So the meeting is done, finished, kaput, right? Wrong! Meetings are like Hollywood horror show zombies. They come back to life and eat those who remain. Determine the next steps, and document them in e-mail. That is the way to make dead meetings stay dead.

Address the e-mail to all attendees and cc: everyone affected by the outcome. Include a short meeting summary of the decisions made, information shared, or ideas generated. Then list the next steps specifying who does what, when. Now, finally you can move on in safety.

See, it's not so hard to respect people's time. Meetings are costly in so many ways. Of course, they are necessary for strong group communications. But if you run them, run them well. Everyone will appreciate it, and you'll get more done.

July 1, 2006: "Stop writing specs, co-located feature crews"

I'm not a Program Manager (PM). I've never been a PM. I'm not likely to ever become a PM. It's nothing personal against program managers. I've known great ones I count among my friends. I certainly have no right to tell PMs how to do their jobs.

That said, PMs should stop writing specs. Period. They are wasting my time; they are wasting my group's time; and they are wasting the company's time. You can almost hear the sound of quiet residual crunching as spec termites chew away at company and customer value. It makes me nauseous.

It's not just PMs though. Developers need to stop writing dev specs. Testers need to stop writing test specs. The madness must stop. The waste must stop. We must regain our senses and take back our productivity, along with our sanity.

> **Eric Aside**   This column was easily among my most contentious in terms of response. As you can see in the next paragraph, I guessed it would be. The biggest misunderstanding about my message was the difference between formal and informal documentation. I argue that co-located, cross-discipline teams need only informal documentation, like photos of whiteboards stored on a wiki with some minimal commentary. Teams divided by distance or discipline need formal documentation, like detailed specifications.

Have you lost your mind?

"Surely you can't be serious?" I hear my conscientious readers say. "You've been preaching quality (see "Where's the beef" in Chapter 5) and design (see "Resolved by design" in Chapter 6) for years. You've been telling devs not to act before they have the spec and not to code before they've thought through the design. Are you saying you were misguided, or even, perhaps, wrong?" No, of course not.

Feature teams must understand the user experience before they create it, and devs must understand the internal design enough to explain it with a straight face to peers before they implement it. But neither of those steps requires formal written documentation.

Why do we have formal written specs? Customers don't need them. Marketing and product planning groups don't need them. Even content publishers and product support get limited use from specs. So who needs these wanton wonders of waste? To find out, throw specs away and see who screams.

Therein lies a dilemma

If we no longer had specs, devs and testers would cry, "How am I supposed to know what the code should do?" Tell them to discuss it with PMs and they'd holler, "PMs don't just hang around my office all day. I need specs written down. I need to review them, change them, and update them."

Ah yes, there's the rub. Not that devs and testers need to review, change, and update specs, but that PMs don't hang around to discuss the user experience, implementation, and test strategy all day. Well, what if they did?

What if PMs stayed all day in the same open area surrounded by whiteboards with devs and testers who were working on the same feature set? Would we still need formal written specs? Wait, I hear more screaming.

Special needs

Without formal written specs, teams that depend on features from other teams would protest, "How are we supposed to use your code if we don't know how it works?" Good point. If PMs are hanging around the feature team all day, they can't also be on call with all the down-stream teams, and we can't fit everyone into the same team room. However, downstream teams don't need a spec—they need a mini-SDK, which component teams should be providing anyway, and which adds great value.

Without formal written specs, the compliance police would bark, "Where's the <insert your favorite bureaucratic suppository here> document?" Another good point. The compliance police keep us out of harm's way. It's an important if thankless job, and they often require formal written documentation to do it. However, the compliance police don't need a spec either. They need complete compliance documentation, which often has different information in a different form than a spec.

> **Eric Aside**   Who are these "compliance police"? They are regular engineers who focus on key areas Microsoft must ensure are correct in our products, such as security, privacy, world readiness (no inappropriate euphemisms or references), and compliance with all applicable laws and regulations. Examples of typical documentation they require include threat models (security), privacy statements, and licensing terms.

In both cases, you don't need formal written specs. Instead, you need specialized documentation that is easier to write because it's not open-ended.

I don't recall

So do we still need formal written specs? I can't remember all the cases, so let's recap:

- PMs spend their days in the team room discussing the user experience, implementation, and test strategy with the feature team.

- The team writes mini-SDKs for downstream teams.

- The team fills out required compliance documentation.

It's good that I wrote that down. Oh wait, that's a problem.

People are forgetful. You've got to write ideas down, particularly when you are constantly switching between projects. Naturally, if a feature takes months from start to finish you might even have people leave the team and lose the information entirely.

Stick to one thing

But what if you worked on only one feature at a time? Then it wouldn't take as long, and you wouldn't be switching between projects. There would be little chance of anyone leaving, and remembering ideas would be much easier. You'd just need to capture whatever was on the whiteboards with a digital camera and paste it into a wiki or Word document.

It's like having specs, only without the mind-numbing tedium. That leaves you more time to think and collaborate at the whiteboard, and less time at your desk pushing pixels and words around.

Okay, you keep the feature team in close quarters with lots of whiteboards. You work on one feature at a time till it's done, documenting your decisions with a camera. You write specially targeted documents that add value downstream. This sounds like Lean software development (which you can read more about in the article "Lean: More than good pastrami" in Chapter 2). Bingo! That's what you get when you cut out the waste.

You ready?

Very few teams could stop writing formal specs tomorrow. They haven't adopted the feature crew concept of working on one feature at a time from start to finish, and they aren't co-located in a team room with whiteboards.

However, that's starting to change. Groups are co-locating because it's faster and easier to get work done. Groups are forming feature crews because you get higher quality faster and leave behind less incomplete work. Take those trends, put them together, and you can kiss specs goodbye forever. It's more than a dream; it's a homecoming to simpler days, but with the wisdom gained by years of hard-fought experience.

February 1, 2007: "Bad specs: Who is to blame?"

Specs, by and large, are terrible. Not only PM specs, but dev and test specs too. By terrible, I mean difficult to write, difficult to use, and difficult to maintain. You know, terrible. They are also incomplete, poorly organized, and inadequately reviewed. They've always been this way and they aren't getting better.

I'd love to blame PMs for this, partly because I enjoy it, but mostly because they are the leading source of awful specs. However, the facts don't support blaming PMs. Everyone writes bad specs, not just PMs. Even PMs who occasionally write good specs, mostly write poor ones. And good specs are still difficult to write and maintain, regardless of who authors them.

If PMs aren't to blame for shoddy specs, who is? Management would be an easy target—another group I'd enjoy blaming. It's true that some organizations, like the Office division, traditionally produce better specs than others. So clearly management has a role. However, Office has changed management many times over the years, so the cause must be deeper than the people in charge.

It's a setup

It's clear that the blame falls squarely on the spec process—how we write specs and the tools we use to write them. The process is cumbersome, difficult, and tedious. The templates are long, intimidating, and complex to the point of being intractable. Basically, we've made writing good specs as hopeless as winning a marathon in a fur coat and flip-flops.

Anal anachronistic alarmists will say, "The spec process is absurdly dysfunctional for a reason. All template elements and process steps are needed to avoid past catastrophes." See, you never have to worry about too much bureaucracy from on high when there's plenty down low where it counts.

Dysfunctional processes always come from the best of intentions. The trouble is that the original goal and intent was lost somewhere along the way. Revive the goal and intent, and new and better ways to achieve it will present themselves.

> **Eric Aside**   I worked in Boeing research for five years. Not all, but most, of the bureaucracy there seemed to come from the top. I've been at Microsoft for 12 years. Not all, but most, of the bureaucracy here seems to come from the bottom. We are free to act independently at the lowest levels. Sometimes that means we're given enough rope to choke ourselves.

Communication breakdown

The goal of all PM, dev, and test specs is to communicate design and design decisions to people across time and location. We want to make that communication easy and robust, with plenty of feedback and quality checks.

In case you missed it, those were four separate requirements:

- Easy
- Robust
- Feedback
- Quality checks

Each requirement can be satisfied with a different solution. The approach, "We'll just add more sections to the spec to cover all requirements," is as idiotic as, "We'll just add more methods to the class to cover all requirements." Instead, let's take on the requirements one at a time.

Keep it simple and easy

The spec needs to be easy to write, understand, and maintain. It should use standard notation, like UML, for diagrams and common terminology for text. It shouldn't try to be too much or say too much.

The simpler the format the better. The generic spec template in the Engineering Excellence Handbook has 30 sections and three appendices. The superior Office spec template has 20 sections. Both are far too complex.

A spec needs to have three sections plus some metadata:

- **Requirements**   Why does the feature exist? (Tied to scenarios and personas.)
- **Design**   How does it work? (Pictures, animations, and diagrams are especially useful.)
- **Issues**   What were the decision points, risks, and tradeoffs? (For example, dependencies.)
- **Metadata**   Title, short description, author, feature team, priority, cost, and status.

That's it. The status metadata could be a workflow or checklist, but that's the limit of the complexity.

"But what about the threat model? What about the privacy statement? The instrumentation or the performance metrics?" I can hear you demanding. Get a grip on yourself. Those items are quality checks I'll talk about soon. The spec structure itself is simple, with no more or less than it needs. It's easy to write and easy to read.

Online materials	Spec template (Spec template.doc)

Make it robust

The spec needs to be robust. It must verifiably meet all the requirements, both functional requirements and quality requirements. "How?" you ask. What do you mean, "How?!?" How would you verify the requirements in the first place? You'd write a test, right? Well, that's how you write a robust spec. In the first section, when you list functional and quality requirements, you include the following:

Unique ID	Priority	Functional or quality	Short description	Related scenario(s)	Test(s) that verify the requirement has been met

If you can't specify a test to verify a requirement, then the requirement can't be met, so drop it. Can't drop it? Then rewrite the requirement till it's testable.

> **Eric Aside**   I believe there is a basic equivalence in solid designs between tests and requirements. Every requirement should have a test. Every test should stem from a requirement. This results in clear, verifiable requirements; more comprehensive tests; consistent completion criteria (all tests pass = all requirements met); and better designs because test-driven designs are naturally simpler, more cohesive, and more loosely coupled.

Get feedback

The more eyes that see a spec before it's implemented, the better it will be and the less rework it will require. You want feedback to be easy to get and easy to give. At the very least, put draft specs on SharePoint, using change tracking and version control. Even better, put drafts on a wiki or a whiteboard in the main area for the feature team.

How formal does your process, feedback, and change management need to be? As I discussed in a previous column ("Stop writing specs," earlier in this chapter), the degree of formality necessary depends on the bandwidth and immediacy of the communication. People working on the same feature at the same time in the same shared workspace can use very informal specs and processes. People working on different features at different times in different time zones must rely on highly formal specs and processes.

Regardless, you want the spec to be fluid till the team thinks it's ready. How will you know it's ready? It's ready when the spec passes inspection by the test team using the quality checks.

Check that quality is built in

Here is where our current specs go farthest off base. Instead of adding security, privacy, and a host of other issues as quality checks, groups add them as separate sections in the spec. This is a disaster, and here's why:

- Specs become bigger and far more complicated.
- Authors must duplicate information across sections.
- Bottom sections get little attention, causing serious quality gaps.
- Designs become incomprehensible because their description is spread across multiple sections.
- Mistakes and gaps are easy to miss because the whole picture doesn't exist in one place.
- Updates are nearly impossible because multiple sections are affected by the smallest change.

Instead, the quality checks that apply to every spec are kept in a list everyone can reference. The first few checks will be the same for every team:

- ✔ Are the requirements clear, complete, verifiable, and associated with valid scenarios?
- ✔ Does the design meet all requirements?
- ✔ Have all key design decisions been addressed and documented?

The next set of quality checks is also fairly basic:

✔ Have all terms been defined?	✔ Are there issues with compatibility?
✔ Are security concerns addressed?	✔ Are failures and error handling addressed?
✔ Are privacy concerns met?	✔ Are setup and upgrade issues covered?
✔ Is the UI fully accessible?	✔ Are maintenance issues addressed?
✔ Is it ready for globalization and localization?	✔ Are backup and restore issues met?
✔ Are response and performance expectations clear and measurable?	✔ Is there sufficient documentation for support to do troubleshooting?
✔ Has instrumentation and programmability been specified?	✔ Are there any potential issues that affect patching?

A team may also add quality checks for their product line or team that reflect particular quality issues they commonly face.

Online materials   Spec checklist (Spec checklist.doc)

The key is that the design section describes the feature completely, while the quality checks ensure nothing is missed. Yes, that means the "How" section could get pretty big to cover all the areas it needs. But those areas won't be rehashes of the feature specialized for each quality requirement (security for the dialog, privacy for the dialog, accessibility for the dialog).

Instead, the areas will be the feature's logical components (the API, the dialogs, the menus). Duplication is removed, each feature component is described as a whole, and all the quality requirements are incorporated into the design in context.

> **Eric Aside**   In an interesting and funny coincidence, the day after this column was published, Office simplified their spec template to a single design section and a published quality checklist. While I couldn't claim the credit for the change, I did feel vindicated.

What's the difference?

With all those checks and tests added, you might ask if I've simplified specs at all. Here are the big changes:

- The number of sections is reduced to three (Requirements, Design, and Issues).
- Designs are described completely in one section.
- All functional and quality requirements can be verified.

I've also talked about opportunities to make specs less formal and easier to understand.

Who's to blame for bad specs? We all are, but bad specs are mostly the result of bad habits and poor tools. By making a few small changes and using vastly simplified templates, we can improve our specs, our cross-group communication, and our cross-discipline relations. All together, that can make working at Microsoft far more productive and pleasant.

Chapter 4
Cross Disciplines

In this chapter:

April 1, 2002: "The modern odd couple? Dev and Test" 62

July 1, 2004: "Feeling testy—The role of testers" 65

May 1, 2005: "Fuzzy logic—The liberal arts" 68

November 1, 2005: "Undisciplined—What's so special about specialization?" . . .72

Software development, when done well, requires a broad skill set. You need to truly understand the customer and the business. You need strong user experience design skills and knowledge of usability (even for API work). You need engineering design skills, software development skills, software testing skills, and tremendous familiarity with the target platform, which could be a server farm.

Sure, you might have all those skills, but how good are you at talking to yourself? If you lack that skill, you'll likely miss important aspects of product development. If you're great at talking to yourself, that could lead to even more serious problems. In all, you are better off developing an appreciation and knack for working well with others.

In this chapter, I. M. Wright tackles relationships between developers and other disciplines. The first column describes the symbiotic relationship with test. The second delves deeper into the role of testers. The third column deals directly with the Achilles Heel of most engineers: how to interact with nontechnical people. The last column questions why and when different disciplines are even necessary.

I spent the first half of my life wondering why people couldn't be more like computers. I've spent the second half being thankful they aren't. Sure, I still get frustrated at times with people who don't think the way I do, but my life is more interesting and my solutions are more creative thanks to the diversity of people that surround me. It's part of why I love the "Hard Code" column; the response is never predictable or boring.

– Eric

April 1, 2002: "The modern odd couple? Dev and Test"

Is there a more classic love/hate relationship than the one between developers and testers? (Okay, maybe between developers and program managers, but I digress.) As a developer, you either see testers as nagging or persistent, nitpicky or thorough, obnoxious or passionate, unsophisticated or customer-focused, doomsayers or cautious.

The same could be said for how testers view developers: brilliant or geniuses, dedicated or hard-working, creative or inventive—uh yeah, right. If the truth be told, testers often think as poorly of developers as we do of them.

Many teams are far from reaching parity and mutual respect between these disciplines. Some steroid-sucking developers out there might respond, "That's fine—lead, follow, or get out of the way. If the test team can't keep pace, can't stand toe to toe, can't flex their own muscle, then they should step aside and avoid the oncoming dev machine."

Big words from small minds. It's time to tear this twisted testosterone tale apart, piece by piece, and reveal how real developers should be working with the greatest allies they have: testers.

How do I love thee? Let me count the ways

So why do development teams often treat their test teams as second-rate and unworthy of respect and cooperation? I'll break down the reasons, one at a time:

- **All testers really wish they were developers; therefore, developers must be better.** Any ridiculous generalization like this can't be true. Not all testers wish they were developers. Some do, certainly, but others want to be golf pros, racecar drivers, product unit managers, program managers, parents, priests—you name it. Some even want to be great testers.

  The real disgrace about this myth is that it shows how insecure some developers really are. A developer who is truly proud of his work and accomplishments wouldn't need to feel that development is a superior discipline.

- **Testers are not as smart as developers.**   Taken as a corollary to the previous fallacy, this is often voiced as, "If testers were as smart as developers, they'd be developers." Again, bull excrement at the most basic level.

  However, even fair-minded people will point out that testers often aren't required to have the same level of education as developers. Black-box testers, in particular, are frequently hired with little or no technical experience. To me, this is purely a case of the chicken versus the egg—there simply isn't enough external training for testers.

> **Eric Aside** Black-box testing treats the product as a black box. You don't have any access or knowledge of the internal workings, so you probe it like a customer would— you use it and abuse it till it breaks. Microsoft has been steadily moving toward white-box testing, in which you use exposed instrumentation to automatically and systematically test every aspect of the product.

Many people inside the company are working hard to correct this inequity through initiatives like the Readiness at Microsoft Program (RAMP) and the Test Lead program. Even a few universities and local community colleges have begun offering courses in testing. But until colleges and universities create standardized bachelor's and master's degree programs in this important discipline, testers won't find quality opportunities to learn more about their field through higher education.

Does this lack of educational opportunity mean that most testers are not smart? Of course not. There are strong and weak testers just as there are strong and weak developers. That's all.

- **Testers wouldn't have much to do without developers.**   The idea that without developers, testers would have nothing to test leads some people to think that developers are better. (Of course, the fact that developers often generate plenty of work in the form of bugs leads many people to think that developers are worse.) Nonetheless, is every upstream discipline considered inherently stronger than the downstream counterparts who depend on them? It is harder to direct a movie than to run the projector, but then again, it's easier to dig up a diamond than to cut and polish it.

  It really comes down to the complexity of the work, and testing products and functionality well is easily as difficult as writing the stuff in the first place. Many of the hard theoretical coding problems have been solved, but many of the hard theoretical testing problems are still waiting for answers.

- **There aren't as many strong test teams as there are strong development teams at Microsoft.**   Based on this presumption, developers might extrapolate that their discipline must be better than testers in general. This is a bad assumption and poor pretext for not doing all that you can do to grow your test team and strengthen your whole group in the process. Testing is not as mature a discipline as development. Using this as an excuse to act condescendingly toward testers only serves to lower a developer's maturity level rather than raise a tester's.

Necessary evil or priceless partner?

We can't ship a product without testing it. Think of the three worst bugs that testers found in your code last cycle and you'll know what I'm saying. What many developers haven't realized yet is how well you can ship a product with the test team's support.

Unfortunately, for many groups, testing remains a necessary evil rather than an integral priceless partner. I know that there are developers out there chiding me saying, "Integral priceless partner, as if! Test is what they've always been: monkeys that bang on the code till it breaks and then whine about it till we fix it."

If that's the way you treat them, then that's what your testers will be. However, there's an alternative approach.

A man's got to know his limitations

It starts with understanding three principal areas where development falls short: writing perfect code, understanding Raid holistically, and working within the customer's environment.

No developer writes bug-free code; even if there are no logic bugs, there may be behavior bugs. No developer lives and breathes Raid; he just uses it as a tool. No developer commonly works in the customer's environment; he works on big machines with tons of memory, processing power, and disk space. Developers also have high privileges, fast networks, the latest operating system and patches, and no legacy code—and they work in their native language. Basically, developers are hopelessly out of touch with what is necessary to move the product from their desk to the customer's.

So guess who's holding the safety net and providing the balancing pole for developers as they cross the tightrope between code complete and release? That's right, it's your testers.

Testers find both the logic and behavior bugs; they live and breathe Raid; they know where you stand and how much work needs to be done; their computers run all the time in the customer's environment and in all the different languages, platforms, and configurations. Testers can tell you how many bugs you need to fix each week without guessing. They know where the problem areas are and can give you gut and metric readings of how far you need to go.

You complete me

Developers can make you say, "Wow!" But testers will save your behind and make you proud of your development efforts.

If you treat your test team like trash, trash is likely what you'll ship and trashy is likely how you'll feel. If you prefer a smooth release and want to ship a great product, make your test team your ally.

The key is for you and your development team to understand and appreciate all that the test team offers you. They cover the areas that you can't or don't want to do. They keep you on schedule and on track. They keep you honest and represent the customer's perspective.

Tell testers how valuable they are to you. Tell them how they can help both your teams ship a great product. Do everything that you can to support them, and they will come through for you.

> **Eric Aside**   I really can't say enough about my respect and appreciation for the test discipline. In the five years since I wrote this column, great strides have been taken at creating parity between dev and test in all areas, but there's still more we can do. As for managers and PMs, I admire and respect them too, but since I live under the darkening shadow of their every whim, forgive me for not stroking their egos.

By the way, if you're already making the test team a valued partner, it's time to do the same with service operations. The same arguments apply, so why not trade in your pain and frustration for synergy and success?

July 1, 2004: "Feeling testy—The role of testers"

I've been carping on code construction quality quite a bit lately. One of the five key methods of removing bugs early is unit testing. (The others are design, design review, code review, and code analysis, like PREfast.) Doing comprehensive unit testing has drawn dubious disbelief from some devs I meet: "Isn't testing a job for testers?" "If devs write the [unit] tests, what's left for testers to do?"

> **Eric Aside**   PREfast is a static analysis tool for the C and C++ programming languages that identifies suspect coding patterns that might lead to buffer overruns or other serious programming errors. Though initially used only internally, it recently shipped as part of Microsoft Visual Studio 2005.

First of all, unit tests are usually focused on isolated components, and testers cover far more than component testing. Their tests include boundary coverage, structural coverage, path coverage, black- and white-hat testing, and a host of system-wide and scenario-based testing, just to scratch the surface.

No, first of all, what the heck do you care if there's nothing left for testers to do anyway? Since when have you abandoned your responsibility to check your own work? Is passing on crappy code some kind of perverse form of charity to you? Do you not give a flying fork about doing your job? Have you no decency or pride?

> **Eric Aside**   When I wrote this column, I initially got stuck for a "second of all" paragraph, so I reread the first "First of all" paragraph. Suddenly, the "No, first of all" paragraph flowed out faster than I could type it. That's always a good thing.

Unit testing drives better implementation design; more testable code; fewer regressions, build breaks, and BVT failures to debug; and better overall construction quality.

Advanced protection

In my article called "Where's the beef?" (see Chapter 5), here's what I said about a dev's responsibility to write instrumentation and unit tests:

> *"NO, this is not a tester's job. Test's job is to protect the customer from whatever you miss–despite your best efforts. The testing team is not a crutch on which you get to balance your two tons of lousy code. You should be embarrassed if test finds a bug. Every bug that they find is a bug that you missed, and it better not be because you were lazy, apathetic, or incompetent."*

However, in fairness to the devs that actually care enough about their peers to consider the impact of unit testing on test jobs, I should discuss more about the role of testers in protecting our customers and how testing may actually evolve if and when devs finally get their acts together.

A change will do you good

In "The modern odd couple? Dev and Test" (which appeared earlier in this chapter), I pointed out three primary ways testers protect our customers:

- Finding bugs we miss.
- Living and breathing quality metrics (mostly from Product Studio).
- Running tests in the customer's environment as opposed to the developer's environment.

Devs writing unit tests doesn't change any of these roles for testers.

But testing is changing nonetheless. Almost all new test hires are expected to know how to write automation code and white-box tests. The more cynical among us may think that there is a secret plan to eliminate testers after all tests are automated. However, the real reason for enhanced automation resides in the time it takes to run all the necessary tests to pass an urgent security, privacy, or reliability update, or even to just validate a build. As teams try to push quality upstream, automated tests are essential to ensure construction quality before check-in.

That brings us to the next key turning point. As the quality of your code at check-in increases, how testers perform their role changes. Note that their role is the same–find missed bugs, analyze quality metrics, and run in the customer's environment. It's how they do it that's different.

The twilight zone

Right now finding bugs in checked-in code is akin to spotting a coffee shop in Seattle–they are hard to miss. Sure, you write a test plan and test cases to exhaust all the different possibilities. But the expectation is always, "Just run the application, the bugs are sure to be there."

As teams push quality upstream, finding bugs after check-in becomes more difficult. At first, teams simply test *buddy drops* as part of their check-in criteria. A number of teams are doing this now, including some in established groups such as Microsoft Windows and Office.

> **Eric Aside**   A buddy drop is a private build of a product used to verify code changes before they have been checked into the main code base. That way the impact of unstable code on other teams is minimized. Developers share the private build only with their "buddies"—that is, their teammates.

But as dev teams begin to use disciplined practices and measurements to predict and control their bug counts, the number of bugs found in a buddy drop should plummet by a factor of a thousand. Thus, the typical Microsoft team of 15–20 devs that produces 3,000–5,000 test bugs per year would instead produce 3–5 test bugs per year. When buddy builds get that solid, test needs to learn some new tricks. (I talk about how some teams have achieved these low bug counts using cool software engineering principles in "A software odyssey," which appears in Chapter 5.)

Commander Data

Remember, test's role is to protect customers by finding bugs that devs miss, analyzing quality metrics, and running in the customer's environment. In a world where code handed to test has only a handful of total bugs, the challenge is to take test's three responsibilities to the next level.

With such low bug rates, testers should no longer be able to easily find bugs in isolated components or common configurations. Instead, they need to focus on full customer system scenarios and realistic customer configurations, further leveraging their unique customer perspective. While test teams do this a fair amount today, it likely will become their primary focus in the future.

The other key change is in analyzing quality metrics. For devs to get low bug rates, they must collect quality data from the beginning of design, through compile and build, and then use it to know what mistakes they are making, how best to find them, and when they can confidently say they've found 99.9% of them. Someone outside of dev needs to be checking the dev's assumptions, ensuring that the data is reliable and accurate, keeping devs honest and customers protected. Of course, that's the ideal job for test.

A side effect of this rigorous dev process is that test will have far more quality data, in far greater detail, than they've ever had from Product Studio. The more data you have, the more there is to analyze and discover. You can almost hear testers salivating.

> **Eric Aside**   Most good testers I know are data fanatics. A perfect afternoon for them is spent up to their eyeballs in Excel spreadsheets analyzing data in different ways.

While devs will do some analysis, this is really a showcase area for testers that entails

- Conducting in-depth statistical studies.
- Noticing key weak spots and trends.
- Finding new ways to improve quality or efficacy even further.

Testers can become the quality process and analysis kings in this new world.

It's quite cool—I assure you

When devs graduate to engineers, testers can start leveraging comprehensive data and process analysis to assure quality. In others words, test becomes quality assurance. Quality control testing doesn't go away, but quality assurance grows into a major role. This same pattern has happened in other industries and is due to happen to software. If we don't make it happen, we will get beat.

So sure, most of this seems like a pipe dream now. Even though some teams are starting to see this level of quality engineering, it's a long way from being part of our largest systems (like Windows). But if your team is beginning to make headway, or if you know forward-looking testers who want to lead the next wave of software quality, suggest that they start learning about in-depth statistical data and process analysis. It could prepare them to take our game to a whole new level.

May 1, 2005: "Fuzzy logic—The liberal arts"

All my life, I've lived among the willfully ignorant—people who might consider knocking wood a silly superstition, yet have no idea how their TV works, how planes fly, or how phones connect. To them, it's all magic. They make up their own mythologies and rituals for getting technology to function. Then these neophytes have the gall to tell you to turn off the lights before you reboot or it won't work.

Before I graduated from college, I had the perfect solution for dealing with these naive fools. I simply avoided and ignored them. Hanging around with techies was right in my comfort zone. That is until I married a "fuzzy"—a liberal arts major. All of a sudden, learning to communicate with the technologically superstitious became enlightened self-interest. We've been together for 20 years now, and I'm beginning to get the hang of it.

Eric Aside   Oh, the grief I got for this column (along with tons of praise). The grief was from techies who were private fuzzies and fuzzies who love technology. Both hated the stereotypes I drew. (Also, people who weren't fuzzy or techie, like art designers, felt left out of the discussion.) As I say below, "Naturally, I've over-generalized here." People are often too polite or hesitant to discuss contentious issues loaded with ambiguity. I over-generalize in every column to bring out salient points and drive dialogue.

It takes all kinds

Why should interacting with the ignorant be any concern of yours? Why not leave the fools to the foolish? I've got three reasons: coworkers, managers, and customers.

Sure, we hire folks for their technical savvy, but we all know that there are people who get it and people who tread water. For every one PM or manager who gets it, there are 5 to 10 who don't. There are a lot of PMs and managers at Microsoft. Any improvements you want to make to your products or practices need to go through them. If you can't communicate with PMs and managers effectively, I hope your geek past has sufficiently prepared you for a life of frustration.

> **Eric Aside**   Many PMs and managers come from the techie ranks. At one point, they understood all the details and took nothing for granted. However, over time it becomes expedient to let go of the details and think more about nontechnical aspects and the "big picture." The world becomes fuzzy. Yes, I'm guilty of this myself.

As for customers, well, we don't get to choose. Customers are customers, and the inability to effectively speak to a customer is career limiting. As I mentioned in my column "Customer dissatisfaction," which appears in Chapter 2, talking to customers is the key to making the right choices for critical product decisions. Customers don't like to be patronized or made to feel small or stupid. I suppose managers and PMs are the same way.

You've got to understand fuzzy folks. You've got to appeal to their best judgment in a way that makes sense to them, makes them feel smart and in control. The alternatives aren't pleasant.

They're not like us

Liberal arts majors are not like us. It isn't just the schools they attended or the classes they took. It's a whole different way of looking at the world that you need to truly grok (a word that might not be familiar to them).

As luck would have it, I've spent the last 20 years trying to understand fuzzy logic. I've discovered some key differences you need to internalize:

- **Liberal arts majors believe rules are rules.**   Techies believe rules aren't meant to be followed blindly; they are meant to be analyzed and understood, then used or altered as needed. Fuzzies believe rules are meant to protect you, and they simply must be obeyed. Even worse, a fuzzy's version of the rules may not match yours. Just remember, if you plan to question or break any perceived rules in front of a fuzzy, you'd better be prepared to explain why it's safe and have an authority figure to back you up. Why? Because...

- **Liberal arts majors respect authority.**   Techies typically don't respect authority, though they do respect achievement. So it might not occur to you that manager approval is that big a deal—but it is to a fuzzy. The good news is that most fuzzies consider techies authorities on technology, so they'll believe most anything you say in your area of expertise. Try not to abuse that advantage. Fuzzies may be different, but that doesn't mean they are stupid or foolish.

> **Eric Aside**   At this point, you might be saying, "Wait a minute, fuzzies have been breaking rules and disrespecting authority for years." They have when they feel justified. In everyday life, fuzzies tend to prefer obedience to uncertainty. Techies prefer to rely on their own reason and logic to determine the rules and authority.

- **Liberal arts majors don't tinker.**   Techies love to tinker; fuzzies avoid tinkering. Tinkering is breaking the rules. It feels risky and unsafe. This difference in attitude is subtle but very important. Fuzzies won't just try stuff. They won't right-click, press and hold, or try different menu items just to see what happens. So don't expect fuzzies to experiment unless they truly know it is safe. Likewise, don't expect a fuzzy to approve a change unless it's well worth the risk and has a safe abort.

- **Liberal arts majors assume everything is simple.**   Techies know nothing is simple because techies focus on the details. Fuzzies focus on the larger picture where everything is simple, and if it isn't, it should be. Neither view is wrong. Everything you do should be conceptually simple and easy to explain at a high level, or chances are good that it will collapse under its own weight. Yet, the devil is in the details. Simple is hard for technical folks who thrive in the details. But...

- **Liberal arts majors don't care about the minutiae.**   Techies love the minutiae; often it's the best part of a project. However, because fuzzies focus on the larger picture, tiny details only confuse the issues at hand. Therefore, if you are describing your idea or project to a fuzzy, you must leave out the minutiae and articulate the simple, high-level concepts and requirements behind your work. Otherwise, you'd better be prepared for no support, and rightfully so. Fuzzies aren't simpletons who need to be babied. They are integrators who will tie your work into everything else going on, if you can provide a clear and simple picture of how your work fits in.

- **Liberal arts majors are not concerned with purity.**   Techies love purity. To them, it is beauty and grace. Purity washes away all the ugly tidbits, leaving the simple core truth of the problem. Unfortunately, all this escapes your typical fuzzy. Fuzzies don't care about the ugly details in the first place. They expect things to be pure and simple. Telling a fuzzy that you've found an elegant, simple solution is likely to get a response like, "Yeah, I should hope so, what did you have before?" If you want to convince a fuzzy to adopt your elegant architecture, don't argue the purity. Instead, talk to them about the customer or business benefits it provides like more reliability and easier maintenance.

- **Liberal arts majors care about feelings and appearances.**   Techies typically don't even realize that feelings and appearances exist. It took my wife years of pointing out the importance of these things before I started understanding them. Fuzzies care tremendously about feelings and appearances. I know that seems stupid and counterproductive, but there just isn't any way around it, so don't bother arguing. Instead, when you propose an idea or plan to a fuzzy, be sure to consider how people will feel about it (assume that everyone is a fuzzy, which is how fuzzies think). Will anyone need to save face? Are you crossing into other people's territory? Are you contradicting someone in authority? You don't need to solve all these issues, but you do need to think about them and point them out to fuzzies. They will be impressed by how perceptive you are and then help you solve the people issues.

Naturally, I've over-generalized here. Not all liberal arts majors have these traits any more than all techies have the opposite traits. But you can't assume everyone thinks the way you do. Just putting your preconceived notions on hold can go a long way toward achieving clear communication.

Getting past security

One of the more important implications of these qualities that make liberal arts majors different is that they tend to surround and protect people in authority. Because fuzzies respect authority and care about feelings and appearances, including their own, they can't let just anyone talk to a senior manager or key customer contact. You've got to work through them. Sneaking past the fuzzy security may be fun and effective the first time, but when they realize what happened, the literary lynch squad will be offended and won't forget it.

Luckily, there are ways to soft-talk your way through. Explain why it's important to talk to the customer or manager. Allow the fuzzy to introduce you and set the stage (appearances, rules). Collect your issues and bring them all at once so the customer's or manager's time is respected and appreciated (feelings, respect for authority). Unless you are asked directly, leave out all the gritty details and cool design (minutiae, purity). Give the customer or manager clear choices of action (simplicity).

Management will love you; the customer will love you; and the crack fuzzy security force will love you.

Making things happen

If you want to drive engineering improvements on your team, you'll need to convince the fuzzies. This isn't easy because improvement means change, change means breaking the rules, and rules are rules. However, you can be an effective driver for change by following this simple strategy:

- First, describe the problem you're trying to solve. Use statistics to make it sound horrible. (It probably is horrible, but fuzzies respect the authority of numbers.) Don't cheat—use real metrics. You want the problem to seem horrible to prove that the current rules are unsafe and need to change.

■ Next, describe what conditions the solution must satisfy to keep the project and team safe—for instance, a rollback strategy, conditional compilation, policy settings, regular reviews, or manager approval. Don't just make this up; think about people's concerns. You must do this before you describe your solution or else you'll get battered by every fuzzy's apprehension. Remember, change has feelings associated with it.

■ Now, describe your solution. Talk about how it meets the safety conditions (which you've previously worked out). Then talk about how it leaves the project in better shape. Suggest statistics that will demonstrate the results (like a percentage drop in regressions or pri 1 bugs or shorter stabilization times). Remember to keep it high level and simple. The statistics are particularly important because there's no other authoritative way to prove you've improved. To avoid the statistics being gamed, always use team instead of individual measures. Be sure to have a celebration when your new rules allow you to meet your goals.

Better together

It's easy to be cynical about liberal arts majors, or about anyone who thinks or works differently than you do. But different approaches bring out different values. Ultimately, we all benefit. It's mushy, but true.

By learning to appreciate the balance that fuzzies bring to our techie world, you can become far more effective. Understand your differences, adjust your approach, tune your message, and respect your audience. In the end, you'll have everything to gain and nothing to lose.

November 1, 2005: "Undisciplined—What's so special about specialization?"

Why do we have testers? Why do we have PMs? Why do we have different disciplines at all? Isn't it wildly inefficient? Why don't we just have engineers who do whatever is necessary to ship quality products that delight our customers? Are programmers incapable of understanding customer needs or executing tests to verify their work? Of course not.

> **Eric Aside**   My introduction to this chapter talks about how important it is to have a team of people with a diversity of skills working together on a project. That doesn't mean those people need to be specialized into different disciplines with mutually exclusive responsibilities.

Yet, we somehow perpetuate these dysfunctional disciplines that create barriers, miscommunication, and conflict—also known as dependency death; handoff hell; black holes of blame;

suffocating, senseless signoffs; and monotonous, mind-numbing meetings. Are we so insecure that everyone has to be "special"?

It's not just ridiculous, it's counterproductive. Devs and testers wait for PM specs, PMs and testers wait for code, and PMs and devs wait for test runs. Sure, there is always other work to do; but if everyone chips in on everything, then everyone is focused on the top priorities, everyone is a customer advocate, and everyone contributes to quality. It's the team way. It's the Agile way. It's old school and it's new school. It's nirvana. What's not to like?

Days of future past

Microsoft didn't always have PMs and testers. We started out in nirvana and yet we strayed from paradise. Why? I've talked to old timers about it. Basically, not everyone wanted to do certain tasks, some people were better than others at certain tasks, and some important tasks weren't getting covered. There was a need, and people started to specialize and fill gaps.

Of course, that was long ago. The market was different, our situation was different, and we were less experienced. But if we went back to everyone doing everything, would history repeat itself, and would people specialize once more? Is there a fundamental principle at work?

Unfortunately, yeah, there is. Specialization is unavoidable and essential.

Before you get too excited one way or another, let me make two points:

1. The need for specialization is subtle; it doesn't always apply.

2. I'm right.

Take it to the limit

How do I know I'm right? Because of a great trick I learned on my high school math team. (Okay, I'm a dork. Let's move on.) Here's the trick: when you need to understand a broad problem, consider the extremes. In our case, the problem is optimal software development role structure. The extremes are coding an interview question and coding Windows Server.

When coding an interview question, you can do everything yourself. You get to know the customer (the interviewer), understand the requirements, spec the solution, code it, test it, and ship it. If you can't, you don't get hired. The moral of the story is that at the simple extreme, there's no need for specialization.

Coding Windows Server requires many more developers. But do some need to specialize? Absolutely, there are parts of the code that are way too complicated for more than a handful of devs to understand. But do you also have to specialize in customer design and testing (either quality assurance or control)? Absolutely, but that's harder to see because the scope of Windows Server is so big. Allow me to present far smaller example: an Xbox football game.

Football is a science

Coding an Xbox football game requires more than one developer. Again, specialization could be essential because of the computer graphics components, the AI components, the statistical components, and so on. But let's skip to the PM and test areas. Do you need specialists there? Absolutely, but not at the tiny feature level.

Writing a football game requires you to know every detail about football: every rule, every play, every formation, every team, every stadium, every player and salary, and on and on. However, not everyone on the dev team needs to know all those things. In fact, most don't need to know any of them. They've got other things to worry about, like computer graphics and AI. But someone needs to know—the game designer.

Someone needs to verify the results of the game. This person must be an expert video game player and football player who knows everything about how the game could be played and should be played. The complexity level is enormous, but it's at a different level of detail than the implementation. The developers who write the code operate at a much lower level of detail. Even the dev architect deals with a different slice of the complexity. But someone must verify the results at the user level—the game tester.

Windows Server is far more complex than an Xbox football game. There are hundreds, if not thousands, of different experiences that must be completely understood, designed, and tested at the customer's level of abstraction. I'd love to say that our engineers have big enough brains to keep all the details straight at every level of abstraction, and that they become refined experts about multiple, entire business models, module decomposition, and detailed implementation, but that's flat out absurd. The moral of the story is that at the complex extreme, specialization is unavoidable and essential.

> **Eric Aside**   This is the part that's lost on many Agile practitioners. Probably because there aren't many Windows-scale products that make the case for specialization so clear cut. Again, I return to the knowledge I gained that projects need to be managed differently at different levels of scale and abstraction. What goes for the hundreds or thousands of engineers at the product level doesn't make sense at the five-to-eight-engineer feature level.

The space between

So, what have we learned? At the simple extreme, specialization is superfluous. At the complex extreme, specialization is essential. Thus, the question isn't, "Should we have specialization?" The question is, "At what level of complexity or abstraction do we need specialization?"

I claim that specialization is a waste of time at the detailed feature level. Devs should understand the requirements of the detailed feature (the spec, scenarios, and personas), then design it, unit test it, and code it. Testers and PMs stay out of specing and testing at the detailed feature level. If devs aren't doing their jobs at that level of detail, then they aren't doing their jobs.

I further claim that specialization is essential at the product level. We need PMs to really understand the customers inside-out, arrange communication between them and the team, and keep the team focused on the ball. We need testers to ensure the customer will be delighted. Not that the product just works, but that it works the way the customer needs and wants it to work.

Stuck in the middle with you

The big argument, then, is where to draw the line in between? When do you stop needing the separate disciplines? Can devs design and test dialogs or APIs? How detailed do you need to go before PMs and testers are overkill and counterproductive? Personally, I think it depends.

Where to draw the line depends on the product. If it's a familiar product with an intuitive purpose, then you probably don't need many specialists. If it's an unusual product with an obscure purpose, at least to engineers, then you need more specialists. Complexity naturally adds to the burden and requires more specialty.

In the end, you should avoid specialization whenever possible. It adds a tremendous burden and drives dysfunction. If you have jobs anyone can do, like check the build or fetch pizza, then everyone should help do them. Anything less is selfish, egotistical, and unprofessional.

When you do need specialists, accept and embrace them. Give them the opportunity to learn, grow, and lead. Our success depends on it. Just don't let it go to their heads. Work to avoid the pitfalls and barriers by using shared spaces, constant communication, and a focus on teamwork and team ownership. Remember: the team comes first, and pizza doesn't fetch itself.

Chapter 5
Software Quality—More Than a Dream

In this chapter:

March 1, 2002: "Are you secure about your security?" 78

November 1, 2002: "Where's the beef? Why we need quality" 81

April 1, 2004: "A software odyssey—From craft to engineering". 87

July 1, 2005: "Review this—Inspections" 91

October 1, 2006: "Bold predictions of quality". 96

Some people mock software development, saying if buildings were built like software, the first woodpecker would destroy civilization. That's quite funny, or disturbing, but regardless it's misguided. Early buildings lacked foundations. Early cars broke down incessantly. Early TVs required constant fiddling to work properly. Software is no different.

At first, Microsoft wrote software for early adopters, people comfortable replacing PC boards. Back then, time to market won over quality, because early adopters could work around issues, but they couldn't slow the clock. Shipping fastest meant coding quickly and then fixing just enough to make it work.

Now our market is consumers and the enterprise, who value quality over the hassles of experimentation. The market change was gradual, so Microsoft's initial response was simply to fix more bugs. Soon bug fixing was taking longer than coding, an incredibly slow process. The fastest way to ship high quality is to trap errors early, coding it right the first time and minimizing rework. Microsoft has been shifting to this quality upstream approach over the time I've been writing these columns. The first major jolt that drove the company-wide change was a series of Internet virus attacks in late 2001.

In this chapter, I. M. Wright preaches quality to the engineering masses. The first column evaluates security issues. The second analyzes why quality is essential and how you get it. The third column explains an engineering approach to software that dramatically reduces defects. The fourth talks about design and code inspections, and the last one describes metrics that can predict quality issues before customers experience them.

While all these columns provide an interesting perspective, the second one, "Where's the beef?" stands out as an important turning point. When I wrote it few inside or outside

Microsoft believed we were serious about quality. Years later, many of the concepts are taken for granted. It took far more than an opinion piece to drive that change, but it's nice to call for action and have people respond.

– Eric

March 1, 2002: "Are you secure about your security?"

I know security is serious sh*t. I know that every time some hacker halfwit exploits a small code or configuration imperfection in a system that he could never dream of writing himself, the dung beetles in the press will feed off this excrement with gleeful abandon, telling our customers that our code stinks—simply because some pockmarked malicious pipsqueak managed to manipulate two lines of code, out of a million, into an illegal perversion. I know this.

Microsoft has millions of lines of legacy code, huge farms of networked servers, and hundreds if not thousands of external partners and dependencies. Each of these has the potential to be the next victim of vile, vindictive, vacuous, vessels of vomit whose mothers still wash their clothes. But which items should we focus on securing first?

> **Eric Aside**   Ah, the good old days when hackers were just misguided youth trying to make a name for themselves or fighting the powers that be. These days, hacking is big business— either preventing it, tracking it, or engaging in it for organized crime. In retrospect, my anger at the early hackers was misplaced. The world isn't a place where you can just hope everyone plays nicely. The early hacker wake-up call set us on the proper path of writing secure solid code.

Beware the swinging pendulum

Some people say that every possible vulnerability must be corrected. That's commendable— but crazy. We can't get so paranoid that our products become unusable.

When I worked at Boeing, people assigned to "black projects" worked in buildings with no windows, were disconnected from the network, and every night removed their disk drives and locked them in a vault. With all these protective measures, these projects were still considered vulnerable.

Even the biggest security hawks probably don't think our customers should be required to blacken their windows, stay off the Web, and remove their disk drives. However, we must raise the security bar far higher than in the past and require accountability for it from top to bottom in our organizations. The key is to remember that this is all about delivering a trustworthy and *delightful* experience to our customers.

Other people say that we only need to focus on securing our firewalls, protocols, and common language runtime. They assume that if these are secure, we have nothing to worry about. This is ignorant and downright dangerous thinking.

Writing Secure Code (Microsoft Press, 2002) by Michael Howard and David LeBlanc (a must read) has an entire chapter on writing secure .NET code, which references almost all of the other 15 chapters. This chapter explains that vulnerabilities are not limited to buffer overruns, insecure protocols, and unguarded ports. Even if these items were the only attack points, firewalls, secure protocols, and managed code wouldn't be enough protection from malicious data.

> **Eric Aside**   I refer to the first version of *Writing Secure Code* in this column. The column was written shortly after the first version was published. Naturally, later versions of the book have even more useful information. Also, Michael Howard has a great Kiwi accent.

Do the right thing

Of course, the right thing to do is to consider every possible vulnerability and rank each in terms of the risk to the customer. Finding vulnerabilities is not as hard as it sounds. By breaking your Web or client application into components and interfaces, you can quickly spot potential issues and classify them with the STRIDE model. By searching your code for dangerous APIs (Appendix A in *Writing Secure Code*), properly restricting permissions, and checking inputs, you can find a ton of easy pickings—the kind that hackers look for. Although a deeper evaluation is necessary to catch more subtle issues, these simple steps will give you a great head start.

> **Eric Aside**   STRIDE is a mnemonic device to help people remember the different kinds of security threats: spoofing, tampering, repudiation, information disclosure, denial of service, and elevation of privilege. *Writing Secure Code* has all the details.

Next you have to assess the risk of each vulnerability. A vulnerability that allows hackers to discover how we keyword clip art is less critical than one that allows hackers to discover a customer's private data. There is a higher probability that a vulnerability will be exploited if you can copy a hack from a Web site and change a couple of values in the script, as compared to a hack that must be tuned to each instance, requires detailed knowledge of the code, and must be written in a low-level language. The more critical the effects, the higher the risk; the lower the probability of exploitation, the lower the risk. Divide the criticality by the chance and you've got your risk assessment. (Table 2-2 in *Writing Secure Code* details this process.)

You're only as secure as your weakest link

Computing security risks sounds simple enough, but how do you calibrate acceptable risk across a big product like Windows? First, your team has to agree on definitions of the criticality and chance ratings. The commonly suggested range for each is from one to ten, where a criticality of ten is highly critical and a chance of ten is highly unlikely.

Next, calibrate these ranges according to your group's agreed-upon sense of importance. Is getting read-only database access to product catalog data a criticality rating of two or eight? What about the same access to user data? If you need to write custom COM code to exploit a vulnerability, is it assigned a chance rating of four or nine? What if that code can be written in VBScript? (One very helpful standard for risk assessment of interfaces can be found in Table 14-1 in *Writing Secure Code*.)

After your group has standard definitions of criticality and chance, a high-level triage or war team can set a balanced risk bar across the organization. We already use this process to settle differences between component teams working on large products and to set a consistent quality bar. The same can and should be done for security issues.

> **Eric Aside**   To differentiate low-level product and feature triage from high-level product-line triage, we have a variety of funny internal names: war room, box triage, and über-triage, to name a few. Personally, I could do without the war references.

Lead, follow, or get out of the way

So are you on board with responding to the security challenge? Do you hate the idea of a group of arrogant, asocial peons pushing us around?

Perhaps you are thinking that these loser lawbreakers should be kept off the Net, and that pandering alarmist reporters and editors should have a sense of decency, fairness, and responsibility, not make heroes of hackers and not vilify Windows beyond all other platforms and systems. Perhaps you are thinking that if these hacking incidents were taken with the proper perspective, then maybe we wouldn't all be going through this fire drill. Unfortunately, this is the world we live in, fair or unfair, true or exaggerated.

Let's face it. No one likes being hacked and few of us praise hackers for their creativity and civic service. But letting snidely, sniffling, scurvy scum have control over the hearts, minds, and computers of our customers is completely shameful.

Sure Linux, Oracle, Sun, IBM, and AOL have as many, if not more, security problems than we do. But as BrianV says, "We are the leader in this industry and we have to lead!" Nothing short of a full commitment is acceptable.

> **Eric Aside**   Brian Valentine (BrianV) was the senior vice president of the Windows division at the time.

November 1, 2002: "Where's the beef? Why we need quality"

This month, Interface focuses on the lessons that we learned from security pushes around the company. What about the lessons that we haven't learned? What about the dumb things we are still doing?

The security fire drill exposed more than security holes in our software. It further exposed the shoddiness of our work and left many folks wondering what the next fire drill will be. Guesses include: privacy, availability, supportability. How about quality? Anyone heard of quality? What the heck happened to quality???

Check-in time on most dev teams is like amateur hour. The kind of garbage that passes as a first cut is pathetic, and fixing it later is like signing our own death certificate. Why? Because we won't fix problems before release that are too superficial, too complex, or too obscure. We won't fix bugs before release that are found too late or simply not discovered until after we ship.

So what, right? We've been shipping this way for years. What is true this year that wasn't before? Oh my, where to begin...

> **Eric Aside**   Much of what I wrote about here five years ago has changed. That doesn't mean we are yet where we want to be. We still fix too much later rather than earlier. However, we've radically increased the amount of unit testing, automated testing, code review, and code analysis we perform both before code gets checked into the main source tree and before we ship. These days we can actually use beta releases for mission-critical tasks and day-to-day work.

Things have changed

First of all, today we are trying to sell into markets that require turnkey solutions—that is, you turn the key and it works. These markets require turnkey solutions because the associated customers do not have the expertise to work around the problems. So if it doesn't work right away, we have to fix it right away.

We have entered two major turnkey markets: consumer products and the enterprise. If you're smart, you're wondering how our competitors have succeeded in these markets.

For the consumer market, our competitors have kept their products small and simple. That way there aren't many failure modes; and if they do fail, the product can quickly restart and recover. We are selling products with far more complexity, and functionality. However, this means we have more failure modes. To stay competitive, our products need to be better with fewer failures and they need to restart and recover faster.

For the enterprise market, our competitors have supplied armies of support personnel and consultants. For many competitors, this is the biggest part of their business—they actually make money on their complexity and failures. When their products collapse, our competitors immediately dispatch their own squadron of people to fix the problems and keep the enterprise up and running.

We don't follow this business model. We sell less expensive products in high volume and provide minimal support in an effort to maximize profits. However, this means that we can't afford to break as often and that we must quickly fix or recover from the few failures that we do have.

> **Eric Aside**   Our "minimal" support has expanded significantly as the Internet provides new models for support, but Microsoft is still a volume software and services provider.

Good enough isn't

The second way things have changed for us as a company is that our key products are now good enough. Actually, feature-wise our key products—Office and Windows—have been good enough for years.

Being good enough means that we've got all the features that our customers need, or at least those that they think they need. This hurts us two ways:

- People stop upgrading to the next version. After all, the current version has everything that they think they need and upgrading is painful and expensive.

- Any software copycat can create a viably competitive product by just referring to our widely distributed, online, fully automated specifications (the products themselves). If the copycat does a better job, making the software more reliable, smaller, and cheaper (say like Honda did to Chrysler), then we've got a big problem.

Think it can't happen? It already has. (Does Linux ring a bell?) Linux didn't copy Windows; it just ensured that it had all the good-enough features of a Windows server. Right now there are developers working on Windows-like shells and Office-like applications for Linux. Even if they fail, you can bet someone will eventually succeed in developing a superior product—as long as we leave the quality door open.

We can't afford to play catch-up with our would-be competition. Detroit has been fighting that losing battle for years. We must step up and make our products great before others catch us.

The good news is that we have some time. Other commercial software companies big enough to copy Office or Windows are poorly run and are way behind us in the PM and test disciplines. The open-source folks lack the strategic focus and coordination that we have; they rely on a shotgun approach hoping to eventually hit their target. We can beat all competitors if we raise our quality bar—ensuring fewer failures, faster restart, and faster recovery—and if we focus on our key customer issues.

Hard choices

But as anyone can tell you, nothing comes for free. If we focus more on quality, something else has to give. At a high level, the only variables that we control are quality, dates, and features. For projects with fixed dates, quality means fewer features. For projects with fixed features, quality means adding time to the schedule.

> **Eric Aside**   Actually, I don't completely believe this anymore. I've seen great efficiency gained by removing waste from the system (as you can see in "Lean: more than good Pastrami" in Chapter 2, "Process Improvement, Sans Magic") and fixing problems early. While it might not be enough to give the company summers off, I believe it is enough for high quality not to cost us features or time. Yes, it's not as quick as the early days when the quality bar was low, but compared to our recent long stabilization periods, doing it right the first time is as fast if not faster.

Before you balk at this thought process, BillG has already made our choices clear in his article about trustworthy computing:

> *In the past, we've made our software and services more compelling for users by adding new features and functionality and by making our platform richly extensible. We've done a terrific job at that, but all those great features won't matter unless customers trust our software.*

The only question is: Are you going to follow through?

There are three principal areas to focus on to improve the quality of our products:

- Better design and code
- Better instrumentation and test
- Better supportability and recovery

Let's break them down one at a time.

Time enough at last

Few developers wouldn't love more time to think through their code and get it right the first time. The trouble is finding the time and having the self-discipline to use that time wisely. So, what would you do if you had more time? As a manager, I would spend more time with my people discussing design decisions and reviewing code.

Two key design issues I'd emphasize are simplicity and proper factoring:

- **Simplicity**   Keeping the design simple and focused is key to reducing unintended results and complex failures.

■ **Proper factoring**   This helps keep each piece of the design simple and separable from the others. It also makes it easier to enforce a sole authority for data and operations, and to maintain and upgrade code.

> **Eric Aside**   Test-Driven Development (TDD) accomplishes both these results for implementation design. You can take a similar approach to TDD for component design as well, though the tests are sometimes no more than thought experiments.

I'd also give devs extra time by pairing them to work on each feature task. This serves to

■ Double the time that each dev has to do the work because you schedule the same task length as if one dev were assigned.

■ Allow for peer reviews of designs and code.

■ Provide each feature with a backup dev in case the primary dev becomes unavailable.

To help my devs apply self-discipline, I'd

■ Schedule completion dates for dev specs (also known as design docs and architecture docs).

■ Make each backup dev as responsible for feature quality as the primary developer is.

■ Measure regression rates and build-check failures to use as feedback on quality at check-in. (Sure, these measures are imperfect, but what did you want? Bugs per line of code?)

> **Eric Aside**   These days I'd use churn and complexity measures instead of regression rates.

Checking it twice

It's never enough to think that you have the code right; you've got to know. Check it from the inside with instrumentation and from the outside with unit tests. The more you do this, both in terms of coverage and depth, the better you can assure quality.

And, NO, this is not a tester's job. Test's job is to protect the customer from whatever you miss—despite your best efforts. The testing team is not a crutch on which you get to balance your two tons of lousy code. You should be embarrassed if test finds a bug. Every bug that they find is a bug that you missed, and it better not be because you were lazy, apathetic, or incompetent.

So how do you prevent bugs from ever reaching testers and customers?

■ **Instrumentation**   Asserts, Watson, test harness hooks, logging, tracing, and data validation can all be invaluable (even instrumental—sorry) in identifying and pinpointing problems before and after check-in.

■ **Unit tests**   Testing can often make the biggest difference between good and exceptional, between barely functional and solid. There are lots of different kinds of unit tests; you, your backup, and your peer in test should pick those that are most appropriate for your feature:

❑ Positive unit tests exercise the code as intended and check for the right result.

❑ Negative unit tests intentionally misuse the code and check for robustness and appropriate error handling.

❑ Stress tests push the code to its limits hoping to crack open and expose subtle resource, timing, or reentrant errors.

❑ Fault injection tests expose error-handling anomalies.

The more you verify, the more code paths you cover, the less likely it is that a customer will find fault in your work.

Physician, heal thyself

Even if you design and code your feature well, and even if you instrument and test it well, there will still be bugs. Usually those bugs involve complex interactions with other software. Sometimes that software isn't ours; sometimes it's old; and sometimes it isn't well designed or tested.

But just because bugs will always occur doesn't excuse you from making bugs rare, nor does it excuse you from taking responsibility when they do occur. You still have to help customers fix or recover from these problems, ideally without them ever noticing.

A wonderful example of recovery is the IIS process recycling technology. Any time an IIS server component dies, the process automatically and immediately restarts. The customer, at worst, only sees a temporary network hiccup repaired by a simple refresh.

Office XP also has a recovery system, though the user is made more aware. When an Office app fails, it backs up the data, reports the problem, and automatically restarts and recovers the data upon request. These solutions are not terribly complicated, but they offer a huge benefit to customers and save tons of money in support costs.

If you can't get your product to automatically recover and restart, you should at least capture enough information to identify and reproduce the problem. That way, the support engineer can easily and quickly understand the issue and provide a fix if one already exists. If the issue does not have a known fix, the failure information can be captured and sent to your team so that you can reproduce it and design a fix for the customer right away.

Capturing enough information to identify and reproduce problems is not as hard as it sounds:

■ Watson currently does a great job of identifying problems, and future versions of Watson will make it easier to reproduce those problems on campus.

■ SQL Server does a great job of capturing a wide variety of customer data, which allows everything from precisely reproducing all the changes to a database to simply dumping the relevant state when a failure occurs.

Step by step

Okay, you follow all these suggestions. Was it worth it? Is the code really better? Did you miss something? If these security pushes have taught us anything, it's that problems aren't always obvious and that ad hoc methods and automated tools don't find all of our issues.

The pushes also reminded us that a couple of missed exploits can cost Microsoft and our customers millions of dollars and lead to a double-digit drop in our customers' perceptions of product quality.

What techniques can we borrow from the security folks? Two immediately come to mind:

■ Decompose your product into components like you would for a threat model, and look for quality issues within each piece. Ask: How should we design each component? How can we make each component instrumented, testable, supportable, and recoverable? Applying more structured engineering methods to improving quality will yield more reliable and comprehensive results.

■ Reduce the failure surface area of your product; that is, reduce the number of ways that your product can be misused. Cut options that allow customers to invent procedures that you didn't intend and that are included just because you thought someone somewhere might desire that option. Simplify each feature so that it performs the one task that you designed it for and that's all. Remember, unnecessary complexity just hides bugs.

Too much to ask?

By now you are surely thinking that I'm insane. There's no way your PM, test, and ops teams—let alone your managers—are going to give you the time to take on everything that I'm suggesting. Actually, it's not as bad as you might think. Many of these practices are tied to each other:

■ Proper design welcomes testability and supportability in your products.

■ Instrumentation helps identify and reproduce problems.

■ Testing shows weaknesses where you need to recover.

To buy more time to do this right, make improving quality a win for the whole team. Define supportability and recovery as features. Get PM, test, and ops into the act.

When we build our products right and customers regain confidence in our work, we will leave our competitors in the dust. They can't match our features; they can't match our innovation and forward thinking; and if we show what great engineers we can be, they won't be able to compete with our quality.

> **Eric Aside**   "Where's the beef" is one of my favorite columns. Five years later I still get pumped reading it.

April 1, 2004: "A software odyssey—From craft to engineering"

Time to weigh in on a development debate for the ages. No, not where to put the curly braces (they go on their own lines). The debate is, "What the heck are developers?" Are we like designers and artists, creative people who need time to think and imagine? Is development a craft and we are craftspeople? Or, as our titles imply, are we "software engineers"? That last suggestion really bristles people. Get over it; the issue has been decided for us.

Oh, there are plenty of people who still think that this is an open debate. I've followed the developer aliases, seen the Web sites, and heard the arguments. Heck, I've made the arguments, claiming forcefully, "We're developers, not engineers." (See "Pushing the envelopes: Continued contention over dev schedules" in Chapter 1).

Developing software is a creative process. It's an unpredictable process, dealing with custom components that have poorly understood properties. Many believe that there's no hope of applying engineering practices to this process in our lifetimes. They contend that we are at worst hacks, cowboys, cowgirls, and reckless amateurs, and at best creative craftspeople. Well, treating software development as a craft is no longer adequate.

Craft a desk, engineer a car

Don't get me wrong, I love crafts. There's nothing like a sturdy hand-crafted table and chairs, an elegant hand-crafted timepiece, or even a well-designed and crafted home in which you can raise your family. I just don't want to drive my car over a well-crafted bridge. I don't want someone to stick a well-crafted pacemaker in my chest. And I don't want to rely on well-crafted software to run my business, protect my assets, or direct my actions. I want well-engineered software for these tasks and so do our customers.

So, what separates a hack from a craftsperson and a craftsperson from an engineer? A hack learns as he goes, acts then thinks, cleans up his mess after someone's stepped in it. Sound familiar? In contrast, a craftsperson studies, plans, uses the best practices and tools, and takes pride in her work. This describes the best of us who develop software. But craftsmanship doesn't quite reach engineering status because you still don't know what you are going to get. Craftsmanship lacks certainty and predictability; you make your best estimate instead of knowing.

It's what you know

Engineering, on the other hand, is all about knowing instead of guessing. It's about measuring, predicting, controlling, and optimizing. An engineer doesn't wonder about things, he looks it up. An engineer doesn't estimate, she calculates. An engineer doesn't hope, he knows. This doesn't mean that engineering lacks creativity or innovation, just that there are known boundaries to safe behavior that must be enforced to achieve reliable results.

But we all know that software is unpredictable. How can we possibly apply structured engineering practices to software? The secret is so obvious; it kills me that I didn't see it sooner. Don't try to predict the software, predict the people who make it. The constant in software development isn't the software, it's the developer. People are creatures of habit and our habits are predictable. That realization may not sound profound, but it changes everything.

To thine own self be true

It may hurt to think that you are predictable, but you are. A little introspection will reveal that truth. You make the same mistakes over and over again. You take about the same amount of time every time to write certain types of functions or objects. You even write them by using about the same amount of code. It's scary but true, and more importantly, measurable and predictable. Holy sh-t.

Okay, so I didn't believe it either at first, but then I spent a couple of weeks measuring myself programming and graphing the results. Like the other 4,500 programmers who tried this before me, I'm an open book. For any given type of function or class, I take roughly the same amount of time, write the same number of lines, make the same number of mistakes of the same kind, and take about the same amount of time to fix them based on type. This insight is embarrassing, but powerful.

> **Eric Aside**   The two weeks I spent measuring myself were part of a course on the Personal Software Process (PSP) from the Software Engineering Institute (SEI). PSP is part of an engineering team approach to software development called the Team Software Process (TSP). I was impressed with their demonstrated results and the theory behind them. My team tried TSP for a while. I'll talk more about how it went shortly.

If you just draw a diagram of the classes that you need to write, you can know with measurably high confidence how long it will take, how many lines you'll write, how many bugs you'll have and of what type. You can also know how many bugs will surface in design review, code review, by the compiler, in unit test, and by the test team.

What's in a number

So what? So this: If you know how many bugs you'll find, you can know to keep looking, you can know when you've looked enough, you can know how many other people should look and what they should look for. You can say, with confidence, we've found and fixed 99.9999% of the bugs, period. In other words, you can know instead of guess. Congratulations, you're an engineer.

Okay, what's the cost? How much crud do I need to track in order to do high-confidence predictions? Here's the full list of the measurements you must collect:

- **Work time spent between checkpoints**   This is the amount of time that you actually spent doing work between each checkpoint. (Checkpoint examples include design complete, design review complete, code written, code review complete, code builds cleanly, unit tests run clean, and code checked-in.)

- **Time and rework spent on check-pointed work**   This is the amount of time spent on reworking stuff you "finished" in an earlier checkpoint, along with a one-line description of what happened and some categorization so that you can reference it later. (This is typically a task like design changes after design complete or code changes for bug fixes or whatever.)

- **Number of lines of code you added, deleted, or changed**   This one is obvious and can be automated easily.

That's it. It's all information that you can get with a decent timer and notepad, although teams are working on tools to make it even easier. You must be consistent for accurate results; but with only these data points, you get more information than you could have dreamed possible.

For instance, you can answer questions like, "How much time did I spend doing real work this week?"; "How many times did we have to change the API, and how long did that take?"; "What percentage of bugs is found in code review?"; "How does the percentage of code review bugs found relate to the time spent in code review?"; "What kinds of bugs are mostly found early vs. late?"; "What kind of bugs take the most time to fix, when are they introduced, and when are they found?"

It's their habits that separate them

So, what's the catch? The data is only good for one person. Everyone's habits are different; you can't compare my data to yours and have a meaningful discussion. This is actually a good thing because managers shouldn't be using data for comparisons anyway. As I discussed in my article "More than a number" (found in Chapter 9, "Being a Manager, and Yet Not Evil Incarnate"), when managers use data against people the measures get gamed.

Although data can't be shared or compared for individuals, it can be aggregated for teams. This is a manager's dream come true. You can do all this prediction and quality management on the team level with little effort and extremely high levels of accuracy. Because aggregated data drives toward the mean, the results for teams are no less accurate than they are for each individual. You could manage 100 people and be able to predict completion dates and bug counts to the level of accuracy of a single individual. Yowza!

Think big to get small

Okay, what's the punch line? Maybe engineering software is possible to some extent. Maybe you can predict code size, bug counts, development time, and so on starting from just a swag at the list of objects in your system. How does that data translate to results? Teams both inside and outside Microsoft that used data like this to target and control their bug counts have lowered their defect rates from the typical 40–100 bugs per thousand lines of code to 20–60 bugs per million lines of code. In other words, the typical Microsoft team of 15–20 devs that produces 3,000–5,000 test bugs per year would instead produce 3–5 test bugs per year.

And yes, those low bug rates include integration bugs. People bicker and moan about how complicated bugs can be in our big software systems. It's true; you do find a large percentage of bugs during integration. But what kind of bugs are they after you find them? Are they wildly complex timing bugs with weird unpredictable multithreaded interactions? Maybe one or two of them are, but the remaining thousands of bugs are brain-dead trivial parameter mix-ups, syntax errors, missing return value checks, or even more commonly, design errors that should have been found before a line of code was written.

Good to great

Of course, the way great teams control their bug counts is by using design reviews, code reviews, tools like PREfast, and unit testing. However, these methods alone only make a developer a craftsperson, dropping bugs by a factor of 10 or so, not by a factor of 1,000. The drop isn't that large because you have to guess where and how to apply your craft; you don't know. By investing in a small number of measurements and taking advantage of your own habits, you can know. You can graduate into being an engineer and earn that factor of 1,000 improvement.

That's a big and necessary step for delivering the quality and reliability that our customers demand. You must also discern the requirements and create a detailed design that meets them, but those amusing subjects will have to wait until next time. For now, dropping your bug counts to around 10 per year would be a nice start.

Eric Aside   So how did my team's experiment with TSP go? Did we achieve a 1,000 times reduction in bugs (rework)? Not exactly. To be fair, my team isn't a typical team and we didn't stick with TSP long enough to get reliable results. The problem wasn't the methodology, though it was unnecessarily burdensome and rigid at times. The problem was the tools—they were unusable and unreliable, and they didn't scale to large teams. Slowly but surely, my team is creating simple modular tools to collect the data and replicate the results that teams at Microsoft and elsewhere have achieved.

July 1, 2005: "Review this—Inspections"

When you get invited to a spec review meeting, what's the first thought that enters your mind? My guess is, "Necessary evil," or "Okay, time to see how bad things are." Perhaps you just let out a resigned groan like the guy who cleans up after elephants at a circus.

How about when you attend a code review? Ever leave feeling uneasy—like you just left your home for a week, but you can't remember if all the doors are locked and the lights are off?

In design reviews, do you just sit there while two people debate a few areas so long that your issues never get heard? Even worse, half the people haven't read the docs in advance, which may be a good thing because the author didn't run a spell check on his Swiss-cheese–excuse of a design.

Well sir or madam, you have a problem. Unfortunately, your team is suffering from a common condition: "Failing to Orchestrate Collective Knowledge Effectively for Design." You're FOCKED.

A bad combination

You get FOCKED when you don't differentiate three activities:

- Generating ideas and solutions
- Receiving feedback on work in progress
- Assessing quality and detecting issues in completed work

Most teams combine these activities into one—a review meeting. Some might call it a clustered version of FOCKED.

Naturally, this is a bad move. By combining three different goals into the same exercise, you not only guarantee failure in every activity, you frustrate and confuse the participants and send mixed messages to the organizer.

How do you avoid consenting to this treatment? Understand what your goals are, and choose the most appropriate and effective method to achieve them. Brainstorming, informal reviews, and inspections are the methods I suggest.

The perfect storm

When you want to generate ideas and solutions, use brainstorming. You can brainstorm in small or large groups or one-on-one in front of a whiteboard. With more than four or five people, use an affinity technique: Everyone gets a stack of Post-It notes. They write down as many ideas as they can and group the notes into common themes.

Regardless of how you brainstorm, the goal is to get as many ideas as possible. There's no bad suggestion. The best solution may result from parts of many initially unworkable proposals.

Brainstorming is great to use early in the design and specing process, before you've written much down. Get together with key stakeholders and feature team members and crank out ideas.

If you can't pick a solution, use the Pugh Concept Selection to decide. This method uses a table to rate each solution against each independent requirement. The rating is positive, negative, or zero, based on fit. Then scale the rating based on significance. The solution with the highest total wins.

> **Online materials**   Pugh Concept Selection (PughConceptSelectionExample.xls; PughConcept-SelectionTemplate.xlt)

Better yet, don't pick a solution. Keep each design idea until you discover some constraint or factor that makes it unfeasible. Eventually, you'll be left with the one solution that optimally meets all your requirements. The Toyota folks call this "set-based design."

Who's in charge?

Be careful not to confuse brainstorming with "design by committee." Although many people may contribute and discuss different ideas, there should be one owner of the design. The owner has the final say; her name is the one on the design.

Having a single owner gives the design clarity and consistency. It creates accountability for meeting the requirements and a champion for understanding and defending the spirit of the design choices.

In contrast, design by committee is for groups of wimps who need others to blame when their spineless consensus crud implodes under the smallest of strains.

So, what do you think?

Sometimes you just need to know if you're headed in the right direction. Reviews of one-page specs can provide this. So can informal peer reviews through e-mail or at team meetings. Reviews of work in progress act as checkpoints against wasted effort caused by early naïve or subtle mistakes.

The problem is that people use this type of review under the guise of issue detection. Informal reviews are pathetic at issue detection compared to other methods. Yet almost all spec, design, and code reviews done in engineering groups are informal reviews.

Trying to use informal reviews for issue detection (like a quick, "Hey, have a look at this bug fix before I check it in") sets up you, your team, and our products for failure. You get a half-hearted review by unprepared reviewers. Your team gets a constant sense of, "Are these reviews really worth it? I feel like we miss stuff." And your products get buggy code that you still end up fixing later—hopefully before you ship.

Teams can get disenchanted or think that they have to work the reviews even harder. The shame of it is that informal reviews are wonderful for getting feedback. They were never meant for quality control or assurance. There's no reason to drag in the whole team, berate them for not reading the docs or code, then slog through an ineffective meeting, all for an informal review.

If you need feedback, ask for feedback. Get feedback early. Make it fun and casual, then thank folks for their help. Walkthroughs (guiding a group through your design or code) and informal reviews are great ways to do this. If you need issue detection for quality control and assurance, you need to use inspections.

It's just a formality

Inspections are for issue detection in completed work. Period. They stink for generating ideas and solutions or for giving feedback. However, if you want to find all the bugs in your designs and code before it ships, you want inspections.

Inspections list all the issues found and give you an accurate estimate of all the issues not spotted. The secret is in the formality. Inspections take no more time than thorough informal reviews, but their formal procedure leaves no unaccounted issues.

> **Eric Aside**   The particular approach to formal inspections I describe here is based on the one used by the Software Engineering Institute's Team Software Process (TSP).

Here's a quick summary of the procedure:

- **Plan**   Ensure that the work is complete, then schedule the meeting.
- **Overview**   Give all your inspectors (that is, reviewers) enough context to understand your work, a checklist of issue types to find, and a copy of the work itself.
- **Prepare**   Tell the inspectors to individually list all the issues they find (based on the issue-type checklist).
- **Meet**   Get inspectors together to merge issue lists, agree on duplicates, determine which issues must be fixed, and decide if the work will require a re-inspection after the issues are corrected.
- **Rework**   Address all the must-fix issues and as many minor issues as you choose.
- **Follow-up**   Learn the root cause of the issues you fixed, and update your checklists to avoid those issues in the future. Repeat the inspection process as required.

The magic of inspections is found in the checklist of issue types and in the issue-list merge. However, before we get there, the work must be ready.

Are you ready, kids?

The point of inspections is to find all the remaining issues in your completed work. If the work is incomplete and full of gaps and basic errors, the inspectors will get bogged down in triviality, lose focus on the tougher checklist issues, and hate your guts for wasting their time.

Before you schedule the meeting, make sure you have a clean spec, design document, or source code. Ensure that specs and design docs cover everything you need to have verified. Ensure that source code compiles, builds, and functions. This includes having a clean PREfast run and completing any other aspects of your group's initial quality bar. Ideally, your team should have someone assigned to verify that the work is complete before scheduling an inspection.

A great way to ensure your work is complete is to conduct a personal inspection. Lots of developers already do this. They look through their own code or designs trying to find issues. Add a one-page checklist of your common mistakes and you've got a personal inspection. You'll want your checklist to contain the most common ways you mess up. Every person's checklist is unique because everyone makes different kinds of mistakes; for example, I'm great with resource cleanup, but I constantly switch parameters around. Update your checklist after every inspection, removing issues you no longer find and adding new issues you start to notice.

Checking it twice

After your work is complete, send it to inspectors (a few days before the scheduled meeting). Attach enough context for them to understand the work, such as a description and the checklist to use.

The team checklist should be one page, like your personal checklist. However, the team checklist should be filled with issue types that concern your team—for example, particular security, reliability, logic, or failure handling issues that your team's software is most prone to have. Like your personal checklist, the team checklist should be regularly updated to remove issues that are no longer prevalent (the team has improved) and to add arising issues.

The inspectors then carefully and independently inspect the completed work for the issue types on the checklist, noting the type and line number for each issue. Often inspectors will find issues that aren't on the checklist. Those issues should be noted as well. Issue types that are prominent but missing from the checklist should be researched for the best way to eliminate them in the future (possibly by updating the unit testing, automated code analysis, or inspection checklist).

There are many approaches to inspecting. One effective technique is to look through the entire work for each issue type, one at a time, then move to the next issue in the checklist. Sure, it sounds monotonous, but the lack of context switching makes it an easy and effective method. Regardless of their approach, after a little practice, inspectors get very good at catching a huge percentage of the issues.

By using the same checklists, the inspectors are ready to merge issue lists and determine how many issues they found in common.

Magical merge meeting

At the inspection meeting, the inspector who found the most issues fills out a spreadsheet, listing all his issues. Often an appointed moderator who is experienced with the process handles the data entry and keeps the meeting on track.

> **Online materials**   Inspection worksheet (InspectionWorksheetExample.xls; Inspection-WorksheetTemplate.xlt)

For each issue found, the group of inspectors note who else found the same issue (type and occurrence). Multiple issues can be found on the same source line. In addition to agreeing on duplicates, the inspectors also mark whether or not the issue must be fixed or if it should be left to the discretion of the author.

When the first inspector finishes his list, the next inspector follows the same procedure, skipping over issues already noted by the first inspector. This continues until all issues are captured in the spreadsheet. The spreadsheet then automatically computes statistics like defect density, yield, the total number of issues found, and the likely number of issues still lurking in the work.

How is that possible? Because everyone looked at the same work for the same issues and you captured which issues were found and missed by each person. So you can accurately estimate how many total issues were missed overall. You are no longer FOCKED.

> **Eric Aside**   The math is based on the old capture-recapture technique used to estimate the number of fish in a lake. You catch *n* fish at various lake locations, tag them, and release them into the lake. Later you catch another bunch of fish at the same locations and note the percentage tagged. Then you divide *n* by that percentage and you have a good estimate for the total number of fish. For inspections, the first inspector's issues are considered "tagged." The other inspectors "fish" for issues in the same design or code "lake." The results give a simple yet accurate estimate of the total number of issues.

Tricks of the trade

Naturally, there are lots of little tricks to help you get the most out of inspections:

- While you can do inspections with large groups, typically you only need two or three inspectors to get great results (not counting the author). Start with three to five inspectors to get the hang of it, and then drop the number as people gain skill.

- Just like informal reviews, it takes time to do inspections right. Plan three to five pages per hour for docs and 200–400 lines per hour for code. These are reasonable rates. Faster and you miss issues, slower and your head turns to mush.

- Don't inspect too much at once. A thousand lines of pure new code will take around three or four hours to inspect. Be kind and inspect it in chunks.

- Do not discuss fixes at the meeting. Inspections are for issue detection, not for generating ideas. Don't let yourselves get FOCKED.

- It helps to have a moderator experienced at filling out the spreadsheet and keeping people from discussing fixes.

- The moderator can also be used to verify that work is complete and ready for inspection. Until people get the hang of it (including people new to your group), you should definitely have a moderator.

- Your team should have a quality bar for how many issues are acceptable to pass on for further testing. If the results of your inspection indicate the number of must-fixes remaining is too high, the authors must have their work re-inspected after fixing the issues found. A nice guideline is: any yield under 75% requires re-inspection.

Getting it right

When used properly, inspections can decrease by orders of magnitude the number of issues released to customers. Teams, both inside and outside Microsoft, have seen these results repeatedly. The key is to not confuse your goals for orchestrating collective knowledge.

If you want to generate some ideas or solutions, run a brainstorming meeting, keeping an open mind and avoiding criticism. If you want early feedback, ask for an informal review, allowing people some flexibility and expecting that some issues will be missed. If you want to assess quality and detect issues, organize an inspection, focusing on the findings and not the fixes. Remember that you can always use brainstorming or informal reviews to help you fix the issues you find.

A little communication and clarity can go a long way. Knowing when to apply which techniques for group engagement can take the failure out of FOCKED, and we all know what a profitable strategy that can be.

October 1, 2006: "Bold predictions of quality"

I've been busy dogfooding lately. It's an ideal diversion for masochists. When it gets to be too much, I can always take respite in a nice horror film. Thank goodness what passes for dogfood now is a vast improvement over years past.

> **Eric Aside**   *Dogfooding* is the practice of using prerelease builds of products for your day-to-day work. It encourages teams to make products right from the start, and it provides early feedback on the products' value and usability.

Years ago, running a dogfood build and having your machine unplugged were almost indistinguishable in terms of productivity. These days, substantial parts of dogfood builds are fully functional, while others remain unusable, unreliable, or unconscionable. This begs the question, "Why?"

Why are some portions of new builds solid, thoughtful, and engaging, while others remain flaky, unfathomable, and exasperating? How can that be? Ask managers and they'll say, "Well, it's tough to tell ahead of time what's going to be good or rancid." Sounds like they're washing down my dogfood with male bovine dung.

Enigma? I don't think so

Software quality is unpredictable? Don't make me gag. Poor-quality software has all the subtlety of a neighborhood ice cream truck. You know it's bad for you; you know it's coming a mile away; yet you can't resist. Managers choose to ignore the signs and buy the ice cream (poor software) because they hate disappointing the children (upper management) and can't resist the instant gratification ("progress").

We've gotten so used to poor software that many people have forgotten the early signs. Let me summarize the rest of this column and make it simple for you. Good software is solid and originated out of complete and critical customer scenarios. Bad software is buggy and originated out of someone's behind.

Twins of evil

How do you spot bad software before it's integrated into the main branch? First, remember there are two aspects to quality—engineering and value. Most engineers get caught up in the engineering side of quality—the bugs. However, flawlessly engineered features can be glorified crud to customers if the ideas came from the wrong place. I talk about this more in "The other side of quality" in Chapter 6, "Software Design If We Have Time."

We're looking to predict both buggy code and code with questionable pedigree. Predicting buggy code is easier, so we'll start there.

The usual suspects

In 2003, Pat Wickline studied the root causes of late cycle bugs in Windows Server 2003. The results were similar to his 2001 study of bugs in Windows 2000 Hotfixes. Simply put, more than 90% of bugs could have been found by design reviews, code reviews, code analysis (like

PREfast), and planned testing. No one method would have found every bug, but the combination nearly finds them all.

In 2004, Nachiappan Nagappan studied measurable attributes in an engineering system that correlated well to bugs found later. Those attributes were code churn (the percentage of code lines added or changed per file) and code analysis results (the number of PREfast or PREfix defects found per line of code).

> **Eric Aside**   He's updated his thinking to focus on churn and complexity measures.

If you want to prevent poorly engineered code from getting into the main branch, have your build track code churn and code analysis results. If those measures go beyond the norms for quality code, then reject the check-in. If your developers don't like it, tell them to do more design and code reviews and write more unit tests.

"What if there's too much code churn, but the feature enables a complete and critical customer scenario?" you might ask. Allow me first to congratulate you on coming up with the only decent reason to not junk the code entirely. Then junk the code entirely. It's time for a rewrite of that section. That's the only way the feature will ever reach your engineering quality goals.

You're gonna love it

Let's move on to predicting questionable feature pedigree. Buggy code is easy to measure and control, though it does require management to set a bar and stick to it. The value of software is harder to measure, but in the end it requires the same thing—management must set a bar and stick to it.

How do you know if a feature or check-in will really be valued by customers? That's easy. If it's part of a complete and critical customer scenario, then users will love it. How do you know if a scenario is complete and critical? That's the hard part.

Luckily, you don't have to do that work. We pay marketing, product planning, and upper management to figure out the complete and critical customer scenarios for a release. No one feature team or product group can do it, because complete scenarios cut across product groups. Instead, engineering's job is to tell the planners what's possible, and then solidly implement the planned critical scenarios from end to end.

Quit fooling around

Of course, overzealous engineers of all kinds, not just PMs, will try to sneak in features that aren't part of planned complete and critical scenarios. While doing so might relieve that engineer's creative constipation, what comes out is predictably putrid for customers.

To trap poorly conceived features before scarce resources get wasted, you must take two steps:

1. Have a clearly documented vision or value proposition that lists the complete and critical scenarios for the release. Prototypes, personas, user experience designs, and high-level architectures also help clarify what's needed immensely.

2. Convene a governing board who owns the vision or value proposition and have them review every feature. If the feature doesn't fit a complete and critical scenario, it's cut. Period. At the beginning of each major milestone, every GPM reviews their list of upcoming features with the governing board. While the board may not review every feature in great detail, they must still ruthlessly and relentlessly uphold the quality, value, and integrity of the release.

> **Eric Aside**   The best groups at Microsoft have been following this process for years.

These two steps precisely correspond to setting the bar and sticking to it. While this bar is more subjective than the engineering quality bar, both require the same disciplined commitment by management to be successful.

Quality is no accident

It's not difficult to predict quality. In fact, it is straightforward. Yet managers at all levels rarely apply the rigor necessary to assure quality.

Maybe managers are afraid assuring quality will add too much time to the schedule. As if doing it right the first time and sticking to only the critical needs takes longer. In fact, when quality is what customers expect, then focusing on quality is always the fastest way to ship.

Maybe managers are afraid engineers won't like assuring quality. As if engineers take no pride in their work or enjoy ambiguity and wasting their time. In fact, engineers take great pride in the quality of their work, prefer to know what's expected, and hate wasting effort.

The truth is that quality is expected, quality is fundamental, quality is central to our success. It is because our customers say it is.

Quality is the right thing to do and the right way to do it. It is the key to our future survival and prosperity. Quality is no accident. You can predict and control it. All you need is a brain and a backbone. Get yours today.

> **Eric Aside**   While they both vigorously advocate quality, it's worth noting the differences between "Where's the beef" and "Bold predictions of quality." The first discusses why quality is needed and the mechanics of getting it. The second describes how to measure and refine your work to push the quality bar higher. We've made significant progress, but quality is an ideal that demands eternal vigilance.

Chapter 6
Software Design If We Have Time

In this chapter:

September 1, 2001: "A tragedy of error handling"..........................102

February 1, 2002: "Too many cooks spoil the broth—Sole authority" 104

May 1, 2004: "Resolved by design"......................................106

February 1, 2006: "The other side of quality—Designers and architects" 111

August 1, 2006: "Blessed isolation—Better design"..........................114

One of the basic questions I have to answer in my current role is, "What software development improvement would have the largest impact on the quality and value of our products?" My initial response would be broad and consistent measurement of desired outcomes, because they tell you the right improvements to make and the impact of making them. It takes out the guesswork and provides positive team-based motivation.

However, if I had to speculate what the measured outcomes would tell us, I'd guess feature crews (lean development) and better design would have the biggest impacts. (We're already doing reviews, code analysis, and unit testing.) I spent the second chapter talking about lean development. It's time to talk about better design.

In this chapter, I. M. Wright exposes the fundamentals and intricacies of software design. The first column starts with basic error handling. The second one denounces code and data replication. The third column outlines the complete design process, including suggested practices. The fourth column focuses on designing great user experiences and making them real; and the last one reveals the true value and purpose of architecture beyond keeping the architect occupied.

Before getting into the columns, I'd like to address the two biggest excuses software engineers give for avoiding design work: the design will emerge, and there isn't enough time. Emergent design claims up-front design is a waste; instead, you should discover and refactor the design as you go. That's great for small code bases (less than 100,000 lines), when refactoring isn't a big deal. However, most production code bases are far larger, and serious rework is extraordinarily expensive. Not thinking things through before you refactor or make other changes can cost you dearly. So take the time now or you're sure not to have enough time later.

– Eric

September 1, 2001: "A tragedy of error handling"

If there is any single aspect of our production code that has been traditionally and uniformly lame, it's error handling. Office made some great strides in this area for Office 2000 with its LAME registry setting for error dialogs. Windows 2000 also improved things quite a bit by working hard at providing meaningful messages with actionable directions. Both Office XP and Windows XP now automatically report severe errors back to us to evaluate and track. However, these efforts only bring us from kicking our users when they're down to apologizing for slamming them in the first place and then perhaps handing them a cane to push themselves upright.

> **Eric Aside**   The internal Office 2000 LAME registry setting added a "lame" button to every Office 2000 error dialog. If you didn't like the dialog, you could hit the "lame" button and your "vote" would be recorded. These days it's been replaced by the "Was this information helpful" link all users can access at the bottom of Office error dialogs.

So why doesn't the code fix the error itself? From my years of staring at our code, I see two main reasons. First, the code has no idea what went wrong in the first place. Second, the error-handling code is not in a position to fix the problem, even if it knew what it was. These two problems are related and pervasive. Let's talk a bit about the typical situation.

The horror, the horror

A dev writes a bunch of code. Another dev adds a bunch more. Then they add code from some other group. Then they add more. Then they realize that they need to handle errors, but they don't want to go back and put error handling everywhere, so they write a Routine for Error Central Handling, or RECH, and propagate errors to it. Then they write the next version that adds more code, maybe written by completely different people. Some folks return meaningful errors, some return a simple pass/fail. Some folks like exceptions; some folks like error codes. The RECH only works with exceptions or error codes, not both.

> **Eric Aside**   I made up the RECH acronym for this column. I have no idea what the actual name is, if any, for the unfortunate practice it references.

If the RECH works with exceptions, then sections of code that return error codes are wrapped with a throw on failure. If the RECH works with error codes, then sections of code that throw exceptions are wrapped with a generic catch that returns an error code. If a section of code returns pass/fail, then it gets wrapped with a generic exception or error code, which might be converted later to an error code or exception. Even if you start with a function that returns descriptive error codes, like much of Win32 or OLE, these calls are often wrapped by a function that either reduces the codes to pass/fail or ignores them completely. All along the way, information is lost...forever.

Taking exception

To add pain to agony, the mixing of exceptions with error codes is a disaster. You can't use exceptions if you don't unwind your stack objects properly. This usually means that anything requiring non-trivial destruction must be an object. That's easy in C#, but it's hard in C and C++.

For example, you must use smart pointers exclusively in code that throws exceptions. However, if some parts of the code use exceptions and others don't, you often get a situation in which an exception-throwing function is called from an error-code-returning function and the catch doesn't happen till you're three levels up. Thus an error generates more errors and corrective action is compromised. It gets even worse in multithreaded apps where exceptions must be handled per thread.

Don't lose it, use it!

You want to use the error information you have in the best possible way. So what do you do? First, pick your poison and go with it.

- If you want to use exceptions, fine, but use them everywhere and make everything non-trivial an object (the .NET Framework model).

- If you want to use error codes, fine, but propagate them in a lossless fashion or handle them at the source.

- If you really must mix metaphors, wrap every exception call inside a return code function with your exception-handling routine, and wrap every return code function call inside an exception function with your return-code-handling routine. Now at least you are not losing data.

Next, you need to plan for action when an error occurs. Figure out the highest level at which you still know what to do if a section of code fails. That level is rarely the top, so stop RECHing.

At that highest actionable level, add your error handling. This will add more than just one error-handling function to your code, but it probably won't add a thousand. The key is to go as high as you can in the stack, but no higher. When using error codes, you may need to add buffers to your application object to hold key information like file paths or flags so that your error handling can fix the problem.

Only as a last resort—or as an act of bravado—report the error to the user. The net result is a system that always seems to work or at least always seems to care. Our customers will love us for it.

February 1, 2002: "Too many cooks spoil the broth—Sole authority"

Segall's Law says, "A man with one watch knows what time it is; a man with two watches is never quite sure." While most people intuitively understand this for watches, it's apparently unfathomable to most devs when it comes to programming. Our code is littered with repetitions of algorithms and data, not only across the company, but also within single applications.

It seems that everyone wants to craft their own watch. We store the same user or system data many different ways with no hope of reconciliation. We copy and paste code all over the place, and then we let it get out of sync. The whole idea of different teams sharing code is ludicrous if we can't even manage to share code within the same application.

A picture is worth a thousand words

Don't believe me? Open Windows Explorer and find a directory with a .jpg or .gif file. Open a blank slide in PowerPoint. Copy the .jpg or .gif file and paste it to the slide background. Now paste it to the text area. So far, so good.

Now drag the .jpg or .gif file and drop it in the background. Next drag and drop it in the text area. Whoops! Try this same experiment with formatted text. Notice that you get a smart tag on paste, but no smart tag on drop.

> **Eric Aside**   It looks like PowerPoint fixed the image bug in Office 2007, but the problem with formatted text remains.

I'm not trying to single out PowerPoint. Try it with other applications and other data. You'll notice how data from a paste is treated differently than data from a drop, and it's not just due to where it's placed. Each of these scenarios should act the same. The data is identical in all cases. In fact, paste and drop do act the same in Word (nice job).

So why does the same data inserted into a document in roughly the same way produce different results? Well, duh! It's a different code path. The irony here is that duplicate code paths are often created by copying and pasting the original code itself.

Does anyone really know what time it is?

Having two code paths to do the same work is just like having two watches. Maybe they behave the same, maybe they don't. Keeping the code paths synchronized with bug fixes and spec changes is a nightmare.

Of course, the solution is to write one routine that does the work and then call that routine from each code path. That's first-year computer programming fundamentals, and yet we make this freshman mistake over and over again.

But the problem doesn't begin and end with functions. It extends to data as well. How many bugs have you fixed that were caused by out-of-sync data values? Could these data values have been derived from one value, but were instead kept separately? And don't even get me started on how often I'm forced to type my e-mail address every day.

Maintaining two watches and keeping them both accurate requires manual synchronization. This is a tedious and error-prone process. It's much easier to have a single watch. Unfortunately, many of us have a watch, a PC, and a Pocket PC, plus we work with a whole mess of people who have their own timepieces.

Luckily, your PC can synchronize automatically with a network synced to an atomic clock. Then your Pocket PC, your watch, and everyone else's can be synced to your PC's time. Automate all that and the problem is solved.

There can be only one

There is a fundamental principle at work here. I call it "sole authority." Every piece of data should have a sole authority for its value. Every operation should have a sole authority for how it is done. Keeping all your timepieces in sync is possible because there is a sole authority for the current time. Consistent user interface is possible if there is a sole authority for how each operation is completed—for things like painting, data input, and message handling.

Every time you copy and paste code, stop and think, "Am I repeating myself or is this really a different operation? What is the sole authority for how this operation is conducted?" Then act accordingly.

When you are about to create yet another registry entry, stop and think, "Is this really a whole new concept to the user or system, or can I derive this value from another authority?"

If you are asked to create a custom control, think, "Is there an existing authority on how this control should work, and how can I use it?"

For you performance geeks out there, remember that caching a computed result is often slower than recomputing the result, due to faster processing speeds and the gating effect of cache hits.

Everything is connected to everything else

Sole authority becomes much more important in the .NET world. We are hard at work giving our users one authority for their identity, another authority for their calendar, one for their address book, and so on. We are betting that the resulting convenience will be a boon to customers and a boost to our bottom line.

But it only works if we use one method to perform all the associated operations. Doing otherwise not only opens us to bugs and makes our users confused and frustrated, but it also can multiply security holes and increase operational costs.

> **Eric Aside**   While the idea of having one authority for identity, calendaring, and so on was good in concept, concerns around trust, privacy, and interoperability caused the notion to fall short in the marketplace.

In software development, too many cooks do spoil the broth. Spoiled broth can give our customers and partners dysentery, not to mention what it does to the cooks. By simply questioning what code or data is the sole authority for every operation or query, we can simplify our code, make it easier to fix and maintain, and give our customers and partners a consistent, pleasant, and intelligent experience.

May 1, 2004: "Resolved by design"

There you are, sitting in front of a whiteboard while some obsessive dweeb goes on incessantly about some design issue. You try to ground the discussion and bring the conversation back to the actual work, but this neurotic nag won't let anything go. "What if this happens?" "We haven't considered this." "We don't know that." "We can't start yet." Analysis paralysis. Meanwhile the clock is ticking and you've got to ship.

We all know design is important. We all know quality design is essential to quality products. But darn it, at some point you've got to code. At some point you've got to ship. The best design in the world is just wallpaper if you can't get it coded in time, and I don't hear many managers saying, "Take all the design time you need."

What is good enough?

Yet the other extreme is just as evil. Jumping in and coding with just a token of forethought on a fleeting whiteboard leads to tremendous rework, tons of bugs, and a fragile framework for future development. Most analysis of defects reveals between 40–50% of them were in the design. Skipping the design step is no solution, but how much analysis is enough? You know when you're done coding—when is the design sufficient to begin development?

To me, the lack of a well-defined design process is the single most debilitating developer debacle. It's not like you don't know it's important—coding is far easier, faster, and dramatically less error prone with a clear and complete design. No worries, no quandaries, no surprises, and none of the infamous Homer Simpson, "Doh!" But did you learn a design process in college? No, they don't teach it. Did you learn one when joining Microsoft? Not likely; most groups are pretty ad hoc about design, and many hardly practice design at all. Ah, but your good buddy I. M. is here to help.

Design complete

The most important aspect of a design process is completeness. Completeness tells you what is enough. You don't want to do too much or too little. Software has multiple dimensions. There are internal workings and external interfaces. There are static concepts and dynamic interactions. All of these dimensions must be covered to create a complete design. Additionally, there are different design tools to help you work with the different areas and levels of abstraction. Here's a table to help make sense of this.

Dimensions of software design

	External	**Internal**
Static	PM spec	Dev spec
	API definition	Test-Driven Development
Dynamic	Use cases	Sequence diagrams
	Scenarios and personas	State diagrams, flow charts, threat and failure modeling

Watts S. Humphrey showed me this table while he was visiting Microsoft once. My team and I filled it in with common design practices and the movement from quadrant to quadrant.

Most design processes spiral inward with a clockwise flow from the lower-left quadrant of the table, starting with the high-level design steps:

- **Scenarios and personas**   Describes at a high level how customers will interact with the software.

- **PM spec**   Describes the external pieces of the puzzle, which include requirements, dialog boxes, menus, screens, data collection, and other features.

- **Dev spec**   Specifies the class hierarchy and relationships, component stack and relationships, and anything else needed at a high level to describe the structure of the implementation. This spec is also referred to as the design document (a misnomer, given its limited scope) or architecture document.

- **State diagrams, flow charts, threat and failure modeling**   Describe and control complex interactions between the objects and components in the system.

A few comments on these initial, high-level design steps:

- Each step has a limited, well-defined scope. By separating and covering all four design quadrants, you won't need to rely on lots of words and repetition to fully describe the design. Be brief, reuse prior examples, and rely on simple diagrams or pictures where appropriate.

- Not every step is necessary in every design. Some designs have little external interface. Some designs don't carry state. Use your own best judgment.

- The external quadrants have a wide audience (all disciplines). The internal quadrants have a purely technical audience.

- Unified Modeling Language (UML) provides ready-to-use diagrams for many of these areas, and there are tools that make creating UML diagrams easy. For example, Visio has a ton of built-in UML diagram types.

- Threat and failure modeling are far easier to get right by reusing component relationship diagrams that you should already have. Use Excel spreadsheets to categorize and rate threats and failures and to specify mitigations.

> **Eric Aside**   We now use a threat-modeling tool to do this work. You can find some on MSDN.

Details, details

Just as each step shown in the preceding table drove the next clockwise turn around the design dimensions at a high level, the same process occurs at more detailed levels. You basically spiral into implementation through the following steps, which are closer to the center of the table:

- **Use cases**   Simple descriptions of how actors use the system to perform tasks. Visio even has built-in shapes for use cases if you like pictures.

> **Eric Aside**   The term *use cases* is often used to describe very high level scenarios, not the simple low-level ones I'm talking about here. Sorry for any confusion.

- **API definition**   When you have the use cases, specifying the application programming interface (API) correctly becomes far easier. This step solidifies the contract between components and objects. Then you can actually start coding the implementation.

- **Test-Driven Development**   TDD provides an ideal framework for methodically and robustly creating a simple, cohesive, and well-factored implementation, complete with a full suite of unit tests.

- **Sequence diagrams**   For particularly complex functions or methods, use sequence diagrams to clarify code constructs.

A few comments on the whole design process I just outlined:

- The process has no unnecessary complexity or added steps. Each step is well defined and leads into the next step with all the information needed.

- As with any process, you may be tempted to skip steps to save time (like skipping straight to TDD without a PM spec, dev spec, or use cases). That's fine if the outcomes of those steps are trivial, but you invite peril if the outcomes are tricky (and around here outcomes tend to be tricky).

- You know what enough is and when you are done.

Show me what you're made of

Okay, so I glossed over two bits:

- How do you get the right scenarios and personas?
- How do you bridge the gap between a PM spec built from those scenarios and personas to a dev spec with a class hierarchy and relationships and a component stack and relationships?

There are two ways to get the right scenarios and personas. One way is through direct contact with customers. The second way is top-down, starting with the following even higher-level steps in the design process spiral:

- Market opportunities and personas (external-dynamic)
- Product vision document (external-static)
- Product architecture (internal-static)
- Subsystem interaction diagrams or flow charts (internal-dynamic)

Then continue spiraling into the scenarios and personas as discussed previously.

> **Eric Aside**   When you've got hundreds of millions of customers, thousands of engineers, and billions of dollars in the balance, I'd advise using a rigorous approach to high-level design. If that upsets you, I'd advise staying away from large successful projects. When that much money is involved, projects are driven by politics or process. I dislike politics.

Mind the gap

Bridging the gap between a PM spec (or higher-level product vision) and a dev spec (or higher-level product architecture) requires mapping functional requirements (like features) to design parameters (like classes or components). There are two straightforward methods for doing this:

- **Design patterns**   Recognize that you've solved this problem before, and reuse the old design.
- **Axiomatic design**   Use this method for brand-new designs and even for cleaning up and evolving old designs. The steps are fairly clear-cut:
  1. Create a table in Excel or Word, with the rows listing the functional requirements and the columns listing the design parameters. The internal cells should be blank to form a matrix. This is known as the design matrix.
  2. Ensure that each functional requirement is written to be orthogonal to the others. This often means breaking up complex requirements into basic pieces. Adding new requirements just means adding new rows (nice).

3. One by one, list design parameters that would satisfy each functional requirement. Often a design parameter (a class or component) helps satisfy more than one requirement. Mark an "X" in each cell under the design parameter column that helps satisfy the corresponding functional requirement. The design matrix should now have Xs scattered throughout the cells.

Okay, so by now we need an example. A simple one is the design for a faucet. The two orthogonal functional requirements are to control flow and temperature. Consider two alternative designs, each with different design parameters: separate hot and cold water taps, and a single lever with tilt controlling flow and rotation controlling temperature. The two corresponding design matrices look like this:

Two alternative design metrices for a faucet

	Hot tap	Cold tap		Tilt lever	Rotate lever
Flow	X	X	**Flow**	X	
Temperature	X	X	**Temperature**		X

4. Rearrange the design parameters so that no Xs appear above the diagonal of the design matrix. You may need to rethink how classes or components can better match to a smaller number of requirements to get this to work.

Notice in our example that the separate hot and cold water taps have Xs above the diagonal, while the single-lever design is nicely factored into a diagonal design matrix. The single-lever design produces a far better faucet.

5. The resulting design matrix will document a nicely factored design. If all the Xs are on the diagonal, the design is completely decoupled and will be a cinch to implement. Any Xs below the diagonal indicate dependencies and can help you guide the proper order of development. Any Xs left above the diagonal that you couldn't remove are nasty, cyclical dependencies that should be handled with great care.

Your recipe for success

So there you are—a step-by-step guide to minimal, yet complete and robust design. It may seem a bit daunting, but really each step is straightforward. By using a methodical approach, you won't miss anything, you can schedule it, and life won't seem quite so open-ended when the pressure is on.

This type of complete approach also cures analysis paralysis. Follow every step and you're done. If people try to add extra steps or bring in extra requirements, you've got documentation to halt their advances.

As I mentioned in my last column, "A software odyssey" (which appears in Chapter 5), dropping bug counts by a factor of a thousand was a necessary step toward meeting the quality that our customers are demanding. The other is discerning the requirements and creating a detailed design that meets them. By using a complete design approach along with an engineering-based implementation, we can exceed our customer's expectations for quality and value, turn around our industry, and stomp our competitors in the process.

February 1, 2006: "The other side of quality—Designers and architects"

Quality. Value. Motherhood. Ideals we can all agree are good things. Not too many people argue against them. But what is quality? What is value? I'd ask about motherhood, but my wife claims I'll never understand.

I've been at offsites where we've been asked to define quality and value. It's offsites like these that make hellfire and brimstone sound appealing. Of course, we get nowhere. If it weren't for the free chocolate chip cookies, the entire time would be wasted.

The trouble is that quality and value are wrapped in perception. Even if we built a product that precisely matched the spec with zero bugs, customers and reviewers might still hate it. If it doesn't work the way they think it should, it's junk. If it doesn't solve the problem the way they expect, it's trash.

At the same time, I-Puke can produce a buggy piece of glorified plastic that crashes twice a day, and it will get showered with praise and command premium pricing just because it reminds people of their pet rocks. Life isn't fair. The market isn't fair. And customers are fickle.

You'll have to do better than that

Of course, whining about unfair markets and fickle customers is pathetic. Microsoft has traditionally dealt with customer capriciousness in two ways: wowing customers with new must-have features and chasing down competitors.

Unfortunately, as the software market matures and broadens, customers get featured-out and computer usage becomes more critical, making customers more conservative. These days, customers often equate more features with more headaches. "Make the features we already have work" is the kind of enigmatic advice customers offer.

Even chasing down competitors has its limits. The strategy works well because you know exactly what customers want. Unfortunately, when you catch up, you are back to being clueless. You have jumped ahead only to fall back behind.

A change would do you good

How do we break the cycle? That's easy—with designers and architects. By designers, I mean the people involved in defining the user experience—the "what." By architects, I mean the people involved in defining the end-to-end implementation approach—the "how." Customer and business needs define the "why" and "when."

There are two sides to quality: design and execution. At Microsoft, we execute like nobody's business. Though we still have a way to go, we are improving the quality of our execution all the time.

> **Eric Aside**   The insight about quality being a combination of experience design and engineering execution is another key piece of wisdom I've gained over the years. Too often people don't separate the two or think of about only the experience or the engineering.

But what good is perfect execution if you produce a product nobody cares about? You need great design, and that's where designers and architects rule.

Good designers really understand the entire customer experience. They think it through, end to end, and design a solution that looks beyond hardware, software, networking, and other technical boundaries. The result focuses simply on how to thrill the customer. Key aspects for designers are simplicity, seamlessness, key scenarios, differentiation from current solutions, customer-driven constraints, and perceived value.

Good designers produce a pipe dream. Good architects make it real.

The man just got it wrong

Many developers think architects are all about diagrams, abstractions, and deep thoughts, instead of practicality, efficiency, and execution. They've met architects who concentrate on purity and elegance instead of being down and dirty in the code. There's a name for smug, detached architects: unemployed.

Good architects have a firm grip on reality. It's what differentiates them from designers. Though, the best designers and architects can dream beyond boundaries, yet live within them. Architects break down the pipe dream created by designers into a variety of implementation options. Each option has its own advantages and issues.

Doing it well

Good architects keep all their options open for as long as possible. As they think through how to translate the current state of technology into the designer's future vision, constraints will arise that restrict their options—constraints like cost, performance, security, reliability, legal considerations, partnerships, and dependencies. Eventually, few options will remain and an optimal, high-level implementation design—AKA the architecture—will emerge.

The next task for architects is to clearly articulate the architecture to all the products and components that together realize the designer's vision. The two most important factors are the interfaces and the dependency graph between the pieces. Often existing components and interfaces must be refactored to avoid circular dependencies or enable new variations of behavior.

Naturally, the lowest-level dependencies must be the most stable and developed first. Part of the job for architects is to devise practical ways of accomplishing this. Often it means first updating the interfaces and leaving them stable while the code underneath is reformed.

> **Eric Aside** At the risk of sounding conceited, I'd say the last three paragraphs are worth another read. They cover the simple steps that great architects follow yet most architects miss.

Next time, try sculpturing

Regardless, before a single line of shipping code is written, the designers and architects must envision and describe the road map to realize customer value. Oh, I can hear naysaying nitwits crying, "Waterfall!" at even the hint of thinking before acting. But the idea is to create a road map, not a full-scale replica. By knowing what you want to achieve and thinking through the pitfalls, you might actually have a chance of shipping a real solution.

Because the road map isn't the real thing, there's still plenty of work for the product teams that are fleshing out and executing the design. What do the designers and architects do during that time? Jump to the next project? Draw more pictures? Present papers at conferences? No, ding-a-lings—that would be disastrous.

Designers and architects must keep the product teams honest and resolve all the conflicts that arise. No one has a big enough brain to think of everything, nor should you waste years trying to do so. Good designers and architects leverage what they know as a foundation and then work with the product teams to resolve the remaining issues as answers emerge.

This means designers and architects must have strong communication skills. They must work well together as well as with the product teams to present a consistent message and guidelines. They must also have large enough brains to keep the big picture in mind as they review the details that make it possible.

Just the right tool

In addition to their vision of the future, the key tools designers use for keeping product teams on track are end-to-end scenarios and critical-to-quality (CTQ) measures. While the practice of defining and testing end-to-end scenarios is gaining critical mass support at the company, CTQ measures are just taking hold. These are the small handful of measures that will make or break the customer's sense of quality and value. They could be performance or reliability measures, like time to complete a task or uninterrupted connectivity. They could be usability features like only authenticating once or consistency of interface. Whatever speaks "quality" to the customer the loudest, those are the CTQ measures.

In addition to the architecture, the key tools architects use for keeping product teams on track are the interfaces and the dependency graph. (The dependency graph could be as simple as a block diagram or as complex as a wall-sized component graph.) The whole idea is to allow hundreds of small teams to work independently while still creating a seamless experience. The pieces will never fit without the right interfaces. The work will never remain independent without respect for clear boundaries between layers.

> **Eric Aside**   The whole idea of small team independence was important enough that I devoted the next column in this chapter to it, "Blessed isolation—Better design."

Beyond these walls

Designers and architects play different roles, but they share one aspect in common: broad, end-to-end scope. Their job is to think across feature boundaries, product boundaries, and even market boundaries to seize opportunities. That's because customers don't see any boundaries. They just see incomprehensible, unmet potential. Designers ignore the artificial boundaries to bring out the value. Architects wrestle the boundaries into submission to make it real.

Sure, we could continue to frustrate customers, play catch-up, or blow years of a lead messing around until we realize that nothing fits together. Or we could take advantage of our breadth and depth to deliver unparalleled and uncompromising value to our customers. It's not hard, but it does require the discipline to think broadly before we act, then the focus to follow through. Achieve that, and we will finally beat our toughest competitor in the market: ourselves.

August 1, 2006: "Blessed isolation—Better design"

I received plenty of what I'll call "feedback" on my last column, "Stop writing specs" (which appears in Chapter 3). According to my critics, design documentation forces design to occur and differentiates a robust architecture from, well, much of our code. Somehow readers got the impression that I was against documented design. Perhaps it was the column's title.

That impression is wrong. I am for design; I am against waste. I believe if you work with a small multidisciplinary team in a shared collaborative space, on one feature set at time from beginning to end, then you don't need to write formal specs. Continuing to write formal specs in such an environment is wasteful and should stop.

But what if your feature set is so big that your feature team has more than eight people? What if your team is spread across floors or even continents? What if you first design groups of features, then implement them all, and then test them all? All these cases call for formal written specs. Without them you can't keep your team on the same page over time or distance.

Breaking up is hard to do

Architecture. Now I can hear naïve naysayers nitpicking, "Then your whole column was pointless. No real product feature is so small or independent that it can be done by fewer than eight people in isolation." Architecture. "You're just like those Agile extremists," the dogmatic dinosaurs would continue. "They talk a good game, but at Microsoft we work on big products for big customers with big issues." Architecture.

Is there a way to bridge the gap between big products and small teams? Why yes, there is. It's called, "Architecture." The whole point of architecture is to break intractable problems into little manageable ones. Architecture, when done properly, delivers the needed isolation.

Doing it well

Unfortunately, there are countless examples of bad architecture and bad architects out there. How do you do architecture right? Funny you should ask.

While creating robust, reliable, and resilient architectures is hard, the process itself is simple:

1.   Collect scenarios and requirements the product architecture must satisfy.
2.   Ensure those scenarios and requirements are clear, complete, and independent.
3.   Map scenarios and requirements to product components that will implement them.
4.   Identify interfaces between the product components.
5.   Inspect the components and interfaces for failures and vulnerabilities.
6.   Document the components and interfaces.
7.   Redesign and refactor as issues and new requirements emerge.

Before I get into the details, which hold all the entertainment value, let's first talk logistics.

There is no "I" in team

I've known architects whose lives are out of control. Because architecture is broad by its very nature, there are loads of people involved. Some architects spend their entire days in meetings with stakeholders, followed by nights and weekends doing the actual architecture work. While the commitment is impressive, it's not advisable and likely unsustainable.

Of course, it's no better for an architect to work alone and ignore stakeholders. A far better model is the architecture team.

The architecture team is composed of senior engineers from each feature team and chaired by the product architect. They meet regularly, as often as daily at the beginning of a project, and no less than weekly thereafter.

The architecture team as a group performs all the steps I listed. One member is responsible for documenting the information collected and decisions made. (That role can rotate.) Instead of the architect traveling to stakeholders, all but the most senior stakeholders come to the team. This vastly reduces travel time and randomization for the architect.

Some product lines have architecture teams composed of product architects and chaired by the product line architect. This hierarchy works well to cover the most complex cross-product scenarios and requirements.

Step by step

Okay, we've got the steps and the people to do them. Now how about those details:

- **Collect scenarios and requirements the product architecture must satisfy.** This one should be a no-brainer. The key is getting stakeholders to review these areas with the architecture team as needed. Remember to consider the impact of quality requirements (like security), as well as functional requirements.

- **Ensure those scenarios and requirements are clear, complete, and separable.** Getting clear and complete requirements puts a burden on the architecture team, but should be clear-cut. (Don't forget performance.) The separable piece is more subtle. You want separable requirements to avoid circular dependencies. However, often multiple scenarios relate to the same underlying requirement. In that case, the architecture team must break up the scenarios into the shared piece and the independent pieces. The shared piece becomes a separate requirement.

- **Map scenarios and requirements to product components that will implement them.** This defines the architecture, the layering of the components, and their responsibilities. Ideally each requirement should be implemented by one and only one component. That would provide pure isolation and make implementation a snap.

  In real life, many components are often involved in many requirements. The components involved in the largest number of requirements are your biggest dependencies. They need to be the most stable and get completed first. Circular dependencies are to be avoided at all costs. Axiomatic design can be a useful tool for doing this difficult mapping step.

- **Identify interfaces between the product components.** Once you have the mapping, identifying interfaces is easier. If two components work together to implement a requirement, they need an interface between them; otherwise, they don't. Generally speaking, only requirement-driven interfaces should be defined at the architecture level.

- **Inspect the components and interfaces for failures and vulnerabilities.** Quality issues around security, reliability, manageability, and so on are often apparent directly in the architecture. Spotting and resolving them or mitigating them up front can save you countless hours later.

- **Document the components and interfaces.**   Yes, I said it. You should write formal documentation for your architecture. Even if your product group works with small multidisciplinary teams in shared collaborative spaces on one feature set at time from beginning to end, those small teams require isolation to function independently. They get that isolation from clearly defined interfaces and component responsibilities. The architecture is shared across teams, time, and distance, so it must be documented.

  Once the component responsibilities and interfaces have been debated, designed, debugged, and documented, the architecture is done. It's done, but it's not finished. The architecture doesn't truly get fleshed out till all the feature teams implement it.

- **Redesign and refactor as issues and new requirements emerge.**   Regardless of how smart or thorough your architecture team is, they will always miss issues and get blind-sided by new requirements. That's why it's important for them to keep meeting every week. Problems that arise get brought before the architecture team, which returns to first principles and refactors the design as needed. The architecture team consists of senior engineers from each feature team, so the problems will be visible and well understood.

> **Eric Aside**   The C# architecture team, led by Anders Hejlsberg, still meets for two hours three times a week, even though the original spec was completed seven years ago. While the number of team members has varied, Anders says it ideally consists of six people plus one PM who takes notes and keeps the agenda.

Dogs and cats living together

Once the architecture is documented and the components are isolated, individual feature teams can engage free from conflict. Should an unforeseen problem arise between components, the architecture team can quickly address it.

There's still plenty of bottom-up design left to do. Because the scope is smaller and the impact confined, there's ample room to experiment and apply less burdensome Agile design techniques, like Test-Driven Development.

Were you to attempt bottom-up design for the whole product, the simultaneous number of conflicts requiring broad redesign would quickly collapse the project under its own mass hysteria. It's one thing to rethink a single component behind a stable interface. It's another to constantly change interfaces and responsibilities across a million-line code base.

By using top-down design just enough to provide isolation and bottom-up design enough to optimize collaboration and quality, you get the best of both worlds. By using architecture teams, you coordinate effort, create growth opportunities for your senior engineers, and achieve blessed isolation. It's a beautiful, peaceful world within your reach.

Chapter 7
Adventures in Career Development

In this chapter:
December 1, 2001: "When the journey is the destination"...................120
October 1, 2002: "Life isn't fair—The review curve".........................122
November 1, 2006: "Roles on the career stage" 126
May 1, 2007: "Get yourself connected" 129

Most of the engineers I know and admire are not overly ambitious. They'd be perfectly happy with the simplest of titles and little fanfare so long as they were given a chance to put their ideas into action and have a positive impact on the world. It's true, I kid you not.

Unfortunately, even the most humble of engineers must actively manage their careers or risk losing opportunities to have the positive impact they seek. It's not because the world is cold and heartless, though it sometimes seems that way. It's because the world is highly populated with talented people who all wish to be heard. It's naïve and foolish to leave your chance at destiny to chance.

In this chapter, I. M. Wright shares the secrets behind developing a happy, successful, and satisfying career. The first column tells managers that ambition does not correlate to value. The second one uncovers what it takes to excel in a competitive world. The third column explains the differences between roles and career aspirations. The last one describes the importance of personal networking to your effectiveness and goals, and how you can best develop and maintain your own network.

The most basic career question engineers face is, "Must I be a manager to be successful?" Simply put, the answer is, "No." If your manager tells you otherwise, he is wrong, ignore him. Better yet, switch groups and work for a capable manager. If your boss suggests you try management, consider her suggestion. Management can be rewarding and fulfilling, and your boss may see unmet potential for you in that area. However, it's a choice, not a requirement. The employee data backs me up, as does my own experience and the experience of my friends. You own your career: you decide, you drive, and you draw your goals within reach.

– Eric

December 1, 2001: "When the journey is the destination"

Do we all have to be superheroes? Is that the Microsoft way? When a dev busts his or her behind for you day in and day out for a year shipping your product, is the message always, "That isn't good enough"? What does it take to satisfy the life-sucking career advancement beast?

There are plenty of folks, myself included, who believe and pontificate that you can always do more, be better, and reach higher. Never be satisfied with the status quo, we say; always push yourself and your team to the next level. We associate this attitude with Microsoft Competencies like self-development, drive for results, and technical passion and drive. Does this mean that if you're happy with where you are and what you're doing that you are a parasite on the corporate host?

A man's got to know his limitations

If you think great but satisfied people are parasites, you are a fool. Not everyone can or even wants to be Bill Gates, much as I like the guy. We all have our limits and priorities, and for many of us, being a VP just isn't realistic or desirable.

Ah, but I know what you alarmists are thinking: Lowering your sights means lowering your expectations. Lowering your expectations leads to mediocrity. And mediocrity is a noxious lesion that grows, infects, and consumes a company, rendering it a mountainous boil of pus. So true.

And yet, it can't be right that great devs with years of shipping experience, plenty of passion for product, and drive for results should be told that they have no place at the company unless they become an architect or manager. Surely we've all known folks like this. They love working here. They love coding. They love the software industry, the new technology, and the dramatic positive impact we all get to have on our society.

There is nothing wrong with the attitude and ambition of these devs. They are the backbone of the company. They are the very foundation that drives us forward and makes us successful. I call these dedicated people "journey developers" (because "journeyman" is not PC, and as you know, I am so PC).

> **Eric Aside**   "PC" in this case means *politically correct*. By the way, this column received one of the most universally positive responses of any I've written.

Vesting but not resting

Don't get the journey developers confused with the "rest and vesters." The rest and vesters have lost their passion for product, their commitment to customers, and their drive for results.

The journey developers still have all these qualities and are totally committed to shipping the best software on the planet, while leaving the people, technology, and design leadership to someone else. Maybe someday they might change their minds and decide to lead by more than just their example and experience. But until then, it is essential that their productive, dedicated, and invaluable contributions be supported, rewarded, and encouraged.

> **Eric Aside** "Rest and vest" was an internal term for employees who stopped working hard and were just hanging around waiting for their stock options to vest. After the Internet bubble burst, the term didn't really apply anymore.

I wish they would only take me as I am

Being a journey developer needs to be a recognized growth path for devs, just as the expert/ architect and lead/manager paths already are. It's true that by choosing to limit their leadership, journey developers necessarily limit their impact and influence. This means that journey developers will rarely be able to rise above a level 63 SDE.

> **Eric Aside** In the United States, the entry level for a Software Development Engineer (SDE) is level 59 (compensation levels vary by region). Level 63 is considered a "senior" level for engineers. Levels beyond that take you to "principal" and "partner."

Some might argue that this is reason enough to discourage this career path, but that attitude shortchanges us all. We need their contribution and experience. We can't afford to hand over many of our best developers to some lesser company. Our compensation package is generous enough to keep our journey developers. We can easily find creative ways to reward their efforts, and at the same time not force responsibilities beyond their level.

Of course, some journey developers will change the path they're on and become our future leaders. For them, and for new developers who want the flexibility, the journey developer career path would provide the time and respect that they need to grow and contribute on their own terms. Being patient and understanding as a company can make all the difference in retaining great contributors and increasing their job satisfaction.

We're in this together

As you might have already surmised, the journey path doesn't just apply to development. There are similar people in all disciplines of work at Microsoft who love their jobs and do them extremely well, but they aren't either ready or willing to take on a leadership role. We can and should understand and appreciate those people who love the company, love their jobs, love our customers, and want to contribute without being forced to lead.

As managers, it's important to push our people beyond their comfort zone at times to get them to exceed their own expectations; we can't and shouldn't lower the bar for anyone. However, that doesn't excuse bullying some of our best people into a job they don't want and making them feel unappreciated or inadequate at the very time they are helping us succeed. Being the world's smartest, most productive, and passionate people working for the best company the earth has ever seen should be good enough.

> **Eric Aside**   The concept of journey developers was implemented a few years ago. Now no questions are asked when a productive senior engineer chooses to go no higher.

October 1, 2002: "Life isn't fair—The review curve"

Two devs, Harley and Charlie, same level, same division. Harley works hard and well; Charlie works hard and well. Harley is smart; Charlie is smart. Harley is a team player; Charlie is a team player. Harley works on a high-profile feature; Charlie works on a low-profile feature. Guess who comes out on top in calibration? Guess who gets the 4.0 instead of the 3.5? You know it's Harley.

> **Eric Aside**   The numbers refer to the old Microsoft rating system, which ranged from 2.5 to 4.5 (the higher the rating, the better the rewards). While a 3.0 was acceptable, most people pursued and received a 3.5 or higher. We've changed the review process, like the rating system, many times at Microsoft, but it's always been about comparing and calibrating your work to the work of others doing the same job at the same level of responsibility.

I can't tell you how many times a Charlie has walked into my office or the office of another manager to whine about how he got shafted. "I worked just as hard as Harley," says Charlie. "You assigned me to the crud feature. I followed what you said and I got the frigging staff. It's not fair." Sorry, Charlie–life isn't fair.

Hear that crashing sound? It's the Charlies of the world leaping out of their seats and screaming, "What the heck do you mean, 'Life isn't fair'? What kind of excuse is that for your poor management! You delegated this crud to me. Am I supposed to blow off your assignment and then drive a truck over Harley and steal his? Who GPF'd your brain, and why am I still working for a manager with a blue screen for brains?"

Welcome to the real world, Charlie. It's harsh and switching managers may not help.

> **Eric Aside**   "GPF" means general protection fault, which crashes old computer systems, causing them to display a blue screen with crash information. As for Charlie's system crash, from his perspective he was set up for failure, when in fact as I describe next, Charlie had choice and opportunity but passively allowed himself to fail.

I'm not going to take this anymore

Sure, management matters (to borrow a phrase), but it's your career and managers have to juggle many different demands. Someone has to create the less glamorous features, and if you are willing to do it, well you've made your own bed. I hope it's comfortable.

But no one says you have to lie down and take it. Wake up, grow up, be your own Harley—hit the throttle and put your career in the passing lane. "How?" you say. Get wise or eat Harley's dust.

The Harleys of the world are either lucky, savvy, or both. Because we've already concluded that your luck stinks, you'd better get savvy. Here's the key: the savvy dev knows the customer and knows the business.

> **Eric Aside**   The names "Harley" and "Charlie" were originally "Hughie" and "Dewey." (I enjoy "Car Talk.") When I came to the critical "Sorry, Charlie" line, I changed names. The only neutral name I could rhyme with Charlie was Harley, as in "Harley Davidson." That set the tone and metaphors for the rest of the column.

Knowledge is power

Sometimes high-profile features are obvious; everyone can point to them from the beginning of the product cycle. However, there are always features that don't look high profile but will be, and some seemingly high-profile features that turn out not to be. To discern the difference, you, Charlie, must understand your customers and understand your business. Typically, most of your team, including management, doesn't.

Why don't many of your peers and managers understand your customers and business?

- Because they think they understand, but are relying on old information.
- Because they think the customer is just like them and the business is to "make lots of money."
- Because they are relying on someone else to understand these things.

You don't need to be so foolish and ignorant.

Taking care of business

To align your work with the business, you've got to research your group's business model. Remember, your boss may not be any more familiar with it than you are. Chances are good that your product unit manager (PUM) knows it fairly well and that your PUM's boss knows it quite well. It's easier to get an appointment with your PUM, so start there.

However, a chat with your PUM may not be enough. A PUM's view of the business model may well be skewed to overemphasize her own products. To really understand the bigger picture, you often need to go to the director, general manager (GM), or VP. As an important courtesy, seek approval from your PUM first, then set up a meeting with her boss.

Uh oh, it's Charlie again: "Why in the world would my director/GM/VP ever want to see me? Don't they have better things to do with their time?" Assuming that they have a free 30 minutes, most of these high-level folks would actually love to see you.

Go ahead, make my day

Sure, a director/GM/VP's life is full; they deal with politics, defend their division and strategy in meetings, put out fires left and right, scrub data to support their positions or find weaknesses, and all sorts of other tasks completely abstracted from the real work that you do—the real work that they did when they started out. Trust me, they miss it.

These high-level folks love to talk to real people. It helps them get in touch with what's happening on the front lines. They love to talk about the business with folks who'll admire them and politely ask them questions that are easily answered. It's a little slice of heavenly pie for these VIPs, and you are the essential ingredient.

One thing to remember is that high-level people deal with problems all day. They don't want to hear you complain; if you use this time for whining, they will associate you with your problems. When you ask for the appointment, make it clear that you want to talk about where you and your team fit into the business.

Reach out and touch someone

So, you've talked to your upper management and charmed them while you learned about your business model. (This will also come in handy at promotion time.) Next you need to understand your customers.

Charlie says, "Isn't that the PM's job?" Sure it is; just don't choke on Harley's exhaust as he rides off with your rating. It is everyone's job to understand the customer, and there are plenty of easy ways to do it:

- Observe usability tests.
- Attend customer visits and focus groups.
- Join an online community.

- Talk to the Product Support Services representative for your products.
- Read reviews of your products.
- Check out reviews of your competitor's products.

Do whatever it takes to get in touch with your customers. Know what they want and what they really care about.

Got lemons? Make lemonade

Now you're ready to slap on some chaps and fire up the hog. If you know the business and know the customer, you can tell which features are juicy and which are window dressing. You'll also know which features aren't getting the attention they need to really win the customers' business.

> **Eric Aside**   "Hog" is an affectionate nickname for a Harley Davidson motorcycle.

Chances are you already work on some not-so-flashy features. Recognize that they have the potential to be key to your product's success. They just need to be focused on serving your business and customer needs. Move them in that direction and you'll become the team hero.

Change your tune

If you find that others have all the sweet assignments, or you just can't stand to work on backward compatibility, legacy support, and setup (which are key but not exciting) anymore, there are other ways to change your fate.

The easiest way is to choose the best features to work on at the beginning of a product cycle. Because most folks are ignorant of business and customers, you shouldn't find it difficult to identify some prime features that others will miss. However, if you're already in the game and feeling shut out, there are two sure ways to get yourself back in:

- Look for late-breaking feature needs. These are the "whoops we forgot that" feature, the "last-minute customer request" feature, the "keep up with our competitors" feature, the "new cool enabling technology" feature, and the ever popular "this critical feature stinks—we need new blood on it" feature. Remember your business and customers to avoid jumping onto a loser; but if it's a winner, get all over it. If the boring, stupid features that you were working on suffer as a result of your new assignments, they should have been cut anyway.

- Become the backup dev for a great feature. Go to your boss and say, "Hey, Harley is working on a pretty critical feature without any apparent backup. If it's alright with you, maybe I could learn more about it, maybe help him fix bugs or something, and then we'd have a backup in an emergency." Bingo, you're in. Either you get to be the hero this go round or you get Harley's feature next go round when he moves onto something else.

The one behind the wheel

Life really isn't fair, and the good assignments don't just get handed to you. It's true that your boss should understand your business and customers, and share the wealth in assignments. But you can't count on your boss's knowledge or generosity to move your career forward.

Take ownership of your career and the work that you do. Know your business and customers well. Apply that knowledge to make your products better and drive your career forward. If you succeed, it won't just be you who wins, we'll all reap the benefits.

> **Eric Aside**   There are three columns that hold a special place in my heart: "Dev schedules, flying pigs, and other fantasies" (my first column, which appears in Chapter 1), "Where's the beef?" (a turning point on the road to quality, which appears in Chapter 5), and this one, "Life isn't fair" (critical topic and a fun read). Many great topics, rants, and word plays followed, but these early columns set the tone for the rest.

November 1, 2006: "Roles on the career stage"

I'm sitting here and I'm tired. It's not long hours. It's not a cold coming on. It's not a lack of sleep. It's the idea of explaining for the thousandth time how someone with three reports can be an individual contributor or why there isn't a special Career Stage Profile for an architect. The answer to both questions is simple: role ≠ career stage. Get it? I didn't think so. Darn, I'm tired.

> **Eric Aside**   Career Stage Profiles are detailed descriptions of the work expected of employees at different career stages for different disciplines. Generally, for each discipline there are three sets of stages: entry stages (for U.S. developers, that's levels 59–62), technical leadership stages for individual contributors (levels 63–69), and organizational leadership stages for leads and managers (levels 63–69).

Look, you're not dumb and neither are the other thousand people I've temporarily enlightened. There's some subtlety to this; words get overloaded and confused. But it really isn't complicated—role and career stage just aren't the same thing.

One, in time, plays many parts

Perhaps some definitions will help. A role is like a part in a movie. Different people can play the same role. The same people can play more than one role. In fact, you can play multiple roles in the same meeting or conversation. It happens all the time.

For example, say you are a dev lead discussing a feature implementation with an old friend who happens to report to you and is also married to your cousin. In the same conversation, you could play the role of manager, friend, architect, relative, peer, mentor, and adversary. That's an extreme case, but perfectly plausible.

Roles can change by the minute, but typically at work we have a primary role, perhaps a secondary role, and a handful of lesser roles. For instance, some architects have a small number of reports. Their primary role is architect. Their secondary role is lead. Their lesser work-related roles include Microsoft employee, peer, tester, designer, mentor, and subordinate.

Stage right

Career stage is quite different from role. Career stage doesn't change by the minute. You don't have multiple career stages—you've got one. You might reference a number of career stage profiles in your commitments because they help define the roles you play. However, you are still only residing in one stage at any given point in your career. (I'll explain why later.)

So what is a career stage? A career stage defines your progress in your chosen growth path. Because you are only in one career stage, knowing which one is important. To validate your current career stage follow these steps:

- Select your discipline: dev, test, PM, UX, and so on.

> **Eric Aside**   "UX" stands for the *User Experience* discipline, mostly designers and usability experts.

- Select your career aspiration: technical leader (individual contributor stages) or organizational leader (manager stages).

- Review the career stage profiles with your manager to fit your skill set, discipline, and aspiration to a career stage. (Your current level and region often provide a clear starting point.)

I aspire, sir

Remember, it's not your current role that matters. It's your aspiration. Say you are in a dev lead role, but you want to be known for your technical leadership, not your management skills. If you are a developer at level 64 and work in Redmond, theoretically your career stage could be either Lead SDE or Senior SDE. However, because your aspiration is to be a technical leader your career stage should be Senior SDE.

"But I'm a dev lead," you say. Yeah, if you want to stay a dev lead or perhaps one day become a dev manager, that's fine. But if you want to become a technical leader, then either switch your career stage to Senior SDE or enjoy being dead-ended as a Lead SDE.

"But I have three reports," you say. Yeah, so one of your roles is a lead. Big deal. That has little to do with your chosen career growth. If you want to grow as a technical leader, then you must choose that growth path. Sure, you still need to be a good manager in your lead role and many of your commitments will still come from the Lead SDE stage, but those won't be your career development goals.

Overqualified

"But what if I'm a level 66 Principal SDE and I'm happy being a lead?" you say. Lead SDE tops out at level 64 in Redmond (level 65 is in the accepted range). At level 66, you are overqualified to be in the Lead SDE stage (though you certainly could still play the lead role).

Why does the Lead SDE stage top out at level 64? Because at Redmond level 64 you should have all the skills and scope the lead role requires. If you are level 66 or higher, you didn't get there because you could manage a small set of individual contributors really well. You got there because of your technical leadership. If you stopped being a technical leader and played only the lead role, you'd be underperforming as a level 66. That's why your career path is technical leader and your career stage is Principal SDE.

> **Eric Aside**   Leads topping out at level 64 was the biggest point of contention about this column. People, important people I respect, thought I was saying that dev leads can't be above level 64. They misunderstood. My point is that if you are above level 64, you must have more going for you than managing a small team. It must be an important team, and you must be providing strong technical leadership. Thus, your continued growth isn't the result of your small-team management skills, it's the result of your technical insight and guidance. You want your career stage designation to match your source of growth, while maintaining your secondary role as dev lead.

I'm special

"So why is there no architect career stage?" you say. Being an architect is a role. You need different career stages for different growth paths, but not for different roles. The growth path for a highly technical specialist is the same as the growth path for an architect. Both are technical leaders, so they both share the same career stages.

Sure, the role of an architect is different from that of a world-renowned expert in database logging. But they must have similar skills and develop in similar ways to advance. Thus, they are both either Principal or Partner SDEs.

There can be only one

"Okay, fine, but why can you be in only one career stage?" you say. If you can play multiple roles, why not have multiple career stages? Because your career stage is tied to your growth path, which is tied to your aspiration.

Most healthy individuals with single personalities have one career aspiration at a time. Yes, it can change from time to time. But at any given point in your life, you have one primary career goal. That one goal determines your career stage uniquely.

Now you could conceivably aspire to be a major technical leader and organizational leader simultaneously, but you'd fail in a miserable way. The reason isn't due to a lack of effort. Enough amphetamines could keep you working 24 hours a day for weeks at a time.

The problem is that being a leader means leading others. That means communicating with them, but not everyone is around all the time. At the end of the day, the availability of others constrains how much leading you can do in a day. To be a great leader, you must focus your efforts.

What do you want to be?

What do you want to be when you grow up? That's the central question the career model asks. You don't need to have the perfect answer. You just need an answer for now that can focus your efforts and allow you to make progress.

"Pick one and go with it" is the advice I prefer. You can switch later if your aspirations change, but meanwhile you'll learn and grow. We don't always become what we set out to be. It's the journey that holds the interest. But you can't just stand undecided at the fork in the road. Choose your path and enjoy the ride.

May 1, 2007: "Get yourself connected"

For many Microsoft engineers, it's a matter of principal. Not *principle*, as in belief, but *principal* as in that coveted career stage when they get more influence, more esteem, and more stock—as if one begot the others. That's ridiculous and naïve. In fact, it's influence and esteem that help you reach the principal stage, with the extra stock as a nice side benefit.

But how do the *unprincipaled* acquire influence? How do they receive esteem? Many engineers feel they are entitled to these gifts because they are smart and uniquely skilled. Okay, their capability and intelligence may be unique among their relatives, but not among their peers. We expect everyone we hire to be smart and skilled. So where does that leave you?

Well, you could become an organizational leader, like a lead or manager. Do those jobs well and influence and esteem are yours from those you manage. But management has its own issues and isn't for everyone. How do you broaden your influence as an individual technical leader when being smart isn't enough? Through your network—networking is fundamental.

It's who you know

The cynical among you might chafe at the idea that who you know is important. After all, aren't your ideas your true value? Yes, of course they are. Now, who are you again? What's your idea? Why does it deserve 20 minutes of my time to understand it, relative to the ideas of the other 27,000 smart engineers at Microsoft, let alone the innumerable smart engineers across the world?

It takes time to comprehend and appreciate ideas, especially from people you don't know because you are missing all their context. Therefore, if you want your ideas to be appreciated, you need to develop relationships with people who can appreciate them. The more people you know, the more people there are who can appreciate your ideas, the more influence you have, the more esteem you receive, the further you will go. Simple.

A strong network can also help you find new roles, get better reviews from peer feedback, and learn more about everything that is happening. Your network makes you look, act, and be smarter. When someone asks you a question, you don't need to know the answer; you just need to forward the question to a smart friend. Even though the smart friend had the answer, the questioner still sees you as the person who got the answer.

But how do you expand the network of people you know? And once you do, how do you keep all those relationships active? Let's face it, most engineers, myself included, are not social butterflies. We also don't have the time or inclination to host dinner parties. Luckily, networking isn't that difficult or imposing. It does involve a time commitment, but not as much as sales or politics.

I use habit and routine

To build a large and strong network, you must acquire certain habits:

- **Be curious** all the time about everything.
- **Be appreciative** of those who help you.
- **Be responsive** to those who ask you for help.

These three habits are essential to building and maintaining a strong network. They aren't complicated. They don't take as much time as personal hygiene. But if you let them slip, your network will disintegrate quickly. So when I say "make them a habit," what I mean is, *make them a habit.*

Aren't you curious?

Most engineers are naturally inquisitive. The trick to building a network is to apply that curiosity to other people's interests. After all, who isn't charmed by those who show genuine interest in what they do?

When you bump into someone you know, or even someone you don't, ask about their work. Find out as much as they are willing to tell within the time available. Make it a habit to do this all the time. You will learn a great deal, and you'll develop a broad network.

It's important to focus on the other person, not yourself. This isn't about you; it's about your acquaintance. Of course, you should answer any questions your new or old friend has about you, but don't stray far from your friend's interests. After all, talking about yourself gives you little value other than feeding your ego. Talking about your friend develops familiarity, and with it, trust. You'll get to focus on your interests when you have the need later.

> **Eric Aside**   A question I received about this column was, "What if the other person is trying to build a network—doesn't one of you need to talk about personal interests?" Yes, of course, the conversation should be balanced. I emphasized not talking about yourself because it's so easy to get lost in your own interests and exploits.

So, next time you're stuck on a bus to some event, stuck in line for food, or stuck waiting for a meeting or class to start, ask the person you're stuck with about their current project. Not just the name of the project, but what it is, how it works, what's tricky about it, what's fun, what's a pain, what are the people like, what is the management like, everything! This isn't small talk—this is genuine curiosity. It's just what you need to engage the person into a mutually beneficial relationship. It works and costs no more than the time you were stuck anyway.

You have our gratitude

Another subtle yet effective way to draw people into your network is to owe them a favor. I learned this reading about Abraham Lincoln, who borrowed books from neighbors who often lived miles away. In addition to getting access to books that were scarce, Lincoln found that asking for a small favor, such as borrowing a book, created a strong bond between him and the lender. The lender would find Lincoln to be trustworthy and appreciative. In addition, Lincoln would be in the lender's debt—a situation advantageous to the lender and one that made a continuing relationship desirable.

So, say you are looking for an opportunity to draw a specialist in media codecs into your network. You know the person's address, but they don't know you. Graciously asking that person for help with a codec issue would be an ideal way to start a relationship, assuming you follow certain guidelines:

- Use a real issue that requires the help of a specialist. Anything less will waste the specialist's time and be met with disdain.
- Be clear and concise in your question, and provide a time frame. Again, this demonstrates that you value the specialist's time. As I've written before, this is important in all communication. (See "You talking to me?" in Chapter 8.)

■ Thank the specialist generously; detail the value you received from their help. You want the entire experience to be positive for the person helping you, making them feel valued for their expertise.

You might say, "But why not do the specialist a favor? Isn't asking the other person for a favor completely twisted?" When you do a favor for someone else, particularly unasked, that person now owes you. The relationship with you is tainted with guilt and associated with burden. But when the specialist does you a favor that you truly appreciate, there is no burden or guilt. Instead, your new friend only experiences feelings of advantage and being valued.

I'll get back to you

Naturally, favors work both ways. That's how networks function. People provide service to you. You provide service to them. If you want to keep these relationships working, you must be responsive.

What does "responsive" mean? Well, how long does it take you to think someone doesn't care enough to respond to your mail? One day, perhaps two? You must respond to mail from your network within roughly 24 hours. Period.

Your response could be, "I'm sorry, I can't get you an answer right now. Can I get back to you in a week?" That response is far better than none at all. No answer means you don't care, whereas the "I'm busy right now" answer means you care, but you're busy.

You might say, "You've got to be kidding! I've got too much e-mail as it is. Now, I've got to answer every stupid question that comes to me within a day?" First of all, maintaining a network is an investment that pays large dividends. Nothing comes for free. Second, answers often come cheap. Forwarding a question onto someone else is just as good as answering it yourself. Why? Because people only care about getting an answer. They write to you and they get answers; that's all that matters. Just remember to appreciate those who answer the questions for you.

Welcome to the world

Where do you find people to be in your network? Everywhere. In lines, meetings, and classes; on discussion aliases; in collaboration spaces like CodeBox and Toolbox; from Web queries; and everywhere else you go at Microsoft. Outside Microsoft, you can find people at conferences, on blogs and forums, you name it. Finding people is easy. Getting them into your network and keeping them is the trick.

When you find people, keep track of them. I keep great e-mails and papers that I read, so I can contact the author(s) at a later date, when there is an opportunity to draw them into my network.

Eric Aside   There are a bunch of personal networking sites now on the Web. While they are very clever and useful, be aware that Brad Pitt isn't likely to be on one, and neither is the Angelina Jolie of your field. These sites are a great place to get started but not the complete solution.

Once you get someone into your network, stay in touch. There's no need to be artificial about it. Building and maintaining networks is highly opportunistic. The key is to take advantage of opportunities. When you bump into someone you haven't heard from in a while, stop and talk even if it's just for a few minutes. Ask them about what they are doing now. Be curious. Draw them back in.

Remember, networking doesn't have to be a great deal of work, but it is a commitment. The payback is expanding your mind and your reach. You will learn more about what's going on and where opportunities are. More people will know and respect you and your talents. Your ideas will be more easily accepted. All that leads to greater influence and esteem. You'll even make some close friends along the way. That's a *principal* worth pursuing.

Chapter 8
Personal Bug Fixing

In this chapter:
December 1, 2002: "My way or the highway—Negotiation" 136
February 1, 2005: "Better learn life balance". 139
June 1, 2005: "Time enough". 142
August 1, 2005: "Controlling your boss for fun and profit" 148
April 1, 2006: "You talking to me? Basic communication" 152
March 1, 2007: "More than open and honest" 156

By the time my professional career started, I had already compared academia and the business world, having experienced graduate school and a number of internships. Academia was far more political. In business, raw measures were there to evaluate your effectiveness. I wondered if I was smart and quick enough to compete and succeed in industry.

It took some time for me to realize that once you got past the entry levels, which prune the dim and slow, intelligence and speed don't make a difference. Your communication skills and how you manage yourself as a human being are what make you effective in the long term. I've known smart jerks and quick rogues who initially succeed, only to fall hard when their luck runs out.

In this chapter, I. M. Wright is your personal help desk, providing both the why and how to correct weaknesses that may be preventing you from getting the most from your job and life. The first column reveals the secrets of effective negotiation between people and teams. The second one tackles work-life balance. The third column provides all the tools and tricks you need to efficiently manage your time. The fourth column tells you how to influence those in power. The fifth column breaks down barriers to clear and effective communication; and the last one exposes the impact of personal and corporate values on our shared success.

It's easy to blame others for your frustration, poor luck, and the outright unfairness the world throws at you every day. The alternative is to look inside. You can't control what happens to you and the things you care about, but you can always control how you respond. Finding ways to be better every day is the most constructive reply you can give.

– Eric

December 1, 2002: "My way or the highway— Negotiation"

People are paying a lot of lip service these days to cross-group collaboration. Our employee survey results show that almost everyone thinks we should collaborate better, but that almost no one does. Gee, whatever could be the problem?

Could it be that groups have conflicts? Conflicting dates. Conflicting visions. Conflicting features. Conflicting requirements. Conflicting priorities, objectives, customer bases, business models, marketing messages, executive direction, budgetary constraints, resources. Hello?!? For crying out loud, most teams have trouble collaborating within their own group, let alone working with other teams.

Yeah, "But I. M.," you say, "Collaboration is good." Bugs get fixed once—in one place. There's no duplication of effort. The user sees one common way to do things; there's only one user interface to master. Developers need to understand only one API. There are fewer openings for a hacker to attack and fewer holes to patch. Groups can share resources and code. People can focus more on design and less on implementation and test. And, and, and...

So we're back where we started. Collaboration can be both good and intractable, as can working with other people in general. The key is good negotiation skills, something far too few of us know or practice. So what do we do? I've seen two basic methods of collaboration and negotiation used at Microsoft....

An offer you can't refuse

The first way is the "collaborate and like it!" approach, which is by far the most common approach used around here. Someone big, loud, and powerful beats everyone over the head until they work together. (Usually an executive tells the groups to collaborate or else.) When that doesn't work, the executive slaps the two groups together so there's no other choice.

This corresponds to the negotiation tactic of yelling louder in an attempt to intimidate people to do things your way. Yuck, how juvenile. No one likes this bullying technique, except occasionally the bully. The worst reorgs are conducted in this way, and they are always nasty. Good people leave the group and sometimes quit the company. Feelings are hurt. Productivity and morale drop like a dot-com stock and take months to recover, if they ever do.

> **Eric Aside**   While forced collaboration is still used, it no longer dominates at Microsoft. These days, teams have agreements with each other as I describe next, or they simply share source code. It's far better, but people often don't understand the reasoning behind the agreement and skip important aspects. This predictably leads to problems, which is why knowing how to negotiate is so fundamental.

Grow up

The second method is a more mature approach to collaboration. It is also a bit subtler. You form a kind of agreement with your partner group. (Yes, I know there are obsessive PMs out there who mess this up by writing detailed and demeaning contracts that demoralize and disengage their dependencies, but you needn't overdo it like that.) Up front you simply agree to what your group and your partner group will do, what your group and your partner group need in return, and what your group will do if things don't work out and likewise for your partner.

This method is analogous to the effective negotiation strategy of discovering and disabling threats while fulfilling needs, thus establishing trust between parties and creating a basis for compromise and collaboration. That was a big sentence with lots of big ideas, so let's break it down.

A shadow and a threat have been growing in my mind

When two groups are okay with the idea of mutually benefiting from working together, the big problem becomes removing barriers, not the collaboration process itself. This philosophy isn't true if the groups want to defeat one another, like we might feel toward our competitors.

However, for groups within Microsoft or when working with our partners, the real challenge to collaboration is getting all of the obstacles out of the way.

Don't shoot the messenger

Barriers to good collaboration always come in the form of threats, needs, and trust. Remove the threats, fulfill the needs, and you establish trust. Everything is downhill from there.

- **Threats**   So, say you would like to use Windows Messenger in your application, but you are afraid that the Messenger team's schedule will not match yours and that they will make last-minute changes that cause your program to break or your project to slip. This is a valid threat.

- **Needs**   You need the Messenger team to grant you a stable code branch around your ship dates, and you need them to verify their builds around your usage of their APIs.

   On the flip side, the Messenger team has needs to be met—they don't want you to cause them grief—no huge feature changes or requests, no additional localization costs. And they want you to use their setup module so that you don't break the other applications that use Messenger. They need you to agree up front to use the component as is, to cover any additional loc costs, and to incorporate their setup module in your application.

> **Eric Aside**   Truly understanding and appreciating your partner's needs and concerns are critical to successful negotiation. Make sure you are in sync by directly acknowledging each other's situation and requirements. No compromises yet, just acknowledgment will go a long way to building trust.

- **Trust**   The contract you make, which can be as informal as an e-mail, documents that your team agrees to use Messenger's setup and cover the cost of any additional loc; their team agrees to give you a frozen code branch around your ship dates (easy with Source Depot) and to use your BVT to verify their drops. You also specify what happens if either of you becomes dissatisfied with the relationship. Then product unit managers (PUMs) from both teams agree to the terms, and you are set to work together as partners.

> **Eric Aside**   A Build Verification Test (BVT) checks if a software build satisfies a set of requirements. Using a BVT to check software drops from other teams before accepting them is a wonderful practice. Even better is giving your BVT to the other team so that they can check themselves. That way, they know when they have met your requirements and you never have to deal with an unacceptable build.

After that, you can work out drop locations and schedules and solicit help implementing the APIs. This becomes easy when you both trust that your concerns will be met.

So happy together

The key to maintaining this level of trust is to keep the communication lines wide open. Ensure that PMs from both sides are talking to each other about schedule or feature changes, problems, and surprises. It's not hard, but if either team forgets, it can spell doom for the project.

> **Eric Aside**   A mnemonic the Harvard Negotiation Project recommends is ACBD, Always Consult Before Deciding, that is, don't make any impactful decisions without first talking to your partners.

When you negotiate this way, by removing threats, fulfilling needs, and gaining trust, you become incredibly effective in all facets of life. A mistake that people often make when negotiating is to jump in with solutions before listening to the concerns of others. If you prematurely present a solution, no one will accept it; they are afraid to get hurt. If you listen well, ask questions, and resolve the issues first, people will be surprisingly open to your ideas.

> **Eric Aside**   Be sure everyone feels like a winner after the negotiation is complete and beyond. Losing is a universal threat. One of the easiest ways to ensure everyone wins is by including everyone on the winning team—for example, "Here's OUR great design."

This method of collaboration is not magic and it's not just for working across groups. Good negotiation skills can help you at home, around the neighborhood, within your own team, and with our partners. So get out there—collaborate and like it!

February 1, 2005: "Better learn life balance"

Warning: Mushy, reflective column follows. Proceed at your own risk.

I didn't want to work at Microsoft. I was happy with my previous job, and they treated me well. Working at Microsoft would mean giving up my life and my family, working outrageous hours, and putting the company before all other things. I had many friends who worked at Microsoft. They often asked me to join them, and I always said "no."

Then I decided I needed a change and entertained an offer from one of Craig Mundie's old groups. I wasn't a young, campus hire. I had a wife, a home, a two-year-old son, and another boy on the way. I had no intention of giving that up. I told my prospective boss that I was a family man. I would only accept a position in which I saw my kids off to school every morning and ate dinner with them every night. To my surprise, he agreed heartily. More importantly, he kept his word.

Balance is key

The subject of work-life balance comes up all the time in discussions that I have with devs around the company. Heck, it comes up with everyone I meet. Many employees I've spoken to genuinely feel that they must choose between Microsoft and their personal lives. The only disparity is the degree of commitment demanded.

That is tragic. Not just on a philosophical level, but often on a personal level. I've seen people get divorced, lose custody of their children, become ill or depressed, and let go of friendships and all semblance of a personal life. I've seen it happen to friends and coworkers from the time I joined the company nearly 10 years ago until within the past year.

> **Eric Aside**   The real tragedy, as I describe next, is that all this grief is unnecessary and not what Microsoft or any decent company wants for its employees.

We are whole human beings. Denying work-life balance denies our selves. There are three ways we commonly cause ourselves grief:

- **We let work trump everything else.**   As I just mentioned, the consequences are clear and devastating.

- **We have different values at work.**   Our values define who we are, and trying to be two different people is wrenching.

- **We try to keep work and home separate.**   Living a double life is stressful and impossible to manage.

Words without action

Our leaders have said that balance is important. Part of Bill Gates' message about changing the world together was "for everyone at Microsoft to develop a challenging career with opportunities for growth, competitive rewards, and a balance between work and home life." Steve Ballmer has talked about the importance of his own home life, especially as his family has grown. Yet this message apparently hasn't become a reality for many employees.

> **Eric Aside**   As I mentioned in the first chapter, Steve Ballmer, our beloved Chief Executive Officer, practices work-life balance himself. I've met him several times while he was cheering on his son at a basketball game or going out to a movie with his wife.

It is easy to put much of the blame for our lack of work-life balance on management. Although almost anyone would say balance is desirable, it is sometimes hard for managers to juggle balance with other business priorities. Even managers who support work-life balance can send contrary messages unintentionally.

For example, during a crunch time, a manager may start ordering dinners for those who "choose" to stay late. So devs who arrive at 10:00 A.M. will stay until 8:00 P.M., working a 10-hour day. But their teammates with kids arrive at 9:00 A.M. and only stay until 6:00 P.M. (nine hours). Then from home, they log on at 9:00 P.M. and work until midnight, working a total of 12 hours. The devs who "left early" feel guilty about abandoning the team, don't get a free dinner, and actually work longer.

This contrived example isn't meant to knock anyone; it's meant to demonstrate a reasonable case where hard-working people can be penalized unintentionally. If managers wish to promote a fair and balanced work environment, they must apply a fair and balanced reward system.

But the responsibility for work-life balance doesn't end with management. Bill's next sentence asserts, "In a fast-paced, competitive environment, this is a shared responsibility between Microsoft and its employees." Given management's focus on results, is taking personal responsibility for work-life balance reasonable or career suicide? Within a certain framework, I have found balancing work and home to be both achievable and respected. If you think my claim is fanciful, wait until you hear about the framework.

I can't even balance my checkbook

Achieving balance isn't easy for your checkbook, let alone your life. Here's my five-step program for an advantageous balance between work and home:

1. **Understand and accept your lifestyle choices.**   The first step is to know yourself. What are your priorities? Does career come before home? What are your limits? Would you give up a parent-teacher conference, but not the school play, to advance your career? You must understand and accept these choices, even if they seldom arise. This

will prepare you to speak with your manager from a position of strength and conviction, one he or she will respect and uphold.

> **Eric Aside**   My experience has been that this step is the hardest. Most people have never had to confront their life choices. Being honest with yourself and truly deciding where you draw the line between work and home can be challenging, but it's extraordinarily important and valuable.

2. **Set ground rules with your manager.**   Every time I begin reporting to a new manager (a common occurrence at Microsoft), I discuss my work expectations: "I see my kids off to school every morning and eat dinner with them every night. If that is unacceptable, I will respectfully seek a different position." We always agree that there will be occasional exceptions, but the ground rules are clear and established. No manager has turned me down, and sticking to my ground rules has not impacted my advancement. However, jobs that require lots of travel are not for me. Many of my managers have told me that they consider my strong convictions and clear values a strength.

3. **Do not compromise quietly.**   Occasional breaks in the usual routine at work are expected, but a two-week trip to Japan would be a big deal for me. When this type of request comes up, I take the opportunity to reassert my constraints. Often an alternative is available; sometimes I just need to go. Either way, my manager is reminded of my priorities and his or her commitment to honoring them. If you compromise too easily, it tells your manager that you don't really care that much. Your manager will likely continue to ask for more and more of you until you finally do care, establishing a new, less desirable limit.

4. **Use RAS and Remote Desktop or OWA as needed.**   Of course, there are crunch times several weeks every year. Before terminal server (Remote Desktop), crunch times meant that I returned to work after putting my kids to bed. These days, I frequently log on from home after they go to sleep—not because I'm always in crunch mode, but because I love my job and like the work. But I spend just as many nights watching TV or movies with my wife. I choose my activities based on creating the balance my family and I need.

> **Eric Aside**   Remote Access Service (RAS) is a means to tunnel into the Microsoft intranet from home. Outlook Web Access (OWA) is an AJAX application that permits you to access your corporate e-mail, calendar, and contacts from any Internet connection.

5. **Drop the schizophrenic pretense of separation.**   For years I had a work life and a home life. That's how I was always told it should be, regardless of how awkward or uncomfortable it got. Now I just have a life. Period. A family health crisis seven years ago forced me to drop the absurd pretense that I could separate work and home. No one can effectively separate their lives in two, unless they have a serious personality disorder. So, live the same at home and at work, within certain limits of decency and responsible behavior.

Balance good...everything good

Being in touch with what we need to live a full life and then living by those standards are wonderful gifts that we can give ourselves. Part of this is graying the line between work and home so that we aren't constantly context switching our values and our souls. This doesn't mean that we spend all our time at work chatting with friends and relatives any more than it means we spend all our time at home working online. It also means that we must honor the privacy and needs of our coworkers. Remember, the Microsoft value is open and respectful, not just open.

But if you do integrate work and home, a beautiful thing occurs. Lessons that you learn at home help you at work. Insights you gain at work improve your life at home. Balance yields tremendous personal growth as well as personal well-being. You may never become a megalomaniacal industry magnate, but the great riches you gain will not be so easily lost.

June 1, 2005: "Time enough"

"Work smarter, not harder." Wouldn't you like to shove cliché-spouting, nonsensical know-it-alls into a meat grinder to give them a more representative look? Especially when the message comes from a middle manager who has assigned 18 "high priority" projects to your team and then joins the rioting mob of inane, inconsiderate ignoramuses who constantly interrupt you to ensure that you can't possibly think.

There is never enough time to keep up with even a fraction of the work that is typically on your team's to-do list. Even if you had a reasonably scoped set of work, the relentless interruptions and meetings would still make completing any real work laughable.

Yet, this is the job of a typical dev lead or manager. Good managers get through each day successfully restraining themselves from strangling half the people in their hallway. Great managers learn to manage their time.

Give it to me straight

There are countless books and organizers for time management. Most seem to me to be embarrassingly superficial, wildly impractical, or written for aliens from a parallel universe where anal retentiveness is an indicator of high social status.

For me, time management comes in three basic varieties:

- Cutting down interruptions and context switches.
- Delegating your work to other team members.
- Careful selection of work items based on priority and leverage.

Pardon the interruption

To be effective, you need to concentrate. Recent studies have shown two interesting findings:

1. Heavy context switching causes a higher drop in IQ than using marijuana.

2. Employees are most productive when they are working on precisely two projects.

The first finding shouldn't be surprising. You can't think if you can't focus due to constant interruptions and context switching. The second finding is more subtle. It says that you need to concentrate on one project at a time, but need a different project to switch to when you get stuck or need a break on the first. The second project is treated as filler—that is, useful but not essential.

Some interruptions are easy to control. I turn off all forms of e-mail notification and I set the ring volume on my phone to its lowest possible level. (The phone just quietly clicks.) As a result, I no longer get interrupted by e-mail or the phone. I reply when I'm ready to take a break, not when someone else happens to click the Send button or dial my number. This does not make me less responsive than I was before; it just puts me in control.

When I do find a good stopping point and scan my e-mail (usually every 10–40 minutes), I try to completely dispense with each message as I read it. Each message represents a context switch. You reduce context switches by reading each message once. (The lean folks call this "single piece flow.") More than 95% of my e-mail can be deleted, cataloged into a folder, transferred to someone else, or responded to immediately upon receipt.

Some might claim that this process puts undue priority on minor items. However, you must read a message to determine if it's minor. After you've read the message, it usually takes more time to context switch back and re-read it later than it would to simply dispense with it now. As a bonus, when your inbox is almost empty, it takes far less time to find specific messages and see what's left to do.

As for Instant Messenger, I don't use it at all. I believe IM was sent to us by the devil to enslave our teenagers and ruin our lives. Of course, that's only my opinion.

> **Eric Aside**   My older son is a teenager now. I stand by I. M. Wright. To my friends on the Messenger team, "No offense."

Find your happy place

Another way to reduce interruptions is to get lost. Go somewhere that no one can find you, and finish some work. Armed with remote desktop and a laptop or kiosk, you can work almost anywhere: meeting rooms, building lobbies, cafeterias, you name it. As far as anyone can tell, you're in a meeting. You can't do this all the time without harming your team, but it's great when you need to catch up.

You can also work when others aren't around. Most developers show up around 10:00 A.M. and work until 7:00 P.M. If you show up around 8:00 A.M., you have two uninterrupted hours. Leave at 5:00 P.M., and if necessary you can log on from home after 8:00 P.M. when things are quiet. I wait until my kids are asleep if I've got extra work to finish.

Finally, you can institute focused time during the week when people are expected to not interrupt you or your team unless absolutely necessary. For this policy to be successful, you must choose a predictable time when interruptions are less likely anyway. One day or an afternoon and evening during the second half of the week is often a good choice because most meetings and fire drills happen early in the week.

None of us is as dumb as all of us

An especially evil form of interruption is the meeting. A meeting forces you to stop productive work and throw yourself into a frustrating, time-consuming, black hole of wasted life from which you can never recover. However, there are several actions you can take to minimize the life-draining effect of meetings:

- **Stop going.**   There are only a few meetings you must attend: your one-on-ones, your project status meetings, and your staff meetings. Almost all other meetings are discretionary. If a meeting feels optional, try skipping it. If nothing bad happens, don't go again.

- **Make someone else attend.**   Try delegating the meeting to someone else. (More on this in the following section.)

- **Run effective meetings.**   As for meetings that are left, make them as effective as possible. Read my column "The day we met" (which appears in Chapter 3, "Inefficiency Eradicated") for tips on running tight meetings.

- **Put all your meetings back to back.**   I know this sounds strange, but the idea is to reduce context switches. First, try to schedule your project and staff meetings early in the week, and then schedule all your one-on-one meetings around them. Sure, the early part of your week will be hellish, but the middle and end of your week will have uninterrupted blocks of time.

A burden we must share

Although cutting down on interruptions is great, the most effective way to get your work done is to give it to someone else. There's a reason why the lives of leads and managers are so busy—you've got a whole team of people to look after in addition to your project work. The balancing factor is delegation. Managers can leverage their teams to lighten their loads.

> **Eric Aside**   Architects can use architecture teams this way too, even though the members of the team don't necessarily report to the architect.

There's a tendency for new leads and managers to avoid burdening their teams. They'd rather take on the stress and load than seem weak or lazy. That's foolish, cowardly, and selfish. The worst thing you can do to your team is stress yourself out. When you are stressed out, you become short with people, you don't take time to think and listen, you make bad decisions. Soon your team follows your lead, becoming stressed and dysfunctional.

You must be the rock for your team. You must keep your head when others lose control. You can only do this when you work within your limits. Hand over all the assignments you can to your team. Remember, they only wish to support and please you.

Why does your team want to support and please you? Duh, you write their reviews and initiate their promotions. They need challenging assignments that expand their scope to get that 4.0 and advance their careers. They need the kind of assignments that you're asked to do. Why hold your people back? Why hoard all the tough, critical tasks? Delegate your work to your team, and give your people what they want and need to advance.

Tell me what I must do

When you delegate your work, it's important to do it right. The trick to delegation is to delegate ownership, not tasks.

The difference is subtle, so I'll give you an example. Say your project depends on Media Player and you're scheduled to meet with the Media Player team. You don't feel like going, so instead you plan to send Anil, a dev on your team who wants to become a lead.

If you just delegate the meeting to Anil, you know what will happen. No matter how well you prepare him, Anil will be asked to answer questions and make commitments he isn't equipped to handle. He'll meet with you later to recap the meeting. You'll ask all kinds of questions that he can't answer, and you'll both be left with the feeling that you should have attended the meeting yourself. The result is frustrating for you and feels like failure to Anil.

Now, let's say that instead of delegating only the meeting to Anil, you delegate the whole relationship with Media Player. You bring Anil into your office and say,

"Anil, I want you to OWN our relationship with Media Player. You ensure that they have our technical requirements and that we can commit to theirs. You own working with their team, understanding their APIs, and designing and coding our end of the interactions. How does that sound? Oh, and by the way, the first meeting is coming soon."

Anil will love it. He'll go to the meeting empowered to answer questions and make commitments. He'll feel a sense of authority along with responsibility. Anil is set up for success. Meanwhile, not only did you get out of that meeting, you got out of every future Media Player meeting. What a difference.

He's just a kid

If Anil is a junior person and delegating ownership is risky, there are several ways you can mitigate the risk:

- Accompany him to the first few meetings, but keep your mouth shut; defer to Anil as much as possible, then debrief him later.

- Assign Anil a mentor who can play a similar role to the one I just mentioned.

- Ask a friend on the Media Player team to look out for Anil and let you know if there are any problems.

- Ask to be on the e-mail threads sent between groups, and have Anil provide regular, detailed status reports.

- Use some combination of these methods.

Regardless of how you proceed, Anil owns the relationship with Media Player and has the opportunity to show his stuff while leaving you more time to focus in other areas.

You deserve a break

The ownership approach to delegation works well for almost every type of assignment. Any time you have a task to hand out, even if it's only to cover for you while you're at the dentist, stop and think about the larger context for the task and assign ownership of the whole scope.

By the way, if you're having trouble getting started with delegation, take a two-week vacation. You'll be forced to delegate all your work—and when you get back, you can let folks keep it. Plus, you get a two-week vacation as part of the package. Sweet!

Everything's in order here

The last major variety of time management is how you select which work items to pursue and in what order. Start by listing all your current tasks and decide which ones to keep.

The work items should fall into a few categories (listed in priority order):

- Tasks that require your personal attention as part of your job (taking care of your team, reviews, one-on-ones, staff meetings, employee issues).

- Tasks that are critical to your personal development goals (training, key assignments, executive or customer engagements).

- Tasks that enable you to stay engaged with your team members and manage them effectively (morale events, project and team meetings, design and code reviews, debugging, triage, and hand-picked project work).

- Tasks you happen to particularly enjoy.

All items in the first category must be on your list. Often there are tasks that overlap between categories; these are high-leverage items and should definitely be on your list. Everything else can potentially be dumped or delegated.

After you've pared down your list of work, you need to order it. Consider the priorities of the categories I mentioned, how leveraged the task is, and the urgency. In the end, you should have only two or three major projects and a few minor items.

Remember to focus on only one major project at any given moment and give it your full attention. Switch to other projects when you get stuck or need a break.

Keeping it real

One of the most highly leveraged work items you can have is direct project work, like owning, designing, and coding a feature. Project work gives you insight into employee issues (build problems, team personalities, cross-group interactions), assists in your personal development by keeping you sharp and current, and engages you with your team and larger organization in a direct and integrated fashion. You'll almost certainly enjoy it, assuming you pick the right task.

Some people debate whether or not a dev lead or manager should still code. To me, direct project work is so beneficial to yourself and the team that you can't afford not to do it. The trick is picking the right task. If you have three or fewer reports, you should have enough time to devote to almost any project assignment. However, with four or more reports, people and project issues will arise frequently enough that your availability will be unpredictable.

Having an unpredictable schedule isn't a problem early in a project. However, as you get closer to the end, your peers across disciplines will demand delivery commitments that you cannot keep with certainty. You'll end up handing unfinished work to your team members, who are already under pressure to complete their current assignments. Plus, you won't have time to transition your work sufficiently, which makes the transfer even more painful. Now your peers hate you, your team hates you, and you hate yourself because you had to give up and give in.

All this changes if you choose project work that isn't critical path. In particular, with more than three reports you should select work that

- Doesn't need to ship.
- Can be easily disabled.
- Is risky, fun, cool, and an unexpected delight to customers.
- Ideally, is well integrated into the product.

When you select an assignment with these attributes and your peers across disciplines demand delivery commitments, you can say, "Honestly, I think I can finish it in the time frame you need, but I can't make promises. However, if I don't get it done in time, I can easily disable it and it won't ship." Now, your peers are comfortable, your team is unaffected, and you are stress free and feeling fulfilled. Oh yeah, it's the only way to go.

By the way, it's not hard to find this kind of project work. Usually risky, fun, and cool features that are well integrated into the product are too scary to make critical path. So you can assign them to yourself and enjoy keeping it real. Management does have its benefits.

Large and in charge

It's easy to let a lead or manager job take control of your life. The interruptions, overwhelming commitments, and disengagement from "real work" can make even the most capable people dream of when they first started working and everything seemed so simple.

However, there is a variety of ways to take back control of your work load, reduce interruptions, create opportunities for your staff that lighten your load, and trim your assignments to only those that provide the most benefit to you and your team. Applying these techniques puts you back in charge. That's exactly the place an effective and engaged leader needs to be.

August 1, 2005: "Controlling your boss for fun and profit"

There's a great gesture you can do to show just how little you care about someone who is wallowing in self-pity. You lightly rub the tips of your thumb and forefinger together saying, "This is the world's smallest violin playing, 'My Heart Cries for You.'"

That's how I feel when people complain about their helplessness in the face of the seemingly invincible power of their manager. "Oh, management will never give us the time to improve our build or change our practices." "I wish our manager took this training. That's the only way we'd ever take up inspections. (See "Review this" in Chapter 5.)" "I'm really uncomfortable with our product's current direction and group's organization, but there's nothing I can do."

Grow up, you weenies. Based on your pathetic excuses for inaction, nothing would ever get done. Don't you think your bosses say the same thing regarding their bosses? If you don't make desired change happen, it doesn't happen. Period. The difference between you and someone powerful is not your level of control; it's your willingness to act.

I have no hand

"Yeah, but my boss won't listen to me," is the common retort. "She has all these reasons why we can't change." Well, good. At least you've made the transition from being pathetic to being ignorant. You're trying to do something about your situation; you're just inept. Relax, most people are.

Unfortunately, influencing without authority rarely comes naturally; it is an acquired skill. When trying to enact a solution, most people jump right in. They go straight to their bosses with their idea, only to get shot down. Sometimes people even do a tremendous amount of preparation, writing a long white paper or presentation, only to be summarily rejected.

What you may not understand is how to prepare appropriately, how to present your idea effectively, and how to get your idea enacted. Let's break it down.

> **Eric Aside**   I gave an internal talk on this topic. Registration filled in minutes. The moral: many people want to know more about influence without authority.

Know the enemy and know yourself

Start with appropriate preparation. I'm going to list a bunch of steps, but they can all be done in less than a day (minutes for small issues).

First you need to scout the landscape. Only fools walk into a minefield without a map. Most people know how they want things to be, but that's an endpoint, not directions to get there.

- **Understand your proposal.**   What is risky about your idea, and how do you mitigate the risks? What can change about your idea, and what are the core principles you can't compromise? Be realistic and honest with yourself.

- **Understand your history.**   What were the reasons for your current processes and organization? Could you regress by changing them?

- **Understand your enemies.**   Who prefers the current state and why? Are any of them strong enough or passionate enough to make change difficult? How would you placate them or even draw them to your side?

- **Understand your friends.**   Who is unhappy with the current state and why? Do they like your idea? How strong, considerable, and passionate is your body of support?

- **Understand your management.**   How is your management being measured or judged? What benefits would be worth the risk from your manager's point of view? Can you increase the benefit to management or reduce the risk?

It sounds complicated, but if you have been paying attention to how your coworkers interact, you and a friend or two can scout the landscape in a candid short discussion. Talking to a few people is often necessary to unearth the history or understand the issues. Regardless, scouting is essential to success.

They succeed in adapting themselves

Now that you know what you're up against, you need to adapt and refine your original idea accordingly:

- **Choose who to please, who to placate, and who to ignore.**   Sure, you want to please everyone, but sometimes it's better to just make sure nobody gets upset and focus on the few you really need to make happy—like your boss. Some folks will be fine if you just keep them from harm. Others can be ignored if they follow whatever your boss decides or simply don't care.

- **To please people, focus on the benefits in their terms and negate the risks.**   Use your scouting information to frame the benefits in ways that impress the key players. If your manager cares about efficiency, talk about productivity gains; customer satisfaction, talk about quality and connection; on-time commitments, talk about predictability and transparency. To negate risks, talk about backup plans, go/no-go decision points, redundancy, and/or clear prioritization.

> **Eric Aside**   This is the negotiation step of removing threats and fulfilling needs I talked about in "My way or the highway—Negotiation," which appeared earlier in the chapter.

- **To placate people, neutralize whatever they find threatening.**   Use your scouting to uncover what's scary. If it's risks, negate them. If they have a competing solution, embed it and give them ample credit and the limelight ("It's our idea"). If they have extra requirements, satisfy them either immediately or in the "next version."

In the end, you'll have a plan with a bunch of backers, no one will be apprehensive enough to fight it, and you'll be aligned with what the key decision makers care about. Now you're ready to present it.

Selling water to fish

Selling water to fish really isn't that hard, assuming their credit is good. You simply need to show them what life is like without water. The same thing goes when you are driving for change. You need to frame the problem before you talk about your solution.

The focus is on the key players, usually management. In the same way you use your scouting information to frame benefits in key player terms, you frame the problems in terms that speak to key player concerns. This should be the first slide after the title in a very short deck.

A few important notes here:

- **Anything about you or your ambitions will poison the proposal.**   The proposal needs to be about the key players, the team, and the customers, not about you and your desires for fame, glory, or a high rating.

- **To target your presentation on the key players, you must slip inside their skin.**   Use their terms, talk about benefits to them, and address their concerns. While the solution may have been spawned by what you care about, the solution will belong to the team, not you. It will be owned by the key players, not you. You must leave your feelings out of it.

> **Eric Aside** Generally speaking, slipping inside the skin of key players and leaving your own feelings behind is the hardest step. It's also incredibly important to success.

- **If you talk about the solution first, no one will care.** If you skip over the problem, there is no impetus to change. If you talk about the solution and then the problem, people will fixate on the problem and forget your solution. Always start with the problem and then move on to talk about the solution.

- **You must keep your presentation short—very short.** Change drives discussion and debate. The debate will expand to fill any allotted time. If you can't get through your ideas in two or three slides, you'll lose all sway over the argument.

Eyes on the prize

Your second and possibly third slides speak to your vision of the future state. The vision should be clear, concise, and practical. The goals should be clearly stated in terms of benefit to the key players. Simply put, you cannot reach a destination if you don't know where you're going.

You'll likely have many more slides with all sorts of data and detail about your vision and proposal. You might even have a 30-page white paper. That material is important to document the basis for the change, but relegate supporting material to appendix slides and resource links. You must be crisp to be successful; everything else is there for reference only.

Your last slide addresses how you get from the current state to the future state, or how to reach your destination. There are only two sections to this slide:

- **The issues section**, which addresses how risks and concerns are mitigated. It's where to put your backup plans, go/no-go decision points, redundancy, and/or prioritization.

- **The next steps section**, which addresses who does what and when. Too often people focus on what needs to be done and not enough on who will do it and when it will happen. Without specific people assigned and specific target dates, the change flounders.

That's it: a title slide, problem statement, future state, and transition slide. Now you are prepared to bring your idea forward. For smaller ideas, you can do all this in an e-mail message, but the preparation is the same.

> **Eric Aside** A number of people doubted you could put all this information on three slides and asked me for an example. My best example was a Microsoft confidential proposal that put all the information on one slide. It had vertical and horizontal lines dividing the slide into four quadrants: problem (four bullets in the upper-left quadrant); solution (three bullets in the lower-left); issues (six bullets in the upper-right); and next steps (four bullets in the lower-right).

Engage

You are now ready to engage with the key players. There are dozens of ways to do this, and none is dramatically better than the others. Sometimes the landscape may suggest one approach over another. In general, there are three basic types of approach:

- **Talk to key players one at a time.**   This works well when the key players don't get along or each has different key issues. It's more time-consuming, but it's usually a safe and effective approach.

- **Meet with the key players together.**   This works well to build consensus and bring out hidden issues. It's also a bit faster, but it works best if some consensus already exists about the problem and the issues. If necessary you can start with the first approach to gain that initial consensus, and then seal the deal with a meeting.

- **Target only the top player.**   This works well when the top player is particularly strong or the organization is particularly compliant. Use this approach when no one really matters but the top player.

Go through your deck and be prepared to own the process you've created. Remember that it's not about you—it's about the team, the product, and the customer. Let people discuss and debate as much as they want, as long as they stay focused on the problem you identified. If new issues or risks arise, be sure to note them and devise mitigations.

Dare to dream

This whole process may seem like a great deal of trouble, especially when there's no guarantee your solution will survive, let alone thrive. You may feel that it's not worth it; that the status quo is acceptable or at least tolerable. Maybe that's true, or maybe you're spineless.

Just don't start complaining about how powerless you are or how management won't listen to you and doesn't care. If the current state is acceptable, then accept it and move on. If it isn't, then do something about it. Regardless of what happens, you will drive awareness of the problem and likely cause change. In addition, you'll gain leadership experience and perhaps even gain leadership responsibility. In the end, you will become more powerful by matching your willingness to act with the courage to focus on your team instead of yourself.

April 1, 2006: "You talking to me? Basic communication"

I read a lot of e-mail. I go to a lot of meetings. I read a lot of code and specs. I go to a lot of reviews. I read a lot of white papers. I go to a lot of presentations. Aside from getting the life sucked out of me, I've realized something: most communication is a terrible, tragic waste of time.

That's surprising because the principal difference between junior and senior engineers is their impact and influence. Because everyone is smart around here, the primary driver of impact and influence is strong communication skills. You'd think people would get it right. Of course, I think that about most things.

I've railed against long meetings (in "The day we met," which appears in Chapter 3), poor specs (in "Late specs: Fact of life or genetic defect?," also in Chapter 3), poor spec reviews (in "Review this," in Chapter 5), and unfocused presentations (in "Controlling your boss for fun and profit," earlier in this chapter). Yet, communication is incredibly important for collaboration, growth, and teamwork. Surely between the days of ancient Egypt and now, people have learned how to effectively converse. But where is the evidence? Our e-mail and meetings are bloated and pointless, our code and specs are indecipherable and inadequate, and our white papers and presentations are self-serving and self-indulgent.

> **Eric Aside**   Naturally, I'm overstating the problem again; there are many examples of great communication both inside and outside of Microsoft. However, if raising the alarm means more concise e-mail, clearer specs and code, more engaging presentations and papers, and shorter meetings, I'm all for it.

Why? What's so hard? Where is the source of the problem that takes what precious time we have and fritters it away so carelessly? After many years of contemplation, I believe at last I have found the answer: people aren't thinking enough about me.

Think about me

Yes, people aren't thinking enough about me, the receiver of their mammoth, malformed musings. What is everyone told the first time they write a paper or prepare a presentation? Consider your audience. It's elementary, yet we still have severe signs of self-serving spew. That's because while people do think about me, their audience, they don't think about me enough.

Traditionally, considering your audience has meant understanding who they are and what they know so you can target your communication appropriately. However, apparently that's vague and insufficient. Here's a concise, complete list of what you should consider about me:

- What do you want from me, specifically?

- When do you want it from me? Do I have a prayer of meeting that?

- Why should I care? Will I pay attention long enough to even listen?

> **Eric Aside**   For this entire column on communication, I'm using "me" to stand for your audience, however large or small it might be.

Tell me what you want

Good communication starts with knowing what you want from me—not what you want in general—I couldn't care less. What do you want from me?

Does that sound callous? Heck no, it's as open, respectful, and honest as you are likely to get. We all have hopes, dreams, and ambitions. It would be fun to discuss yours and mine over beers sometime, but right now I'm at work and I'm busy, so try to stick to the point.

Do you just want to keep me informed? Save it. If your information doesn't have a purpose, then I don't need to hear it. You say it's important that I know? Why? What actions do you want me to take later based on the information? How should I use it?

Seriously, what do you want from me? If you don't know, then I certainly don't. And if neither of us know, then we're just wasting each other's time.

Put what you want up front, in the first few lines, the first few slides. Be clear, not bashful. Use bold and my name to highlight what concerns me. I really want to care, but I can't until I know what to care about.

You want it when?

Do not bother asking me for something I can't provide. It's insulting to me and useless to you. I charge big money for miracles, so seek them elsewhere. Don't only think through what you want, think through when you want it and what impact that time frame has.

Sometimes your time frame is long. In that case, don't ask too soon because you'll only have to ask again later. For e-mail, I can simply delete pointless requests; but premature meetings, specs, code, and presentations can really cost me time, not to mention all your wasted effort.

Sometimes your time frame is short. Don't pretend it isn't. I don't mind people asking me for favors, I just mind them taking me for granted. Know when the ask is big and appreciate it when people come through.

Sometimes your time frame is a mystery. If you don't say when you want it right up front, you might as well have not asked in the first place.

Got a short little span of attention

Now that you know what you want from me and when, how about we stick to it? Let's face it. People's attention spans are short and I'm no exception. You need to grab my attention and keep it till I both understand what you want from me and I care enough to actually help you.

Here are techniques for grabbing and keeping my attention and for making me care:

- **Be concise.**   Provide essential context, but get to the point. Don't let my mind wander. If it's e-mail, put everything in the first three lines (the ones that appear in auto-preview).

If it's a meeting, make it short with a small agenda. If it's code, keep the function on one screen. If it's a presentation, use one slide per concept and only provide details I care about, not what you care about.

> **Eric Aside** An example of "put everything in the first three lines" of an e-mail: "Mr. Galt, though you make good points, your last few e-mails have been overly long. Please shorten your communication to a paragraph or less by next week."

- **Be focused.** Stick to the point. (Note the "die" in digress.) Stay on the agenda. Invite only those you need to a meeting, and include only those you need on an e-mail thread. That means don't "Reply all" without editing down the list. Keep function code, white papers, specs, and presentations coherent. If you are taking me down a path or building up to a climax, it had better be worth it. Just know what you want from me and be singularly focused on it.

- **Be simple.** If I have to squint or read it twice and your name doesn't rhyme with "fates" or "calmer," then your cause is lost. Three bullets per slide, five pages per paper, one idea per function, one decision per e-mail, and one feature per spec. Use pictures and stories; pretend I'm five years old. If you can't explain it to a five-year-old, then it's doomed to failure and isn't worth my time.

- **Be organized.** E-mail should read like a news article, with the overview and ask up front, followed by detail as needed. Longer documents should tell a story or follow some other familiar pattern. (Steal from good examples.) Meetings should have an agenda. Presentations should tell me what you're going to tell me (outline), tell me (tight slides), then tell me what you told me (summary). Dull? Only if you make it that way. Add zingers and funny pictures, and be passionate and playful, but stick to the structure. There's a reason why we have these story patterns—they work.

- **Be respectful.** Don't ask obvious questions that anyone with a Web browser could answer. Anticipate objections and questions, and respond to them before they are raised. Don't pretend you know something that you don't, especially laws and patents. If you don't know, say, "I don't know." Choose your words carefully when communicating directly to customers, competitors, executives, and people who may be feeling a bit emotional. When presenting, don't go over your allotted time and do leave time for questions. Don't read your slides, and don't tell someone they asked a good question—I can read for myself, and my question was just as good.

- **Be smooth.** Use proper grammar and spelling. Have someone review your e-mail, particularly if it's sensitive or if you are, let's say, emotional. Use clear variable names and common terminology. Practice your speeches—it's a physical activity. Take steps to relax before you present. There's no presentation hall without a bathroom—use it for quiet time and mother nature, then focus on what you want from me and make me believe. At the end of your speech, conclude clearly with, "Thank you, any questions?" and accept the applause you richly deserve.

■ **Serve me.** Communication isn't about you. You already know what you know. Communication is about me, your audience. Tune your message to my concerns and the type of information I care about. If I ask for data, give me the facts and spare the stories about your grandma. If I have a "bad feeling" about your idea, then skip the data, show me a demo, and have your grandma reassure me. If my boss won't like it or it doesn't fit our process, then convince my boss or change my process and stop wasting my time. Remember, different people are convinced in different ways and care about different things. For more pointers, read my column, "Controlling your boss for fun and profit," which appears earlier in this chapter.

Are we done?

Communication is a big subject, and I'm covering a lot of ground here. Take your time, practice your communication skills, and get good at them. Microsoft is full of smart people like you. To truly differentiate yourself, learn to communicate effectively.

Thank you, any questions?

> **Eric Aside**   And thanks to Jim Blinn, for his advice and closing line from "Things I Hope Not to See or Hear at SIGGRAPH." (You can find an excerpt at http://www.siggraph.org/s98/cfp/ speakers/blinn.html.)

March 1, 2007: "More than open and honest"

Our corporate values are slightly off. I can't disagree with them. It's hard to argue against integrity, honesty, passion, openness, respect, challenge, self-improvement, and accountability. Those are all good things, to be sure.

But are these corporate values the right ones for Microsoft? Say our contact with a key dependency, we'll call him "Deadbeat," tells me his team dropped a critical feature a month ago because their priorities didn't match ours. Is it okay because they are being "honest"? Do I feel consoled because their triage was "open"?

No, Deadbeat is dead meat as far as I'm concerned. I don't care if his team is truthful about breaking its promises. I'm not impressed that their catastrophic decisions are made in public. Our team is now knee deep in sewage with no nose clip and little time to recover.

That's no excuse

People use Microsoft values to excuse themselves from guilt. Deadbeat says, "I know we agreed to ship that feature, and I respect your passion about it. It was a challenging decision, but we're accountable to our dates and had to cut somewhere. I'm just being honest with you.

Yeah, we should have told you earlier, but the triage meeting was open. I guess communication is an improvement area for us."

Now, don't you feel better? They were just exemplifying Microsoft values. Whoop-de-do. We are still in deep trouble with no advance notice. What went wrong?

You could say it was a lack of accountability, but they were accountable to a date and a set of priorities. Those other accountabilities just trumped ours.

The problem is more subtle and has a serious impact on how we develop software, collaborate across teams, and run our business. It starts with our first value, "Integrity and honesty."

I'll be honest with you

People think integrity and honesty are synonyms, but they're not. Honesty means you don't lie. Integrity means your beliefs, words, and actions match.

> **Eric Aside**   I later found a marvelous quote comparing honesty and integrity. "Honesty is…conforming our words to reality. Integrity is conforming reality to our words." — Stephen R. Covey

You can be honest with no integrity ("Yes, I'm the one that back-stabbed you."). You can be dishonest with strong integrity ("I'm okay with postponing the bug, I understand."). Personally, I respect honesty, but I value integrity. You can believe someone who's honest, but you can count on someone with integrity.

Deadbeat and his team were honest but lacked integrity. They agreed to ship the feature, but didn't follow through. When they needed to cut our feature, Deadbeat didn't contact us. He didn't offer us alternatives, redress, or an apology. He didn't take his word seriously.

It's not easy

Honesty is easier than integrity. No one can blame you for being honest. Integrity requires courage and conviction. You must risk upsetting others, including your management and your peers, in order to stand by your beliefs. It's far easier to compromise your standards, assuming you have any. That's why integrity is so valuable.

It's not easy, but when you demonstrate your personal integrity in difficult situations you gain people's admiration. They may not agree with you, but they will know you are a person of character and substance; a person not easily bought or manipulated; a person to be respected.

Honesty is not a strong enough value upon which to hang our partnerships and our business. We must have integrity. Compromise on prices, plans, and particulars, not on principles. When you give your word, keep it. When you can't keep your word, apologize, then make it right.

They seem to have an open door policy

But integrity is not enough to make cross-team collaboration and partnerships work. You need transparency. Transparency doesn't even appear on the company values list.

People think open and transparent are synonyms, but they're not. Open means you're public, you have no secrets. Transparent means you share the who, how, what, when, and why of your decisions and actions.

You can be open without being transparent ("I don't know why we made that decision, but the meeting was open."). You can be closed yet be transparent ("The negotiations were behind closed doors, but this is our consensus decision and here's why we made it and who was involved."). Personally, I value transparency far more than openness. You have access to someone who's open, but you can rely on someone who's transparent.

Deadbeat and his team were open but not transparent. They didn't share how or why they cut the feature we needed. In fact, they didn't share the decision at all till it came up a month later. Had we known when the decision was made, we could have at least argued our case and then adjusted our plans.

> **Eric Aside**   Naturally, consulting all your partners before deciding, or even informing your partners promptly about decisions, is easier said than done. You must have a list of partners at the ready, and a process for notifying them that doesn't get bogged down or bottlenecked. I recommend the SCR process described in "Late specs: Fact of life or genetic defect?" (which you can find in Chapter 3).

No place to hide

Openness is easier than transparency. It's safer to conduct yourself in public, where social norms protect you. Transparency exposes your weaknesses. You don't get to pick and choose what you will share. You must own up to your true situation and risk disapproval. It's far easier to be open and hide behind, "All you had to do was ask." When you are transparent, everyone always knows the score. That's why transparency is so valuable.

It's not easy, but when you are transparent even in crisis you gain people's trust. They may not be happy with you now, but they will never doubt you. You become known, understood, and reliable.

Openness guarantees communication can happen, but not that it will. Transparency ensures our teams and our partners have the information they need to deliver on commitments. Make your schedule and status public. Share your bug queries, acceptance criteria, and build results with your partners. Celebrate promotions and successes, and talk candidly about failures and necessary improvements. Give those who work with you reason to believe in you.

> **Eric Aside**   We've had an interesting internal debate recently around making people's career stage transparent in the e-mail address book. On the positive side, promotions, role models, and who you are calibrated against become public. On the negative side, a class system is exposed, entry-level opinions may not be respected, and senior people may get differential treatment. It's a tough call, but groups are tending toward transparency, which at least exposes the class system so that impropriety can be handled appropriately.

Not what I had in mind

You're probably saying, "Of course, integrity and transparency are important, but so are honesty and openness. Aren't you making a big fuss over minor word differences?" Don't be so sure. Remember, I said the problem is subtle and has a serious impact on how we develop software, collaborate across teams, and run our business.

When people think honesty and openness form the bar, bad things can happen. While I've never regretted upholding my integrity or being transparent, honesty and openness can cause trouble even with the best of intentions.

Honesty can be cruel and heartless, but more importantly it can be deceptive and dysfunctional. That's because people often don't know the real truth, just what they currently believe. They can speak with sincere conviction yet be completely misguided. This leads to misunderstandings, wasted effort, and often animosity.

Openness has the same kind of issue. People don't do everything in public for a reason. How you behave depends on who is there to see. I behave differently in private with my family or my team than I do in public meetings or talks. It's not that I have something to hide; I don't. It's that my family and my team have context that the general public doesn't. That's why negotiation must be done in private in order to be effective. It's intimacy and confidentiality that breed candor and flexibility.

Getting it right

My plea for integrity and transparency doesn't mean I'm against honesty and openness. These are all exemplary values for us to follow. In particular, openness also means being receptive to the thoughts and ideas of others. The world would benefit greatly from an increase in that kind of openness.

But being honest and open falls short of what we need to be successful and can sometimes lead to unintended trouble. We need the integrity to mean what we say, say what we mean, and honor our words and beliefs with our actions. We need transparency in our decisions, our policies, and our projects to allow us to operate and collaborate knowing where we stand.

These may be small requests, but they have huge impact. There are people at Microsoft who feel threatened by transparency or lack the courage to uphold their integrity. They should look deep inside and change either who they are or where they work. For Microsoft to continue as a great company, our values need to mean more than words on a page.

Chapter 9
Being a Manager, and Yet Not Evil Incarnate

In this chapter:

February 1, 2003: "More than a number—Productivity"....................162

September 1, 2004: "Out of the interview loop" 164

November 1, 2004: "The toughest job—Poor performers" 169

September 1, 2005: "Go with the flow—Retention and turnover" 173

December 1, 2005: "I can manage"..177

May 1, 2006: "Beyond comparison—Dysfunctional teams" 181

Part of Microsoft culture is that you don't complain about something unless you've got a constructive suggestion for improvement. Well, I complain regularly about management. What's worse, I've been a manager at the company for 8 of my 12 years. Do I have any constructive suggestions for manager improvement? Funny you should ask.

Today there is considerable support for new managers, but when I first became a lead my experiences with prior managers were my only preparation. I did okay, but I learned a great deal on the job and from mentors. After five years, I joined what became my current organization. My top priority was providing new leads and managers the kind of effective and concrete help I wish I had received. Much of I. M. Wright's writing on management came directly from the materials I created for new managers.

In this chapter, I. M. Wright describes how to manage effectively without becoming demonic. The first column instructs managers on the proper use of metrics and the attributes of a great engineer. The second covers interviewing and recruiting. The third column takes you through the sensitive business of managing poor performance. The fourth deals with retention and turnover. The fifth column divulges the minimum you need to be a good manager, plus how to go from good to great; and the last one provides the secret to transforming a dysfunctional team into a healthy and productive one.

Frankly, I never wanted to be a manager. For 17 years I had been a successful individual contributor and architect. I became a manager because I had my own product ideas and wanted to learn how to run a business. To my surprise, I found managing people to be more engaging and gratifying than programming. Perhaps part of that was the result of being a dad–raising children is similar in ways to growing a team. But mostly it's because compared to people, computers are predictable and unresponsive. Oh sure, computers can surprise and delight you, but not to the degree people can. I still love programming, but I find serving people far more rewarding.

– Eric

February 1, 2003: "More than a number—Productivity"

Is it just me, or have aliens taken over the brains of our managers, convincing them that a number can accurately represent the quality of a product or the value of a developer? Exactly how much data entry, analysis, and forecasting crud must we endure just to placate misguided managers enough to leave us alone so that we can do our jobs? Am I the only one with a deep visceral sense that if we actually were allowed to focus on coding we'd get a lot more done?

Yet the trend is to "measure" more and more of what we create and how we create it and to use these measures to determine the goodness of our products—and of our people. As if disengaging our brains were advantageous. Do you realize how many otherwise intelligent managers could easily second-guess their own best judgment about a person and rely on a "coding success metric" to rate the members of their teams?

> **Eric Aside**   I was asked by the *Interface* editors to write a piece about metrics. I don't think this is what they had in mind, but deadlines are deadlines and I provided the word count they requested.

Careful what you wish for

The *Interface* article "Measuring developer productivity" nicely balances information about the various metrics used to measure devs against the weaknesses of using measures at all. Primary among these weaknesses is that metrics are easily "gamed." Managers will basically get what they ask for. If more lines make the metric better, they'll get more lines. If fewer check-ins makes the metric better, they'll get fewer check-ins. Not because the code is better or the developer is better, but because it makes the measure look better.

As long as people believe that they are being judged by a number, they will do whatever is necessary to ensure that the number makes them look good, regardless of the original intent of the measurement system. After all, why go out of your way to do the right thing if it doesn't improve your standing?

Are all measures useless? Not if they are used to track team and product progress against well-defined and accepted goals—like performance, regression rates, find and fix rates, and days to customer problem resolution. Measures can help drive teams forward and give objective meaning to achievements. However, they never take the place of good judgment.

> **Eric Aside** I've since learned a great deal more about constructive metrics. You want them to measure desirable outcomes—ideally, team-based desirable outcomes. Outcomes focus on what instead of how, which provides freedom to improve. Team metrics drive shared purpose instead of competitive dysfunction. "Lines of code" is rarely a desirable outcome. However, "shortening the time to produce a high-quality feature from start to finish" is a desirable outcome, and it depends on the whole team, not an individual.

Rather than attempting to place a number on individual developer productivity, managers should be answering the question, "What makes a good developer?" If it were as simple as assigning a number, theorem-proving machines would have replaced all of us a long time ago.

Playing a role

The key to measuring the value of developers is to think about development teams, not just individuals. Different people bring different strengths to a team. Consider the role that developers play on your team when judging their contributions. The best developers to have are not always the ones who code the best or fastest.

You don't want a team full of architects any more than you want a team full of leads or a team full of code grinders. Each team needs a balance of talents to be most effective and productive.

The makings of a great dev

But enough skirting around the issue of "measuring a dev." Here are what I consider to be the defining characteristics of great developers:

- **They know what they are doing.**   When you ask great developers why any given line or variable is there, they have a reason. Sometimes the reason isn't great ("I took that code from another place, and it used that construct"). But the reason is never, "Aw, I don't know, it seems to work."

- **They don't believe in magic.**   This is a corollary to knowing what they are doing. Great developers don't feel comfortable with black-box APIs, components, or algorithms. They need to know how the code works so they don't get burned by a false assumption or "leaky" abstraction (like a string class with simple concatenation that hides allocation failures or $O(n2)$ time to execute).

  > **Eric Aside**   Kudos to one of my favorite "Joel on Software" columns, "The Law of Leaky Abstractions," which you can find at *http://www.joelonsoftware.com/articles/ LeakyAbstractions.htm*.

- **They understand their customers and business.**   I talk about this in detail in "Life isn't fair," which appears in Chapter 7, "Adventures in Career Development." Great developers know what really matters, and they can prioritize and make proper tradeoffs.

- **They put customers and the team before themselves.**   No task is below a great dev; no customer is unimportant.

- **They have uncompromising morals and ethics.**   Although individual preferences may vary, great devs care about how they accomplish their work and how they act toward others. Whether in the algorithms they choose or the e-mail they write, they set the bar high for themselves and will not waver from their core values.

- **They have excellent people and communication skills.**   Although not many developers would make good game show hosts, great developers work well with others, respect others, and communicate clearly, effectively, and appropriately. They don't choose to bully or intimidate (although they could), but instead collaborate. (More on this in "My way or the highway," which appears in Chapter 8, "Personal Bug Fixing.")

- **They have a wide, supportive network.**   Great devs recognize greatness in others and are drawn to each other. They quickly develop a network of contacts that support one another and that allows them to be far more effective than any single individual.

Other specific aspects of the general characteristics I've listed include focusing on quality, mentoring others, and displaying exceptional design skills.

None of these characteristics that define a great developer can be simply measured.

You be the judge

When push comes to shove, you as a manager must judge your team as fairly as you can in the roles that each member plays. Having examples from other teams helps give you perspective on your own developers; this is why calibration meetings are so valuable, instructive, and worth the agony.

But remember that no calibration or rating can hope to represent an individual. People are far too complex, and even the most objective metrics are distorted by perspective. Knowing and valuing people as real human beings is the key to unlocking their full potential.

September 1, 2004: "Out of the interview loop"

Recruiting is like a huge vacuum sucking up all my time on campus. But quickly hiring a quality candidate is worth every minute. Luckily, I'm not dependent on anyone for most of the recruiting process. This keeps my candidates rolling through. That is, until the interview loop.

Man, if I could only skip the interview loop, I'd have it made. No scheduling hassles; no multi-week delays for a time slot; no horrible interview questions; no disappearing feedback; no "borderline" hires; no vague, gut-based garbage criteria; no freight train of duplicate thinking; and no last-minute cancellations.

But you can't skip the interview loop–ever. If Bill Gates wanted a job on my team, I'd put him through a loop. No offense. Just put him through the loop and make sure he's going to be a successful addition to the team–then brace myself if he's a no hire.

Blaming the help

Some of you hiring managers may take exception to my statement that I'm not dependent on anyone until the loop. You may say, "What about my recruiter? My recruiter doesn't give me the time of day. My recruiter hasn't sent me a resume in months. My recruiter is the bottleneck." Man, am I glad that I'm competing against you for hires. If it weren't for you lazy, incompetent fools, I'd have a heck of a time stealing all your strong candidates.

Your recruiter is your partner, your friend, and your resource–not your servant. Recruiters have WAY too many positions to fill. Unless your VP thinks your open position is critical, your recruiter cannot do all your grunt work. So get over yourself, get over to your recruiter's office, and get all over their stack of resumes. Otherwise, move over while I get my positions filled.

> **Eric Aside**   Today all the resumes are online, of course. (They pretty much were back then too.) However, the point remains that if you don't find your own candidates, your candidates will find some other job.

Ninety percent preparation

Now, back to the interview loop. (I'll have to save general thoughts about recruiting for a future column.) So many hiring managers get the interview loop process wrong that I'm just going to lay it out for you. A successful loop is 90% in the preparation, and the rest lies with your As Appropriate interviewer. The preparation falls into three steps:

- Prepping the interviewers.
- Prepping the recruiter.
- Prepping the interviewers again.

Anyone who can interview should prepare in advance by

- Taking interviewer training.
- Developing strong interview questions.

Without interview training, your junior people won't learn the proper technique and your senior people won't learn what bad habits they've acquired. Without strong interview questions, you might as well hire Jason Voorhees.

That is the question

Ah, the interview question. What makes a strong interview question? After many years of interviewing, I've decided there are only two types of worthwhile interview questions:

- Questions that expose personality traits.
- Questions that demonstrate how the candidate will perform on the job.

Brain teasers are worthless, background questions are a yawn, and "How would you do this job" questions are mindless regurgitation. Rarely do these types of questions directly expose personality traits or truly demonstrate performance. That is, unless you use the very best follow-up interview question of them all, "Why?" Not once or twice, but repeatedly until you get to that key personality trait or performance characteristic.

Even better, start with a "why" question. For instance, "Why do you want this job? Why are you leaving your old job? Why are you still working for Microsoft? Why do you want to work for Microsoft?" Again, these questions are useless if you stop asking "why" after the first response.

You are looking for how this person aligns with our key competencies, particularly passion, follow-through, flexibility, integrity, and professionalism. Anyone can show these on the surface. Keep asking "why" to get below the surface and find real evidence one way or the other.

The whiteboard compiler

Aside from "why" questions, there are coding questions (or other similar technical problem-solving questions) that try to uncover how candidates will perform on the job. These can be strong interview questions. The issue is coming up with the right questions.

Rather than bore you with countless examples of bad, overused, Web-publicized questions, I've got a step-by-step guide for coming up with your own great new questions:

1. Choose two or three real problems that you or your team have worked on over the past 18 months. The solutions should fit on a single whiteboard and involve at least three different variables. This ensures that you are selecting challenges with short and nontrivial solutions. In general they are small functions, pieces of a design problem, or particular test cases.

2. Break down each problem into a simple core issue, and use that as the first question. As a candidate builds confidence, add more complications that increase the difficulty. For instance, have the candidates look for more optimal solutions, introduce new cases, or ask for a more robust "production-quality" solution.

3. Call out areas that are gray in their analysis, and push the candidates for answers to see how they respond to questions outside of their safe zones.

4. Be prepared for multiple problem solutions, and point out real issues from your real problems.

Discard problems that are over two or three years old. You always encounter new problems, so rotate old problems out. It makes interviewing more fun for you and more relevant for the candidates. It's also much harder for candidates to read the answers on the Internet.

> **Eric Aside**   There is a huge tendency to hold onto old problems because it's easier and you've already learned how to gauge candidates' solutions. Get over it. Recent problems are better.

The goal is to see how each candidate approaches and solves the problems, not to get the right solution. There are a wide variety of things that could keep great candidates from finding a solution during the few minutes that they have with you. Instead, look for how they display core competencies while they are problem solving, such as the following:

- Did they identify if a strategy isn't working?
- Are they asking you questions to help them get on the right path, and do they listen to your hints?
- Did they analyze their process and results?
- Did they apply multiple strategies?

Be present in mind and soul when each candidate is at the whiteboard. You aren't looking for the answer; you are looking for how they get there.

Much of this information can be found in the Interviewer Toolkit, a great resource that HR put together with the help of a number of dev managers, including myself. You can also share and critique questions with your friends and dev team, but be careful not to duplicate their questions or soon the solutions will be published on the Web.

> **Eric Aside**   These days I often need to assess competencies that don't lend themselves to whiteboard problem solving, so I use role playing instead. The basic premise is simple: if you want to evaluate how well someone can code, have them code; if you want to evaluate someone's confidence in their decision making, question their decisions.

> **Online materials**   Interview Role Playing, a how-to guide (InterviewRolePlaying.doc)

Prepping the recruiter

After your interviewers are prepared with potential questions for candidates, you must prepare your recruiter. Send your recruiter the job description (including title and level information) and a long list of prepared interviewers. The longer the list, the easier it is to schedule interviews.

If you are just staffing up, borrow interviewers from your peers' teams and spread around the interviews to avoid creating a high burden on any one individual. Then be prepared to pay back the favor. Regardless of how you find the potential interviewers, let your recruiter choose from many names.

Present your interviewers like a menu: For the first interview, choose from one of these fine selections; for the second interview, indulge in one of these excellent choices. And so on. You can repeat names and be creative, just make it as easy as possible to schedule and you'll get more loops scheduled faster.

Prepping the interviewers (again)

Finally, the day before the interview comes and, with it, the interview feedback instructions thread. Reply to this thread right away with your instructions for the interview loop. Tell your interviewers about the position, what you are looking for in this particular candidate, and how you want the interviews conducted.

Each candidate can bring different things to the position. Each candidate may interest you in different ways. You must describe this to the people in the interview loop as well as describe your sense of the candidates' strengths and weaknesses.

Next, tell the interviewers what type of competencies you want each of them to focus on. Each interviewer should have a clear mission with as little overlap as possible. Leave room for a late interviewer to follow up on issues raised earlier in the day, but make sure every interviewer has a role. This prevents repeat questions, wasted time, and painful oversights.

A gentle reminder

Finally, remind the interviewers of the following:

- Speak briefly and privately to the next interviewer before that interview starts. Talk about the candidate and your hire/no-hire decision. Let the next interviewer know what kinds of questions you asked and what kinds still need to be asked.

> **Eric Aside** Given that interviewers each have a clear mission with little overlap, you may wonder why it's necessary to tell the next interviewer your impressions or what you asked. It's because life is unpredictable and humans are human. Maybe your interviewer changed things around. Maybe the interview got off on a tangent. Maybe some interesting character trait arose that deserves special attention. Who knows? Being flexible is a good thing.

- Write and send feedback promptly after the interview.
    - ❏ Start with your hire/no-hire decision.
    - ❏ Follow that with a short summary of your impressions, both gut and substantive.
    - ❏ Add concrete examples from your interview that back up each of your impressions. Quotes from the candidate are especially useful.

❑   Include what questions you asked and what questions still need to be asked.

❑   Conclude as you wish.

■   Do not use the word "borderline" in your hire/no-hire decision; make your choice and then defend it. By default, a borderline hire is a no-hire.

■   Do not be afraid or embarrassed to disagree with the prior interviewers. Say what you really feel, what you really saw and heard.

The last puzzle piece

With this preparation, the people on your interview loop should be ready to give each candidate a strong interview and reveal real insight into how successful the candidate could be in your open position.

The last piece of the puzzle is your As Appropriate interviewer, the last interviewer in the loop. Like the rest of the loop, you should have a few As Appropriate interviewers available on your interview loop menu. The As Appropriate should be

■   At least as familiar with your position and expectations as your recruiter. Ideally, you should discuss the position with the As Appropriate personally.

■   Engaged in the interview process all day, gathering late feedback, correcting and illuminating poor feedback, and focusing on trouble areas.

■   Prepared to sell your position and the team if the candidate is a strong hire.

> **Eric Aside**   The last interviewer at Microsoft is called the "As Appropriate" because he or she is a senior person and will do the last interview only if it's appropriate—that is, if the candidate shows real promise.

With a good set of interviewers, strong preparation on all fronts, and an aggressive recruiting effort, your interview loops will become your strength instead of your weakness, your propellant instead of your weight. You'll get your positions filled quickly, with great people, and be back at full strength, ready to deliver.

November 1, 2004: "The toughest job—Poor performers"

Reviews are over, and you may have pondered whether or not you'd be better off on a different team. You know, the kind that gives out more 3.5s and 4.0s. The kind where you'd be surrounded by lame wannabes and get a promotion faster. You've probably decided against that kind of move— a wise decision. However, you may be wondering why this inequity exists. Where did those lame wannabes come from? Why are they here? What's being done about it?

> **Eric Aside**   Actually, lame teams get exposed within a year or two, but it would be better for everyone involved if they never got started. That's the point of this column.

Well, take a look in the mirror. Have you allowed poor performers to slide by, thus giving your group easy annual 3.0 targets? Have you let entry-level employees stay entry level for years? Have you passed mediocre employees on to another manager or team rather than deal with them? Guess what? You are the problem.

What did you expect?

The poor performers aren't the problem. As far as they can tell, nothing is wrong. Sure, they aren't excelling, but they are getting by, and that seems to be enough. You haven't driven higher expectations for their performance. As a result, the poor performers stay. They find groups where they can be more comfortable. They hire mediocre folks like themselves. Finally, they drag down their orgs, then scatter like rats from a sinking ship.

But it's not their fault; it's your fault. You must expect more from them. I know it is hard. Poor performers aren't necessarily mean and nasty. They are often kind and thoughtful. They have families and obligations. They care about doing a good job, and they try to do the right thing. Telling them that caring and trying aren't good enough isn't easy.

Get over it and get over yourself. Going easy on mediocre employees is disrespectful and distasteful. You aren't doing them, yourself, or the company any favors. In fact, you are cruelly and selfishly harming all three.

Why? Because you are setting up your underperformers for failure. You've managed to create a situation where every workday your employees wake up, get dressed, and head into a job in which they will fail. Do you know what that feels like? You owe them the decency of explaining where they stand and what they can do to improve.

> **Eric Aside**   I'm being overly harsh here to make a point. If managers said nothing, that would be setting up poor employees for failure; however, managers do typically discuss performance with employees. Unfortunately, they often aren't as clear and firm as they should be, because they don't want to seem cold-hearted or cruel. Actually, being clear and firm is the kindest, most constructive thing managers can do.

Bite the bullet

So, say you've got employees who aren't meeting your expectations in one or more areas. What do you do? Simple. In your weekly one-on-ones, talk to them about your expectations, where they are falling short, and what meeting your expectations would look like. Tell them not to worry about writing it down, you'll send an e-mail.

Why send your expectations in an e-mail? It's all for the lawyers, right? Wrong! You write down your expectations so that they are clear and unambiguous.

One of the biggest problems with performance issues is inherent miscommunication. If your employees were clear on expectations, there wouldn't be a problem. When they are falling short, your employees must be crystal clear on why and what they can do to improve. A short e-mail will do; include bullets on each of your expectations, where they are lacking, and what success would be.

Seeking professional help

But what if you don't see improvement? What if you feel a 2.5 may be in progress? Contact your HR generalist immediately. Your generalist will work with you to ensure that your employees are getting the right information and the right help if they need it.

> **Eric Aside**   In Microsoft's old rating system, ratings of 2.5 and 3.0 were undesirable. Ratings of 4.0 and 4.5 were highly desirable. A 3.5 rating was readily accepted and the most common.

Sometimes performance issues are caused by personal matters. Depending on the situation, Microsoft may have an obligation to accommodate employees through such times. Your HR generalist will know all the options and can properly get your employees the help they deserve. Do not play psychologist, doctor, or lawyer for your employees. Leave those matters for your generalist to refer employees to qualified agents.

Failure is not an option

If the performance issues persist, your generalist can help you find the best course of action. While there are cases of re-leveling or changing roles, the more common situation comes down to presenting employees with three choices:

- Voluntarily leave the company
- Improve
- Involuntarily leave the company

Microsoft is very good about helping employees make the transition, which is why having your generalist involved is so beneficial. Often when presented with clear options and failing expectations, employees will be relieved to leave the company and find a new opportunity where they have a better chance of success. This is the second best result, and it happens more often than you might think.

> **Eric Aside**   Not every employee with performance issues gets the same choices. HR can help you tailor the proper response to each unique situation. Here I'm describing a common set of choices.

The goal is success

The best result is when your employees improve their performance enough to meet or exceed your expectations. You get back great employees. You don't need to fire anyone. You don't need to spend months hiring someone new. You don't need to bring new people up to speed. Your employees keep their jobs and their esteem, and they become successful. It's a huge win for everyone.

So, if your poor performers choose to improve, you must believe that they can and be part of their success. Even if you are sure that this person has no chance of turning his career around, you must trust that he will somehow overcome the obstacles.

Why? Because it's better if he succeeds, and because he knows if you doubt him. People can tell when you don't believe in them, and they assume it means that they don't have a chance to succeed at Microsoft. Remember, if you don't believe that your employees can change, you are setting them up for failure. That can have tragic consequences.

Ask and you shall receive

To set up your employees for success, you must go back to setting clear expectations for solid performance. Your expectations must be in writing to minimize misinterpretation and misunderstanding. Review these expectations weekly, and discuss in writing and in person where there is improvement and what remains to be done.

Often poor performers will show an initial spike in improvement. Managers get excited about this and tell the employees that they are pleased, only to have the employees top out or even regress. The problem is that the employees get the sense that they are exceeding expectations, when in fact they are doing better but still falling short.

You must be supportive, but focus on success by saying, "Hey, it is so great to see your significant improvement. I really appreciate your efforts. By continuing this trend and improving in these other areas, you will begin to meet the expectations of your assignment and be on the road to success." This reassures an employee that you notice and care, while still setting a clear bar.

Often a poor performer who doesn't have what it takes to turn things around will realize her shortcomings after she puts in her best effort and still falls short. If you support their success, employees can leave voluntarily on good terms knowing that you treated them fairly and with respect. You gave them a real chance.

You can't always get what you want

In cases where poor performers are too stubborn or prideful to admit that they can't meet your expectations, you will have all the proper documentation needed for an involuntary resignation (firing). Your HR generalist will help you and your employees through this difficult step.

If you do need to fire an employee, you'll have to send out the awkward e-mail to the group, "[Employee] is no longer with Microsoft and will be pursuing other opportunities." The most difficult aspect of this is that you can't say anything about why it happened. You must protect your former employee's privacy, even if that employee chooses to tell people a different story.

It is common for members of your group to wonder what happened. They'll ask you why an employee left. Although you are not permitted to tell them anything about the private situation of your former employee, you can answer their real question. When people ask about someone else's situation, they almost always are truly concerned about their own job security. That's selfish perhaps, but also quite natural.

Use the opportunity to give them feedback that will help them perform better and to reassure them about their own standing. You can also reassure them that Microsoft has strong expectations of employees because the company knows that we will only succeed when we have extraordinary people performing at their best in a healthy and supportive environment. That is a message we all can be proud of.

September 1, 2005: "Go with the flow—Retention and turnover"

Review season is here. As entertaining as that can be for managers and employees alike, it's just a primer for what follows: musical product groups. The music starts when review numbers are released. A whole bunch of engineers get up out of their office chairs and try to find an available chair in a different group. The music stops when all the interesting positions get filled. The same game gets played at the end of product cycles, but product cycles aren't quite as predictable (different problem).

It's tough on the folks left without chairs. Often they get alienated from their current teams for trying to jump ship. Tough luck? I don't think so. Managers should encourage their people to pursue new opportunities, including people they like. Anything less is selfish, stupid, and shortsighted, not to mention destructive, delusional, and deplorable. When managers make business decisions that put their interests ahead of Microsoft's, they've clearly stopped working for Microsoft. I think Microsoft should stop paying them.

Don't tell me, "Oh, but the project depends on this person. It's necessary for me to alienate him and stifle his personal development. It's for the good of the company." That's a crock-load of dung. What you're trying to tell me is that you didn't plan for turnover, and now that it's come, you want to avoid all the work to recover, recruit, re-educate, and reassign people. In other words, you're brain dead and lazy, but you're making up for it by being selfish and self-serving. Only ignorant nimrods are unprepared for turnover.

> **Eric Aside**   Okay, I've held back till Chapter 9, but I have to say it, I love re-reading these columns. Writing them has always been a cathartic experience. Reviewing them for this book has allowed me to relive the satisfaction of unmitigated rage directed at behavior I truly despise. It's nice in its own twisted way.

I'll just walk the earth

Good managers should expect around 10% turnover a year. Bad managers should expect more, but they probably don't recognize it, and I certainly don't care.

If you're a good manager of a group of 20, you should expect two people to leave your group each year, sometimes more, sometimes less. Even a lead with five reports should expect at least one person to leave every couple of years. People leave for all kinds of reasons, many of which have nothing to do with you or your team: friendships on other teams, new technologies, a change of scenery, and relationships outside work to name a few. You shouldn't take it personally.

Nice dam, huh?

But how should you deal with turnover? Some managers go to extremes to prevent it:

- They blow tons of money on extravagant morale gifts and events, when having more frequent, cheap events would be far better.

- They promise larger roles and promotions—promises they don't completely control, promises they can't keep.

- They deny permission to interview for everyone on the team, which poisons morale and makes the team feel like indentured servants.

> **Eric Aside**   Microsoft has since changed its rules so that managers can no longer refuse to allow their employees to interview. Only vice presidents still have that privilege.

Trying to prevent turnover is like building a dam to prevent a river from flowing. It works for a short time until the dam breaks or overflows and your team gets washed away in a torrent of transfers. What's worse, such measures lower morale and make your team less attractive to the new members you'll soon need.

Flowing like a river

Instead, the best way to deal with turnover is to expect it and embrace it. How? Think flow, flow, floooooooow.

Think of your team as a river instead of a lake. A lake stagnates. There's no energy or impetus to change. The same is true of groups that stagnate. They cultivate mediocrity and complacency; they abhor risk. A river is always running and changing with lots of great energy. You want a river.

A river depends on the flow of water, and your team depends on the flow of people and information. You can think of the people divided into three groups: new blood, new leaders, and elders ready for a new challenge. Here's how those groups should balance and flow:

- The largest group should be the new blood. Not all of them will become technical or organizational leaders.

- Sometimes you'll have more new leaders than elders, sometimes the reverse, but ideally you should maintain a balance.

- For flow, you want a steady stream of new blood becoming your new leaders, and new leaders becoming elders.

- The key to flow is new blood coming in and elders moving out. For this to work, you WANT your elders to transfer before they clog the stream and disrupt the flow of opportunities for others.

Not all technologies flow at the same rate. Central engines, like the Windows kernel, flow slowly, while web-based services, like MSN Search, flow quickly. You need to adjust for your situation, but even the most conservative technologies do change and flow.

How do you successfully encourage and maintain a healthy flow?

- Keep a constant supply of new people.

- Instill information sharing as a way of life.

- Shape the organization and roles to create growth opportunities.

- Find new challenges for your elders.

Fresh meat

For a constant supply of new people, nothing beats interns and college hires. Obviously, you'll also recruit industry candidates and internal transfers, but interns and college hires should be your primary choice for their fresh perspectives and long-term potential.

Your number of annual college hire slots should be at least 5% of your total staff, counting open positions. So if your team has 20 devs, you want at least one college hire slot, more if your team is increasing headcount. Even in a flat headcount organization there is still at least 5% attrition, so look for young talent to fill openings even if none are currently available. College hires sometimes don't start for nine months; anything can happen over that time, so plan ahead.

Interns are the next best thing to college hires, but they take an extra year to join your team. Therefore, you want as many intern slots as college hire slots. DO NOT plan on shipping interns' code. At best, they should be pair programming shipping code. However, DO NOT give interns menial labor either. Instead, give interns strong mentors (people who'll be your next leads) and exciting projects (buddy them up on the coolest features or incubation work). You want to measure them as future full-time hires and convince them that there's no better job in the world than working for you at Microsoft.

Sharing is caring

When you have new folks on your team, you want them to grow into your new technical and organizational leaders. The only way this happens is through sharing information and knowledge. There is a cornucopia of ways to do this. Here are just a few:

- Keep an online knowledge warehouse of how your group works. It can be a big, versioned Word doc; a SharePoint site; or a wiki—whatever works best for your folks. The key is to make it easily accessible and up to date. The first month's assignment for a new person should be to update the content.

- Use buddy systems for all projects and assignments. The arrangement can be anything from mentoring to assigned reviewer and backup to full-on pair programming. The key is to have no one working alone, no information isolated.

- Get people together regularly, ideally daily, to discuss progress and issues. Nothing encourages sharing of information like regular high-bandwidth communication, even for as little as 15 minutes a day.

Buddy systems are particularly important for growing your new leaders and transitioning your elders. It's never safe for an elder to leave if you lose key knowledge and capability in the process. By constantly sharing information, you release the stress-inducing stranglehold on your elder team members, and you make flow and transition a positive and natural experience.

Room to grow

Just like with repotting plants, you need to give your people room to grow. You can encourage this through how you structure your organization, how you issue your assignments, and how you design and promote growth paths for people to follow.

First think about growth paths. The new career models provide excellent and detailed guidance. How do growth paths apply to your team? You should know every employee's desired growth path and current stage. Then you and your leaders should discuss if those desired growth paths are available for everyone, and if not, how will you adjust?

Often how your group is organized blocks your employees' growth. All your senior people may be on one team and newbies on another. Change it, fix it, rebalance, reshuffle. The longer you leave your org unbalanced, the more trouble you'll cause and risk you'll carry.

Restructuring your organization can create dozens of new opportunities for growth. It's critical to take advantage of them. Give your people assignments and new responsibilities that stretch them out of their comfort zone. Naturally, buddy them up with more experienced partners to reduce the risk and enhance the learning, but don't just have the same people do the same things. Choose the assignments based on desired growth paths, and everyone wins.

I must be traveling

Of course, no one can move up if your most senior people stay put. Unless your group is expanding, the only way to make room for growth is to have your elders transfer out. Luckily, that's exactly what they need. If they've been in your group long enough to reach the senior positions, then the only way for them to keep growing is to take on new challenges elsewhere.

Because you've focused on flow, losing your senior employees is no big deal. They've already shared their knowledge and experience. Their project buddies are already familiar with their work. Now all they need to do is find a good fit elsewhere with you supporting them every step of the way. This kind of loyalty and support will not only be appreciated by your senior people, but will be returned in loyalty and respect by the whole team.

Remember, the whole team watches how you treat your most senior folks. It's an indicator of how you'll treat them some day. Nothing wins over a staff like seeing the elder members being treated fairly and generously; leaving the group with praise, well-wishes, and a great future ahead. The message: "Stay with this team and you'll be well rewarded."

Surrender to the flow

When you fight turnover or let it catch you unprepared, you risk your project and the effectiveness and health of your team. When you embrace turnover, it becomes just a natural consequence of life. No fear, no worries, just healthy flow for an effective team.

What's more, driving for flow of people and information in your team creates growth for Microsoft people and value for Microsoft customers. Less stress, more opportunity, greater flexibility, compounded knowledge, higher morale, and a stronger team. What more could you possibly ask? It's time to surrender to the flow.

December 1, 2005: "I can manage"

What do weddings, travel, and managers have in common? Talk to any adult about these topics and you are sure to hear a horror story. At weddings, it's the drunken guest, bad weather, or untimely faux pas. During travel, it's the lost baggage, disruptive passenger, or transit foul-up. With managers, it's the frigging incompetent, clueless, arrogant, insensitive, conniving, beady-eyed, spineless, self-serving jerk who used to be your boss. Not that I'm bitter or anything.

Skipping the extreme cases, most wedding and travel horror stories can be retold with a smile and shared laughter. The same can't be said for manager horror stories. Sure, everyone will have a good laugh at the stupidity or absurdity of an old boss's actions, but when you look into the eyes of the employee who suffered, there is always simmering contempt. That employee has not forgiven or forgotten what that former manager did.

The gift that keeps on giving

Why do people so easily let go of wedding and travel mishaps, yet clench tightly to manager malfeasance? It's because at the end of weddings, the couples kiss. At the end of a long trip, you finally return home. Bad managers stay. There's no happy ending. Bad managers are there every day, day after day, making one bad move after another.

Even when you finally escape a bad manager's grip, his legacy hangs on with lost time, lost opportunities, and lost results. His comments and actions haunt you. His past callousness compromises your current perceived and real sense of worth. You become distrustful of managers in general. It can take a decade to repair the trouble caused in a year—and that's just for one person.

The damage done to the company is even greater. Rotten managers generate lost productivity, waste and rework, poor quality, blown commitments, and disgruntled employees who quit and complain or stay and sabotage. Rotten managers also generate potential lawsuits, but that's a whole other subject.

Good enough for me

"Hey, give managers a break," some might whine. "Being a good manager is hard." No, no it isn't. Being a great manager is hard. Being a good manager is easy. A good manager only has to focus on two things—two very simple things that anyone can do:

- Ensure her employees are able to work.
- Care about her employees.

That's it. No magic, no motivational videos, no 24-hour days are necessary. A good manager just needs to ensure his employees can work, and he must care about them.

Easy does it

Ask even the most pubescent managers how to ensure that their employees are able to work and they'll say, "Remove roadblocks." It's obvious, isn't it? But ask, "What kind of road-blocks?" and they'll say, "Tracking down dependencies," "Hounding PMs for specs," or "Demanding decent repro steps from testers." So misguided.

Why is a frontal assault on cross-group barricades misguided?

■ When managers try to be heroes, they only manage being idiots. They track down dependencies, resulting in rushed, lousy drops, instead of collaborating on BVTs, API designs, and having realistic plans and contingencies in the first place. They hound PMs for specs instead of collaborating on all aspects of the design. They demand decent repro steps from testers instead of providing instrumentation that allows for easy debugging of failures from any source. In other words, misguided managers make themselves part of the problem instead of part of the solution.

■ Cross-group barriers are hard and time consuming to break. Managers need to give their teams workarounds before undertaking valiant quests.

■ Misguided managers allow cross-group roadblocks to distract their attention from more immediate, basic concerns.

Of course, cross-group issues are important to resolve. But there are usually straightforward ways to help with or work around the issues, and more basic problems to address first.

> **Eric Aside**   I'd say that one of the top mistakes new managers make is focusing on removing complex roadblocks rather than the simple ones I describe next. The other top mistakes new managers make are continuing to think of themselves as individuals instead of team representatives and not delegating properly. (See "Time enough" in Chapter 8.)

I want to work

So what basic necessities should managers provide to ensure their employees can work? As I said, that's easy. Engineers don't need much, they just need

■ A desk with a phone

■ Power (light, heat, electricity)

■ A computer with a keyboard and display (some don't even need a mouse)

■ Network access and privileges

■ A healthy environment (safe, relatively quiet, with breathable air)

■ Work to accomplish

Who could mess this up? Maybe finding work for people could be complicated, but usually that's not a problem. However, there are plenty of managers who allow employees to go for days without a computer—managers who don't have an office ready for a new team member.

What happened the last time your network went out or the noise got too loud? Did your manager drop everything and do whatever it took to fix the issue? If not, she failed utterly in her role as a manager. Nothing is more basic than ensuring your employees can work.

What about providing a safe environment? Is there any hostility on your team? What is your manager doing about it? This is why anti-harassment training is necessary. It's because there is nothing more critical, more essential than ensuring everyone is given an opportunity to work in a safe environment.

I'm not an object

The second simple thing a good manager must do is care about his employees. This doesn't mean warm hugs or greeting cards. You don't even need to like them. You just need to care about your employees, seeing them for what they truly are: fellow human beings.

Again, who could mess this up? How hard can it be? Yet managers commonly think of their employees as resources instead of people. They label their employees as the "good ones" and the "bad ones." They turn their employees into objects instead of seeing them as human beings.

Ever have a manager play favorites? It hurts, doesn't it—even if you are one of the favorites? That's because you're always one false step away from being shunned. A manager who plays favorites is a manager who has stopped seeing her employees as people and started treating them as collectibles.

Taking the time to know and appreciate your employees as real people isn't complicated, but it is a commitment. You need to set aside your own preferences and prejudices and let others know you so you can know them. I realize this is mushy stuff, but good managers respect their employees as real people, they don't treat them as abstract headcount.

By the way, you don't need to say or do anything to show you care. In fact, no amount of words or deeds can convince people you care about them if you really don't. People simply can tell. You can yell at them, praise them, criticize them, and even disappoint them—employees will see through it all and still respect you if you respect them.

Remember, all you need to do to be a good manager is ensure your people can work and treat them as human beings.

> **Eric Aside**   It's a necessary and sufficient condition—meaning if you ensure your people can work and you care about them, you are a good manager (really one of the better managers). If you don't ensure they can work or you don't care about them, you are a bad manager regardless of your other herculean efforts.

Good to great

The world and our company would be a better place if all managers were at least good managers. However, Microsoft is a competitive place, so you're probably wondering what makes a great manager.

Many books, journals, and graduate schools have been dedicated to defining great managers. To me it comes down to three aspects:

- **Be a good manager.**   Don't start by being great; start by being good. The moment you forget the basics is the moment you lose the respect and effectiveness of your employees.

- **Have integrity.**   This means align your words and actions with your beliefs. If you believe in a strong work ethic while maintaining a clear work-life balance, demonstrate it. If you believe quality comes first, make it first. You set the bar. You define the team.

- **Provide clear goals, priorities, and limits.**   Clearly communicating your goals, priorities, and limits up, down, and across your organization is essential for highly effective teams and individuals. Goals can take the form of expectations, commitments, or vision statements. Regardless, they show where to go. Priorities show how to get there. Limits provide the safe boundaries within which to travel. Without goals, it's easy to go nowhere. Without priorities, it's easy to get lost. Without limits, it's easy to stumble.

Being a great manager is difficult. You must stand up to the pressure to compromise your beliefs. You must clearly and strongly communicate a consistent message about your vision, what's important, and what's not acceptable. You must do all this while not losing sight of the humanity of your people and the small, but important, things they need to be productive.

I serve

That's all there is to being a good, or even great, manager. It all comes down to service. You are no longer the one doing the work. Instead, you subjugate yourself to the service of your team members so that they can be successful. Management, when done well, is about selflessness. There is no higher calling.

May 1, 2006: "Beyond comparison—Dysfunctional teams"

This column is for leads and managers, but I'll bet you report to one, so feel free to share.

How often do your employees rant about each other? Do they form "secret" alliances? Is the air thick with tension in your team meetings? That must be tough for you; my teams always get along great.

Does your team have lunch together? Are your morale events strained? My team eats together once a week and messes around at a morale event once a month. We laugh almost the whole time.

When your team is stressed, do they fracture? When one of your employees falters, do the others take advantage of the situation? Do they just stand back and enjoy the moment?

Or does your team look after each other? My employees always band together and support one another.

If we reported to the same manager, how would you feel about the job you are doing? What would our manager say? Would she tell you to be more like me? Would she throw my team's survey, retention, and productivity numbers in your face? How would you feel, especially at review time?

Trying to pick a fight

Think I'm picking a fight? Darn right I am. If our manager compared my team to yours and shoved the facts in your face, you'd want me dead, or at least bucked off the high horse the boss handed me. You'd probably try to sabotage my success and make me look like a dimwit.

Sound familiar? If your team is dysfunctional, that's what is happening. Members of your team are sabotaging each other and pressing their own agendas to improve their relative standing. Teamwork is for people uninterested in mortal combat.

Who or what is the culprit? Are your people too competitive? No way, I've got highly competitive people on my team who used to be on yours, only now they get along. Is it the review system that pits people against one another? No, I use the same system. Is it the stress level? No, my people shine brightest when they are challenged.

What's the difference? Why do my teams function so well? Want to know? Here's the answer: I never compare my people to each other; I compare them to their own potential and my expectations. That's it. That's the secret.

Go ahead, try to deny it. It can't be that simple, right? Besides, I have to compare them to each other; it's part of reviews, right? Wrong. It is that simple, and reviews don't have to be destructive.

> **Eric Aside**   I took a dangerous tact of being directly confrontational with my readers and seeming quite conceited for this column. It was deliberate; I wanted my readers to relive that visceral animosity they felt as children against their rivals. Since I. M. Wright is an arrogant son of a female dog anyway, I figured his reputation wouldn't suffer and trusted people could handle it.

This is not a competition

I wish I could claim to have discovered this secret on my own, but I'm not that smart. I learned it from a parenting book, *Siblings Without Rivalry: How to Help Your Children Live So That You Can Live Too* by Adele Faber and Elaine Mazlish (HarperCollins, 2004). The premise is simple: children want your love and attention, and if you compare them to each other, you've declared it a competition. However, it isn't a competition unless you are a really sick parent. Therefore, don't compare.

The same goes for employees. They all want the admiration and appreciation of their supervisor. If you compare employees to each other, then you've declared it a competition—but it isn't. Yes, employees compete for rewards division-wide, but at that scale the competition isn't directly between your team members.

Yes, there are donkeys posing as managers who insist their employees should compete for rewards at the team level. However, that is so far from reasonable, respectful, and rational that I'd like to personally report every case to HR. Donkeys like that shouldn't be allowed to manage people. They should be relegated to walking in endless circles by adults in clown suits while screaming children pull their hair.

When teammates don't compete against each other, their best chance to achieve success is to work together. Life is good.

I'll give you a hint

To maintain a high-functioning team, a key challenge is to avoid making comparisons between team members. Don't give them any excuses to compete against each other. But how do you avoid comparisons? Use these simple pointers:

- **Describe what you like.**   An employee asks your opinion of some work: "How does this compare to Pat's?" This is a trap, so don't mention Pat. Instead, describe what you like: "That's a great implementation. It's clear and concise, easy to test, and uses all the right security protections."

- **Express confidence in your employees.**   An employee complains about a teammate: "I'm blocked until Joe checks in his code, but he doesn't want to check it in till it's perfect. Can you get him moving?" This employee, perhaps unwittingly, wants to look good while making a teammate look bad, so don't fall for it. Instead, express your confidence in your team: "Wow, you are blocked, but Joe's trying to do a quality job. Sounds like a tough tradeoff. I'm sure you two can talk it through and work out a reasonable compromise."

- **Focus on fulfilling needs, not on being "fair."**   You promoted an employee and a peer is jealous: "How did Jane get promoted and I didn't? It isn't fair, we both worked hard." It's easy to get caught up in fairness on many issues, but life isn't fair. Instead of comparing the haves and have-nots, reaffirm your employee's needs and talk about fulfilling them: "I wish everyone could get promotions at once, but the business doesn't work that way. Let's talk about what you need to do for a promotion and put a plan in place to get you there."

- **Talk about behavior instead of people.**   The employee you looked over for a promotion isn't satisfied and wants details: "But why did Jane get promoted instead of me?

How is she better than me?" This is another trap, and one that is well supported by our review system. Focus on behaviors rather than people: "Jane demonstrated leadership of the feature team in designing the solution that was used for a key scenario and then fully implemented by the team. That kind of leadership is something you are still developing. Your design skills are strong, but you haven't shown the leadership necessary to get consensus on your design and see it through implementation."

Focusing on behavior also works well in review calibration meetings. Instead of saying, "Jane is better than Pat," you say, "Jane has reached this skill level as demonstrated in these ways. Pat has not shown those skills." While there is a comparison, it is not competitive. Pat isn't trying to be better than Jane; Pat is trying to attain Jane's skill set. It's a subtle but important difference.

One for all

Having a cohesive team pays huge dividends. They perform better, are more resilient, and have higher morale. Retention is better, communication is stronger, and the team is easier to manage. Being a good manager means caring about your people and other aspects I wrote about in my article, "I can manage" (which appears earlier in the chapter)—but those don't guarantee a cohesive team.

You need to keep your team from competing against one another. That comes from seeing your employees as individuals, understanding their potential, and focusing on their specific needs and your specific expectations for them. Care about your employees without judging them against each other.

When you remove individual competition, you only leave team success. Sure, there will still be quarrels and complaints, but your team will see those as inhibiting their shared success, not improving their personal standing. And nothing beats a team working together to make each other great.

By the way, we've had kids for ten years and still no signs of rivalry.

> **Eric Aside**   If you like behavioral books, also try *Don't Shoot the Dog* (Ringpress Books, 2002) written by Karen Pryor, a former dolphin trainer. She covers everything from quieting your dog to taming your mother-in-law. If you want something even more comprehensive for business, *Human Competence: Engineering Worthy Performance* by Thomas F. Gilbert (Pfeiffer, 2007) is the seminal text for what I do.

Chapter 10
Microsoft, You Gotta Love It

In this chapter:

November 1, 2001: "How I learned to stop worrying and love reorgs" 186

March 1, 2005: "Is your PUM a bum?" 189

September 1, 2006: "It's good to be the King of Windows" 192

December 1, 2006: "Google: Serious threat or poor spelling?" 197

April 1, 2007: "Mid-life crisis" 200

There are three sides to management: the people side, the project side, and the business side. I've already covered people management and project management. It's time to tackle how Microsoft runs its business.

It's easy to be cynical about capitalism and huge corporations like Microsoft. Microsoft must turn a significant profit to stay in business. The company can't make decisions based purely on idealism or what's best for the customer. Staying in business must be a factor or we soon won't have customers. Unfortunately, idealists don't last long in a big company. Luckily, I'm pragmatic and willing to live with some imperfection if it means I get to spend more time with my family. Of course, I still get to ridicule the inevitable foibles of the world's largest software company.

In this chapter, I. M. Wright analyzes and overcomes the challenges of running a successful software business. The first column finds hidden merit in reorganizations. The second identifies the proper role of middle management. The third column accepts the challenge of directing one of the world's largest engineering teams. The fourth compares Microsoft's business strategy with that of Google and other competitors; and the last one examines Microsoft's growing pains and suggests ways to smooth its transition to middle age.

Given my monthly ranting, it's a common misconception that I don't like Microsoft. People think I like getting paid, but if I was in charge I'd change far more than I'd keep. At the risk of alienating all the Microsoft bashers out there, I must be honest. I love Microsoft. Having worked for academia (RPI), the government (JPL), small business (GRAFTEK), mid-size business (SGI), and large business (Boeing), Microsoft is by far the best place I've been. For all its faults and gaffes, Microsoft has three amazing strengths:

- *The people in charge earnestly want to make the world a better place...through software. At every other company I've known, the approach is the opposite: be successful in a field and hope it improves the world.*

■ *The people in charge hire the best and then fundamentally trust them at the lowest levels to make decisions and run the business. Naturally, this has led to some problems over the years and forced checks to be put in place, but empowerment is more than a nice buzzword.*

■ *The people in charge embrace and encourage change and then have the patience and perseverance to see it through. So many companies fight to keep their comfortable status quo. Microsoft fights its size and legacy to constantly improve and adapt to the world it helped shape.*

I love Microsoft and work every day to make it better. It's not perfect, nothing manmade ever is, but if I were in charge, I'd build from its strengths not refashion it from my own imperfect image.

– Eric

November 1, 2001: "How I learned to stop worrying and love reorgs"

This issue of *Interface* talks about some of the technological changes and opportunities for delighting our customers that are rising from the .NET initiative. But the changes haven't ended there for most of us. I'm speaking of the dark side.

Yes, it's the dark side that comes seemingly with each and every change in company and group strategy: reorgs, frigging reorgs. Frigging wastes of time, energy, and momentum. Just the physics of them makes you want to duck, cover, and hold onto your desk for fear of it being moved to another building.

> **Eric Aside**   This column on reorganizations (reorgs) is targeted at managers, as are all the early *Interface* columns.

Down the Tower of Babel it goes

As the reorg message travels down successive layers of management, it gets diluted until finally the mail from your boss says, "Just keeping doing the great work you're doing; nothing changes for now."

Of course, things will change for your group within three to six months. Maybe you'll simply move offices; maybe your management team will change; maybe your group will merge with another or just be cut loose. Who knows? Certainly not your staff, because you wouldn't want to tell them even if you did know. Why? Because plans could change five or six times between when you inform your staff and when change actually happens, and because of all the unease and distraction it would cause your folks.

> **Eric Aside**   You shouldn't hide it from them either, as I discussed in "To tell the truth," which appears in Chapter 1. If anyone asks about reorg rumors, you tell them the truth: "I have no idea what will happen or whether anything will happen at all. I do know what will happen if we can't stay focused on the work at hand."

Life in hell

Meanwhile, your life as a manager becomes a living hell. Even if you don't tell your staff about the coming changes, rumors start flying. Soon you can feel the panic building in your junior staff, while cynicism leaches into your senior staff. In addition to actually doing your normal 60+ hours per week job, you need to

- Calm and reassure your junior staff.

- Convince your senior staff to care about the changes.

- Grapple over offices and seniority on move maps.

> **Eric Aside**   Two quick pieces of advice for office moves: avoid the southwest corner of a building, it gets hot; and use a purely objective, transparent method for choosing office assignments. (Microsoft uses time on the job, also known as seniority, down to the second you signed.)

- Play political death match with new groups that cross yours.

> **Eric Aside**   If two groups merge, each can have only one product unit manager (PUM), group program manager (GPM), dev manager, and test manager. A highly politicized battle can ensue.

- Conspire with your manager to rephrase your group's current plans to match those specified by the new upper management.

- Fight the tendency to play philosophical Ping-Pong with your conscience and peers over making the right changes to your products that match the new company direction as opposed to meeting your ship dates.

- Provide yet another educational series for your new upper management about what your group does.

How can this much nonsense be worth it? Why must we go through organizational self-mutilation every 9 to 18 months? I've got a theory, and it's not the classic "We must always keep at least one large group moving because we don't have enough office space" theory. Here goes...

The road less traveled

What makes big companies like IBM and Boeing as agile as a cashier on quaaludes? IMHO, old orgs are like old habits taking the path of least resistance. It's hard to teach an old org new tricks. Why? Because people deal with folks they know much faster and easier than with those they don't. If an org has been around awhile, no matter how sharp the people are who run it, they will still tend to work with the same peers repeatedly, rather than deal with someone new.

This is a recipe for making middle management stagnant and ineffective. The longer the same managers are in the same org, the more likely it is that they will make decisions based on people they know instead of what's necessarily best for the company or the customer. It's an insidious disease that infects even the smartest people and goes completely undetected. Their lives seem easier and more familiar, while their choices become more restricted and perverse. Total disaster.

How do we keep our managers alert to new possibilities and away from following old habits? We move them around—constantly. Short of getting rid of all middle management, which may seem tempting but really isn't reasonable, the only way to keep our big company acting like a small one is to keep people moving—literally. Yeah, there's pain in dealing with misinformed or apparently clueless new management, but it beats the "old boy" network every time for agility, flexibility, and forward thinking.

> **Eric Aside**   The other solution is to flatten the organization—that is, remove layers of management by having larger numbers of people reporting to each manager. Microsoft has flattened a bit since I wrote this column, and a few groups are experimenting with flattening in the extreme. Going too far concerns me for the same reasons I don't have 15 kids—lack of attention and lack of oversight—but it's worth trying and learning from the result.

Of course, reexamining what you are doing and trying to explain how it fits into the corporate vision is a healthy exercise, and learning about people and projects in different orgs is always a good thing. Thus, I have learned to stop worrying and love reorgs.

Part of the problem or part of the solution?

Sure, we are in a highly competitive market where change is constant and new technologies, architectures, and platforms require us to adapt our strategies. But if all we do is shift focus and not people, our company will get organizational arthritis and stiffen till it becomes a corpse.

The question is, are you or your group part of the problem? If you've been in the same org too long, maybe things seem a little too comfortable and maybe it's time to switch. If your boss has been in the same org too long, maybe it's time to worry.

Regardless, the next time you get that mail from SteveB saying, "I'm as excited as I've ever been about the opportunities these changes will create," suck it up and say, "Steve, I'm as excited as you. Keep up the good work and bring on the new org!"

March 1, 2005: "Is your PUM a bum?"

At the risk of insulting some of my wonderful, former bosses, I think most product unit managers (PUMs) are bums. They pace the hallways, spewing crazed, detailed theories of how things should be—completely out of touch with reality—while living off the kindness of strangers who work in nearby offices. What value do they bring? What purpose do they serve?

> **Eric Aside**   I certainly don't want to insult bums with this comparison. Only a fraction of bums are mentally disturbed. Many live independently in the life they choose. As for PUMs, keep reading…

PUMs are the first level of managers truly removed from any real work. They don't write the specs or the code or the tests or the content. They don't localize or publish or operate or design. They just manage the people who do, along with their budgets. Managing multiple disciplines and their budgets is challenging, but so is dealing with a disconnected, delirious, and demanding boss. Neither should be a full-time job.

> **Eric Aside**   Kudos to a former team member, Bernie Thompson, who suggested this topic, and now runs an interesting site on lean software engineering with another former team member, Corey Ladas.

The man with a plan

Of course, your typical PUM will tell you he serves a critical role. For convenience, we'll name him "Clueless." Clueless spends hours in meetings discussing business development strategy. He fosters key strategic relationships with partners and customers. Clueless discusses these strategies at his staff meetings and at off-sites. He presents his three-year strategy quarterly to his boss, VP, and overall team. "Strategic planning is critical to our success," claims Clueless. "Now all we need to do is execute."

And yet, Clueless seems somehow detached. Perhaps it's because he isn't involved with the day-to-day struggles of the team. Perhaps he doesn't receive enough information from his staff. Perhaps he's more passionate about being a PUM and a leader than he is about the actual work. Or perhaps he's so wrapped up in some abstract strategy that the means of shipping the product seems superfluous. Clueless had it right when he said, "All we need to do is execute." The trouble is that he left himself out of the equation.

I can't wait to operate

Every business plan has two sides:

- **The strategic side**   What are we going to accomplish, for whom, and when?

- **The operational side**   How are we going to accomplish it?

Clueless has the strategic side covered. For someone who isn't going to do the work, the strategic side seems more fun and relevant. Setting a strategic vision is important and must come from the top, so Clueless feels wanted and needed when he focuses on strategy. As for the operational side—well, he can leave that to his competent staff.

But theory without application is merely self-gratification. Architects who don't stick around to solve issues when the building is built or the software is coded are soon marginalized. And strategists who ignore the operational side become nothing more than figureheads who can't understand why the strategy isn't working out the way they planned. In other words, they become Clueless.

The devil is in the details

The strategy is set; yet six months into the project Clueless can't understand why things are already deteriorating. So Clueless starts attending all the meetings, asking questions, demanding results, and driving his staff and his team completely insane.

Micromanagement can get the job done if Clueless is sufficiently obnoxious and amphetamine-rich. However, he will be despised and with good cause:

- **No one likes to be treated like a baby.**   Clueless has a good staff; he should let them do their jobs.

- **Everyone curses the bottleneck.**   When Clueless gets involved in every aspect of the project, all decisions must go through him and he becomes a factor that blocks progress.

- **Opportunities for growth dissolve.**   Clueless is taking on all the decisions and all the risk. He's shut out everyone else from stepping up, while he gets all the credit. Yay, Clueless!

- **The big problems are left unresolved.**   By focusing on the details, Clueless sidesteps the big problems related to how the team operates and he leaves them broken. The entire team becomes dejected and demoralized. Ignore improving the engineering system and the entire project is set up for failure.

There's a better way for a PUM to drive a team to successfully execute on a strategy. It's called *an operating plan*.

The rules of the road

An operating plan describes how your team is going to execute on the strategic vision. As a PUM, you don't need to lay out all the details and make all the decisions, but you do need an operating plan that will adapt and adjust as the project iterates toward the desired goals. Just like the strategic plan, the operating plan should be built by the PUM in conjunction with her staff. Before the strategy is finalized, the team leadership needs to know how they're going to implement it.

For a product unit, the decisions are around people, processes, and tools. Here is a sampling of the kinds of questions you want answered:

- **What will your org look like?**   Who are the leads? Who are the feature teams? Who are the experts and architects? What is the succession plan if people leave?

- **What processes are you going to follow?**   What are you going to do better this time? What's your scheduling process? What are your quality goals, and how do you intend to hit them? How will decisions get made for triage and changes to the plan?

- **What tools will the team use?**   What's your build system? What improvements are you making? What languages and components will you use? How will you automatically and objectively measure your quality goals and give the team feedback on its status?

When an operating plan is in place, team members can easily get the information they need to get on track and stay on track. The PUM can quickly understand the status in context and know where to focus her attention and direction.

Back on course

Both the strategic and operating plans will need adjustments over the course of a long project, but the team will always be in a position to succeed. That's because the strategic plan provides the vision and priorities that tell them where to go, and the operating plan provides the goals and limits that tell them how to get there.

People who do the real work, like you, often complain about not getting management support for making improvements or doing things right the first time. Well, were those improvements part of the operating plan? Is your PUM holding the team accountable for executing on that plan, or is the team only accountable for shipping all the PUM's favorite features on the date he told his boss? Don't just complain—point out the gap and take action.

Is your PUM a bum? Does he just provide strategic direction without also setting clear goals and limits? When things go wrong, does he become Clueless? If so, it's time to get your PUM to step up and define not just what he wants done but how he wants it done. Provide him with your guidance and wisdom. Help him make good decisions about what team goals to measure and what tools to use to drive your success. Then your PUM won't be a charity case, and you'll have all the support you need to do things right.

September 1, 2006: "It's good to be the King of Windows"

The Windows Vista project is nearing its end. It seems like a day doesn't go by without someone announcing they are moving to a new group and someone else announcing, "I am tremendously excited to be joining [fill-in your favorite organization]."

Yes, life is uncertain, and change leads to ambiguity and chaos, but I love reorgs. I even wrote a column about them ("How I learned to stop worrying and love reorgs," which appears earlier in the chapter). How does one stay sane while dealing with misinformed or apparently clueless new management? One of the more amusing pastimes is to imagine you are the new one in charge.

How would you change things if you became King of Windows? What would you do? Do you have the guts to stand up and be heard?

What's that? What about me? I thought you'd never ask...

> **Eric Aside**   I wrote this column shortly after my senior vice president, Jon DeVaan, got reassigned to run the core Windows division. I asked him if he wanted to review the column because people knew I worked for him. Jon said, "I think it would be best if I didn't edit you.... I am sure I. M. Wright would not listen to me if I tried :)."

Have you any last request?

Here's what I'd do if I became King of Windows:

- Oh sure, I'd talk to everyone and all that. Yeah, yeah, yeah. Then...
    - ❏ I'd make the organizational structure match the architecture.
    - ❏ I'd determine the architecture based on the user experience.
    - ❏ I'd drive the user experience based on key scenarios in each usage category.
- But before selecting the key scenarios, I'd select my staff.
- My staff and I would analyze and establish the key scenarios.
- I'd assign staff members to lead the user-experience and architecture efforts.
- When these steps were completed, I'd set the organizational structure and assign leaders.
- I'd devote the first milestone of the new organization to quality and building out the engineering system defined in the architecture.
- I'd set feature priorities based on scenario priority and critical chain depth.

- I'd manage the release by minimizing feature completion cycle time in priority order.

- I'd demand that complete features meet or exceed the dogfood quality bar enforced by the engineering system.

Note that I don't mention any specific methods here, like Test-Driven Development or feature crews. While excellent methods like these should be supported and encouraged by the engineering system, they shouldn't be top-down edicts. Team dynamics should be driven from the bottom up.

Now let's break down each piece, since the details hold all the interest.

Prepare the ship

Talking to everyone and all that. This is more than a gratuitous gesture to the existing staff. Later I'll need to select my own staff, so I need to understand both the current situation and who I have available to serve. The key word here is "serve." I'm not looking for people to serve me or themselves. Either kind would poison my staff and our goals. I'd sooner see them fired. I'm looking for people to serve Microsoft and our customers.

> **Eric Aside**   If there's anything I would change about management at Microsoft, or any company, it's the criteria used to judge who's available to serve. Yes, the best managers serve the company and our customers, but mixed in are managers who serve themselves, their superiors, or only their own organizations—and that is unconscionable.

Making the organizational structure match the architecture. You want the org chart to look like the architectural layout. This allows groups to operate with local control and independence as defined in the architecture. It also makes enforcing architectural boundaries easier. Naturally, you can't do this until you have an architecture. However, you can still think through what the structure would look like. I'd have product groups defined by the major components of the architecture. Each group would have a product unit manager (PUM), architect, group program manager (GPM), dev manager, and test manager.

Determining the architecture based on the user experience. This begs questions around timing and responsibility. Clearly, defining the Windows user experience and architecture must happen before any product groups are formed and any work begins; otherwise, you couldn't set up the organization based on the architecture.

However, even after the experience and architecture are defined, they'll be constantly reexamined, improved, and refactored. For this I'd have the user experience (UX) organization reporting directly to me under a UX director. I'd have a product-line architect with all product unit architects dotted-lined to her, and all of them meeting regularly as the Windows architecture team.

I'd also have directors of program management (PM), dev, and test reporting to me. They would be responsible for the engineering system and the long list of quality requirements like security, privacy, reliability, performance, maintainability, accessibility, globalization, and so on. The directors of PM, dev, and test would have all the product unit discipline managers dotted-lined to them. As such, my staff would drive engineering across the division.

Set a course

Driving the user experience based on key scenarios in each usage category. What makes a key scenario? It's one that creates compelling customer value that differentiates the next version of Windows from all previous versions and all competitors. Naturally, we have marketing and technical research people to tell us what value would be compelling within each market segment. Heck, there's no shortage of opinions on such things. However, my staff needs to choose our bet, what's called our "value proposition," because we are the ones who must believe in it and commit ourselves and all our resources.

Selecting my staff. Choosing my staff will be the most important thing I do. As I mentioned earlier, I'm looking for people whose whole focus is serving Microsoft and our customers, not me and not themselves. They may have career aspirations, but they figure if they serve Microsoft and our customers well, their careers will take care of themselves. As for their personal lives, I would expect my staff's priorities to match my own: serving my family, friends, and community first, Microsoft and our customers second, and my own interests third.

Analyzing and establishing the key scenarios. Once my staff is in place, we start the hard work of defining the value proposition for the next version of Windows. This will mean long days filled with heated debates and detailed analysis. The result will be a clear vision for Windows and the centerpiece of our success.

Engage

Assigning staff members to lead the user experience and architecture efforts. With the value proposition in place, the work starts in earnest on the user experience and architecture. These teams should work closely together, informing each other of what's possible and what's impractical. At the end, we should have prototypes that key customers have validated and a product-line architecture that gives us confidence our goals can be achieved. The teams my UX director and product-line architect put together will form the core of their expanded teams once the organization is built.

Setting the organizational structure and assigning leaders. With the architecture defined, we can fill out the organization. My extended staff who helped create the value proposition, user experience, and architecture would have first choice at key leadership roles. After that, my staff would assign or acquire the rest. The full transition would be timed to occur a week or two after the Windows Vista ship date.

Devoting the first milestone of the new organization to quality, and building out the engineering system defined in the architecture. One of the critical pieces of the architecture is the definition of the engineering system—that is, the set of tools and processes that enable the engineering team to build and ship our products. Often a new architecture will require new technologies and new methods. Hopefully, we also apply lessons from past mistakes. The first milestone provides an opportunity to focus on unresolved quality concerns and building out improved tools, measures, and processes.

> **Eric Aside**   Many Microsoft product lines now devote the first division-wide milestone to quality and building out the engineering system, including Windows. That trend got started well before this column.

Navigation

Setting feature priorities based on scenario priority and critical chain depth. When the quality milestone is completed, the engineering staff will be ready to create new customer value. Creating that value in the right order is critical to shipping on schedule. I'd set the order based on scenario priority (do the most important features first) and critical chain depth (do the most critical dependencies first). This priority ordering and the way it was determined must be transparent to the entire engineering staff.

Managing the release by minimizing feature completion cycle time in priority order. How I choose to manage the release will be the third most important thing I do. The most important is choosing my staff; the second most is defining "done," which I'll describe next.

As for managing the release, I choose to minimize feature completion cycle time in priority order. In other words, I want features completed in priority order and in the shortest amount of time from when the feature team starts talking about the spec to when the feature is ready for dogfooding.

> **Eric Aside**   *Dogfooding* is the practice of using prerelease builds of products for your day-to-day work. It encourages teams to make products right from the start and provides early feedback on the products' value and usability.

Naturally, I'd use proven project management practices to track progress across Windows, but the division's ability to ship quickly and reliably is tied directly to each feature team's ability to do the same.

I will not specify how feature teams are structured or what methodology they follow. That is best determined by the teams themselves. But I will insist that we produce customer value efficiently, ensuring complete high-quality features get delivered as quickly as possible.

This will help everything we do, from early customer feedback to last-minute competitive responses. If lean methods like Test-Driven Development and feature crews happen to produce the fastest feature completion cycles times, all the better.

Demanding that complete features meet or exceed the dogfood quality bar enforced by the engineering system. The most important thing I do, besides choosing the right staff, will be demanding that features not be called "complete" until they meet a high quality bar. The quality bar I'd choose is that of being ready for dogfood. I'd enforce this quality bar within the engineering system and by always installing the latest dogfood build on my own machine. That way, my staff and I will keep a constant eye on whether or not the engineering system is applying the right metrics to maintain standards. Simply put, if your feature doesn't meet the quality bar, it can't and won't get checked into the main branch (or "main").

> **Eric Aside**   Feature crews typically work on branches of the source code from the main branch. This allows them to use the source control system to manage conflicts and builds, without impacting anyone beyond their small team. When the feature is fully developed and tested, ready for dogfood, the feature crew branch is merged and checked into the main branch. Of course, other feature crews check into main, so the longer a feature crew stays on a branch, the more difficult it is to merge at the end. That's another reason why you want to minimize feature completion cycle time.

Accountability

Having a bulletproof definition of complete is a key part of an overall philosophy of account-ability without blame. Architectural boundaries are upheld because they match organizational boundaries. The right value, scenarios, and experiences are delivered because we enforce a priority ordering based on delivering that value. There is little wasted effort because we measure and reward those who deliver completed value the fastest. High quality is built in because you don't get credit for completing anything until it meets the bar.

There's no blame because the system, not an individual, enforces the requirement that quality, value, and a robust architecture are delivered efficiently. The only way to break the architecture, value, or quality is to clearly and transparently break the rules in collusion with your management. Maybe doing so is the right thing to do, maybe it isn't. Either way, the accountability is clear.

Windows, the next generation

There it is, 12 steps to a new Windows. Nothing too complicated or harsh—a few timing issues, perhaps, and some tool and measurement work to construct—but overall, I think it would be both doable and effective. Alas, I am not the king. At best, I could hold his bucket.

However, with change comes opportunity, and there's plenty of change afoot. Make your own voice heard. If you're not a king, send this to someone who is with your own thoughts and ideas. Who knows, we might even start a revolution.

December 1, 2006: "Google: Serious threat or poor spelling?"

Perhaps I'm ignorant, but Google's attempt to compete with Microsoft is pathetic. Microsoft is far from perfect, but unless some company steps up and takes a real crack at us soon it will be tough to overtake us. That company certainly isn't Google.

> **Eric Aside**   This was one of my most controversial columns. Many people inside and outside the company believe Google's approach to Web-based services will do to Microsoft what Microsoft did to IBM's mainframe-based services. I agree with their points about the Web changing the world and our legacy businesses (Windows and Office) making it difficult for us to be as agile as Google. However, I respectfully disagree with their conclusion.

Don't get me wrong, I'm quite impressed with a few things Google has done:

- They created a dominant Internet search engine.
- They created a powerful revenue model off a context-driven ad service with the help of two acquisitions.
- They created an engineer-friendly work environment to attract and retain strong talent.

Those are all great achievements.

However, those accomplishments aren't worth much in the long run. If Google is lucky, it will remain a successful niche player like Apple. If Google isn't quite so lucky and resourceful, it will join the ranks of Borland, Netscape, Corel, Digital, and others. Yeah, some of those companies are still in business, but they are shells of the competitors they once were.

They falter, we flourish

The foolishness and short-sightedness of our competitors never stops amazing me, and Google is no exception. It's almost too easy. Perhaps they think their collective incompetence will lull us into such arrogance, carelessness, and outright laughter that we'll forget who we are and what we do.

> **Eric Aside**   Okay, that was over the top. I wrote this when I felt the pendulum had swung too far in the direction of Google adulation and it was time push back a bit. By the way, I have friends I admire at Google and other competitors. It's the business direction of these companies that I question, not their people.

We're certainly guilty of the arrogance, carelessness, and laughter. I'll be the first to admit it. But thank goodness we haven't forgotten who we are and what we do:

- We empower every person and device with software.
- We continually improve our products.
- We continually improve ourselves.

We follow these principles because we care about every customer. We want to change the world.

Failure by design

Given all the success Microsoft has had, you'd think our competitors would follow the same principles, but they don't. It's not that they fall short trying; it's that they specifically choose not to do it.

Most of our competitors stop improving their products. They move on, satisfied with the current version like we mistakenly did with Internet Explorer. That allows us to catch them and beat them by the time we get to our third version. Google is trying to correct this mistake right now. They've overemphasized new ideas to the point that their top executives are now telling engineers to pull back on creating new products and refocus on the ones they have.

Most of our competitors also stop improving themselves. We outspend all our rivals by a wide margin in research and development. But as old competitors fall behind, new ones take their place.

In addition, we've got a long way to go before we meet our customers' higher expectations for mature product quality. Lucky for us, while Google's practices are sound, they aren't explicitly focusing on quality engineering. Their biggest challenge to us outside of their excellent yet mostly stagnant products is their engineer-friendly work environment. In time, our dedication to continual improvement will beat them in both areas.

Smart people, smart clients

But let's say Google gets its act together and starts continually improving its products and itself. Google has done an excellent job of attracting and retaining strong engineers. They could decide to refocus their efforts on customer value, product quality, integration of services, and multirelease plans. Wouldn't they be a threat, especially with their fantastic ad platform that practically prints money?

No. At best, Google will be a niche player like Apple. Why? Because of our first principle—which Google, like Apple—has chosen to disregard: "We empower every person and device with software."

Apple wants to empower only the people and devices they choose. The strategy has its advantages, but it structurally limits their market. Too bad, they'd be a tough competitor otherwise.

> **Eric Aside**   I wrote my dissertation on a Mac. I love Apple's dedication to design and user experience. Over time, dedication to quality experiences, along with quality engineering, has been the growing source of our own success in old and new areas.

Google wants to empower every person with software, but not every device. They'd rather keep the smarts on the server or in generic snippets on the client. It's the old "network computer and dumb client" story. It's remarkable how many times this losing strategy has claimed victory over the smart client.

Microsoft brings the power of software into every person's office, home, and hands. The closer you can bring that power to people, the more extraordinary and valuable their experience becomes. Google will lose as long as they limit their reach. How badly they lose depends on whether or not they can manage to at least hold onto a few server-based scenarios.

> **Eric Aside**   Some might argue that AJAX provides enough smarts for a client, or that Google has been shipping smart clients, like Google Earth (which I love). However, AJAX is limiting, and Google's software development process, which many consider its strength, is optimized for Web delivery. Google would need to make big changes to focus on smart clients, much like the changes Microsoft has already welcomed to focus on Web services.

Staying vigilant

Just because Google has doomed themselves, that doesn't get us off the hook. We have to keep improving ourselves, creating an environment that attracts and retains great people, including Google employees when they abandon ship. We have to keep improving our products and services, providing more compelling value than Google with integrated, exceptional experiences.

We must stay vigilant because some day—perhaps starting now in someone's garage, perhaps in India or China—there will be a competitor who understands our principles. They won't have our baggage of legacy code and legacy engineering methods. They will focus on lean, high-quality practices and products, starting small and slowly expanding their influence. It's happened in every industry, and it can happen to us.

Staying out in front

What's different is that we have sensed this change in advance. We know the market has matured. We know we must transform our engineering systems and approach in order to produce higher quality products and services that provide more value with greater predictability and efficiency. Our principles of continually improving our products and ourselves are slowly making that transformation a reality. It takes time and patience, but we're really good at taking the time and being patient.

We know in the end we'll win. You can be a part of this exciting time. You can dedicate yourself to improving our engineering and our products. You can put quality and customer value first, for everyone on every device.

Change is difficult. There are always those who prefer the status quo, especially when it comes to old habits. But with change comes opportunity, opportunity for you to define and even lead the new status quo. Grab it while clueless competitors like Google are giving us the chance.

April 1, 2007: "Mid-life crisis"

Recently, I put a significant deposit down on a sports car—a two-seat Tesla Roadster convertible that goes from 0 to 60 in four seconds. It's an electric vehicle that travels over 200 miles on a 3.5 hour charge. A couple of months from now, I'm taking my sabbatical to travel abroad. I know what you are thinking. You're guessing I'm in my mid-forties.

> **Eric Aside** You can read more about the Tesla Roadster at *http://www.teslamotors.com/*.

Yes, I'm having a mid-life crisis, or as I like to call it, the time of my life. Still, my wife and I are happy together; I love my kids and have no intention of leaving them; my job is great and I'm as passionate as ever about Microsoft. I'm just preparing to travel the world and buying a hot electric sports car. What gives, and more importantly, why should you care?

What gives is that my situation has changed, providing new opportunities and new pitfalls. Why you should care is that Microsoft is in the same situation.

> **Eric Aside** I've also been using my sabbatical to assemble this book. At Microsoft, your vice president can award you a sabbatical after a certain number of years of consistently excellent contributions to the company.

You've changed

Up to this point in my life, a sports car was unthinkable. Before I had kids, I couldn't afford such a thing. Once I had kids, a two-seat roadster wasn't practical. Now my kids have grown, as well as my savings, so for the first time a sports car is feasible.

Of course, just because it's feasible doesn't mean I want a sports car. But this is an electric, blow-your-doors-off, twist-your-neck-loose car. Such a car didn't even exist till last year. The technology has improved, the business climate among other things has changed, and I put down a deposit.

Likewise, before now, taking a sabbatical didn't make sense. It took me a while to earn the sabbatical. Once I did, between my kids and my job, taking that much time off was unthinkable. Now, my kids don't need me as much and I've grown my staff to the point where they can cover for me. So taking the sabbatical is viable.

Microsoft has grown up too. We used to be struggling to establish ourselves. Even once we were successful, we had to work diligently for years to be taken seriously. Now we hold a leadership position, have money in the bank, and find ourselves at a crossroads.

Just another tricky day

So is this a crisis? Not for my personal life. My job and relationships are stable. My finances aren't in jeopardy. There are people willing and able to cover for me. All this "crisis" amounts to is an opportunity to indulge myself.

What about Microsoft? People describe our situation as a crisis. They say we've forgotten how to ship; that we are bogged down in process "taxes"; that our approach to managing people and projects is antiquated; and that our competitors are more nimble and relevant in today's market for talent, products, and services. They are right. What went wrong? We're crawling when we should be cruising.

> **Eric Aside**   I don't think it's as bad as some critics say, but their concerns are valid.

How bad is Microsoft's mid-life crisis? I'd say it's worse than mine, but better than the one an old officemate went through. He divorced his wife, left his kids, and remarried a woman half his age. IBM's mid-life crisis was kind of like my officemate's mid-life crisis. Apple's mid-life crisis involved two divorces before returning to their first spouse. While both IBM and Apple pulled through, they definitely suffered.

How does Microsoft avoid suffering through this time of transition? We don't avoid it; and, as it turns out, we haven't. We are suffering, and we'll continue to suffer. Transitions are hard. However, there are things we can do to minimize the pain and maximize enjoying the opportunities that change brings us.

Leave little to chance

Let's take the conversation back to me. Remember, I'm the one taking a long vacation and then returning to a cool electric sports car and the family and job I love. Why isn't my wife leaving me? Why are people willing and able to cover for me? I've had my share of good fortune, no doubt, but my situation isn't an accident, nor is it assumed.

Had I bought a speedy two-seater years ago, my wife probably would have tolerated it, but it would have caused my family grief. The costs to buy, insure, and maintain it would have put stress on our finances. I wouldn't have covered half the driving duties after work because the kids couldn't safely sit in the front seat. What's worse, I would have missed opportunities to connect with my kids.

But I didn't buy the sports car earlier. As a result, my relationships with my wife and kids are stronger, and our finances are more secure. Thus, getting one now isn't a big deal. As an added bonus, new technology has provided an electric alternative.

The moral: Don't prematurely commit to exciting new areas just because they're there—make sure you establish your dependents and can manage the risks. You might even find that technology improvements by then are far more favorable.

> **Eric Aside**   By the way, this is no judgment on people with sports cars. Each person's family and job situation is different. This is more about how a certain approach has helped my family, how it has helped my job, how I successfully weather the changes life has presented, and how that approach could help Microsoft do the same.

I don't think the boy can handle it

Had I taken my sabbatical when it was awarded years ago, I would have compromised my family, my team, and even the quality of my vacation. The family aspect is simple. Today, my kids are older and more independent. This means less work for my wife and less guidance needed from me. As an added bonus, we have more flexibility for where and how long we travel.

The impact on work is even greater. Years ago, my team was new. I hadn't had the time to hire the right people and develop them sufficiently to step into my role. I also hadn't established the practices and guidelines we needed to provide reliable results. Today, while the situation isn't perfect, I've got a strong, experienced team behind me who are eager and able to cover my duties.

The moral: When you invest in developing good people, practices, and guidelines, it gives you the freedom to explore new areas without worry or compromise, while giving your people the chance to continue your work and make it their own.

Not getting any younger

By now, many of my readers are seeing how this relates to Microsoft, but in case you are living in a state of blissful ignorance or denial, allow me to elaborate.

Microsoft is entering middle age:

- **Our market has matured.**   We are taken more seriously by customers, partners, and governments. This is good for us, but it also raises expectations for what we deliver and how and when we deliver it. We can't afford to be careless or impetuous.

- **We carry around tons of legacy baggage.**   Without the extra weight, our competitors can be more nimble, taking advantage of new technology and revenue models faster than we can.

- **Our senior management, middle management, and college recruits all come from different generations.**   This generation gap is quite serious. Senior management never had to ship software with a thousand engineers. Middle management doesn't know agile from fragile. And college recruits haven't a clue about production-quality, world-ready code. This leads to conflicting expectations of development time and engineering approach, as well as to poor decisions based on misinformation.

Don't panic

What do we do? First off, don't panic. We are rich, famous, and darn good looking (from a portfolio perspective). There are worse situations.

Second, remember we're not a human being. We're a company. We only get old and decrepit if we get set in our ways, preventing innovation and keeping the next generation from taking our place. We can learn and renew ourselves if we just choose to do so.

Applying the first moral, we must establish our dependents and manage our risks before we commit. We're too old to be screwing around with unstable base components, like we did with Windows Vista. Aggressively investigate new technologies and innovate our products, but don't commit till dependencies are solid and the risks can be mitigated.

> **Eric Aside** We ended up cutting back some new technologies in Windows Vista because they weren't stable enough to ship with high quality. That's more than a shame. It cost us time trying to put them in, and it cost us more time removing them later.

Applying the second moral, we must invest in developing good people, practices, and guidelines. We're too old to be devastating and demoralizing our staff with death marches (which you can read more about in "Marching to death" in Chapter 1. We must be patient, allowing folks to learn and grow on their own, while teaching them the lessons we've already experienced. This means letting go and trusting our next generation to prove themselves, but having the right guidelines in place to prevent a catastrophe.

Nobody's perfect

We've been less than perfect in establishing our dependencies, managing our risks, developing our people, and having the right practices and guidelines in place. Transitions are hard, and there's no getting around it.

What helps is maturity at all levels. In other words, acting our age:

- No responsible adult drives around in a car with bald tires or builds a house on a fault line. That's foolish. We need to stabilize our dependencies before we depend on them. We can't compromise on quality.

- No decent parent still tells their grown kids what to do. That's childish. Management needs to provide engineers with knowledge, experience, and guidelines; clearly explain the expected results; supply feedback that warns of danger; and then trust engineers to make it happen however those engineers see fit.

Taking these simple steps will do more than make us act our age. We'll develop new leaders to step up when the old generation steps down. While the younger generation continues our work and makes it their own, we can explore new areas without worry or compromise.

Getting older as a company doesn't mean getting old. We stay young and agile by growing, protecting, and trusting our youth to keep us young. I can't wait to take delivery of that electric sports car.

Eric Aside   If current actions are any indication, we have learned many lessons well. We've avoided telling engineers how to work; instead, we have focused on the results we expect. We've changed our approach to dependencies and shipping, making ourselves more lean, agile, and reliable. Sure, Microsoft still has work to do, and I love being part of the solution. I also love that I was trusted to represent Microsoft fairly and honestly when publishing this book. Thanks for taking the time to read it; I hope it was both enjoyable and helpful. By the way, I should be taking delivery of my Tesla Roadster in May 2008.

Glossary

2.5, 3.0, 3.5, 4.0, 4.5 (also known as ratings, the review system, the curve)   Microsoft's old rating system, which was changed in the spring of 2006. Ratings of 2.5 and 3.0 were undesirable. Ratings of 4.0 and 4.5 were highly desirable. A 3.5 rating was readily accepted and the most common.

BillG, or Bill   Bill Gates, the Chief Software Architect and Chairman of the Board of Microsoft.

black box testing   Testing that treats the product as a black box. You don't have any access to or knowledge of the internal workings, so you probe it like a customer would—you use it and abuse it till it breaks.

BrianV, or Brian Valentine   Brian Valentine, former Microsoft senior vice president of the core Windows division.

buddy drop (also known as private build or buddy build)   A private build of a product used to verify code changes before they have been checked into the main code base.

bug, or work item   Internally, we use the term *bug* to refer to anything we want to add, delete, or change about a product, what most people generally call a *work item*. Naturally, this includes code mistakes, the more traditional kind of "bug."

Build Verification Test (BVT)   Checks whether a software build satisfies a set of requirements.

Career Stage Profile (CSP)   Detailed descriptions of the work expected of employees at different career stages for different disciplines. CSPs also outline individual contributor and manager growth paths.

CodeBox (also Toolbox or CodePlex)   A repository for shared tools and code. CodeBox is an internal code-sharing repository. Toolbox is an internal repository, mostly focused on tools and scripts. CodePlex is an external code-sharing repository.

code complete   The stage at which the developer believes all the code necessary to implement a feature has been checked into source control. Often this is a judgment call, but on better teams it's actually measured based on quality criteria (at which point it's often called "feature complete").

dogfooding (also known as "eating your own dogfood")   The practice of using prerelease builds of products for day-to-day work. It encourages teams to make products correctly from the start, and it provides early feedback on the products' value and usability.

external bug, or external   A bug in code not owned by the team. These bugs should never be ignored unless there is a straightforward workaround.

feature   A self-contained collection of functionality needed to provide incremental value to a product. Although features can be large, ideally a feature is work broken down to the point of requiring no more than five weeks of effort to design, develop, and test.

Feature Crew   A small, cross-discipline team tasked with a single feature, or closely related small features, to design, spec, develop, and test together from start to finish. Feature Crews are typically virtual teams: the team members don't all report to the same manager.

milestone   Project dates that organizations (from 50 through 5,000 people) use to synchronize their work and review project plans. The term *milestone* is also used to refer to the work time between milestone dates. Milestone durations vary from team to team and product to product. Typically, they range from 6 to 12 weeks each. Calling a "milestone" a "sprint" does disservice to both terms.

PREfast, or Code Analysis for C/C++   PREfast is a static analysis tool for the C and C++ programming languages that identifies suspect coding patterns that might lead to buffer overruns or other serious programming errors. Though initially used only internally, it recently shipped as part of Visual Studio 2005.

Product Unit Manager (also known as PUM, Group Manager, Director)   The first level of multidisciplinary management. Typically, the PUM is in charge of a self-contained collection of functionality, such as Excel, DirectX, or ActiveSync.

program management, or program manager (PM)   The engineering discipline primarily responsible for specifying the end-user experience, including the overall project schedule, which determines when that experience will release.

project, or release   The entire collection of work necessary to release a specific version or service pack of a product.

RAID (related terms include Product Studio, bug database, work item database)   RAID is a database and client for tracking work items, which can include feature work, bug reports, and design change requests.

reorg   Short for "reorganization." Typically, a reorg starts at the top and works its way down over a period of 9 to 18 months.

RDQ, or PSQ   A work item database query used to determine the state of work for a project.

scenario   A description of an end user accomplishing a task that may or may not be implemented in the current product. Scenarios typically involve using multiple features.

Software Development Engineer (SDE)   A software developer. This refers to the people who write the code and construct the customer experience.

Source Depot, or source control   Our large-scale source control system that manages hundreds of millions of lines of source code and tools, including version control and branching.

specification (spec)   Documentation that specifies how a product should be experienced, constructed, tested, or deployed.

SQM (also known as Software Quality Metrics, Customer Experience Improvement Program)   SQM is the internal name for the technology behind customer experience improvement programs for MSN, Office, Windows Vista, and other applications. These programs anonymously aggregate customer usage patterns and experiences. (Please join when you install our software; it lets us know what works and what doesn't.)

SteveB, or Steve   Steve Balmer, the Chief Executive Officer (CEO) of Microsoft.

STRIDE   A mnemonic device to help people remember the different kinds of security threats: spoofing, tampering, repudiation, information disclosure, denial of service, and elevation of privilege. *Writing Secure Code* by Michael Howard and David LeBlanc (Microsoft Press, 2002) has all the details.

Test-Driven Development (TDD)   An Agile methodology in which developers write tests for code before the code is written.

Toolbox (also CodeBox or CodePlex)   A repository for shared tools and code. Toolbox is an internal repository, mostly focused on tools and scripts, not code. CodeBox is an internal code-sharing repository. CodePlex is an external code-sharing repository.

triage (also known as bug triage or issue management)   A regular meeting toward the end of development cycles to manage issues. Typically, these meetings are attended by representatives from the three primary engineering disciplines: program management, development, and test.

Trustworthy Computing (TwC)   The Microsoft initiative on security, privacy, reliability, and sound business practices.

User Experience (UX)   Refers to the User Experience discipline, which includes mostly designers and usability experts.

Watson (also known as Crash Watson or Windows Error Reporting)   Watson is the internal name for the functionality behind the Send Error Report dialog box you see when an application running on Windows crashes. (Always send it; we truly do pay attention.)

Watson bucket   Each "Watson bucket" represents and stores a customer issue that thousands, sometimes millions, of customers have experienced. Engineers inside and outside of Microsoft can query which buckets came from issues in their software.

white box testing   Testing that uses instrumentation to automatically and systematically test every aspect of the product. Microsoft is steadily replacing its black box testing with white box testing.

zero bug bounce (ZBB)   The first moment in a project when all features are complete and every work item is resolved. This moment rarely lasts very long. Often within an hour, a new issue arises through extended system testing and the team goes back to work. Nevertheless, ZBB means the end is predictably within sight.

Index

A

ACBD mnemonic, 138
accountability, 196
affinity technique, 91
agendas for meetings, 50, 155
Agile methods. *See also* eXtreme Programming; also
    Scrum; TDD (Test-Driven Development)
    breaking down myths, 36–37
    continuous integration, 38
    customer feedback, 31–32
    for overproduction, 25–26
    for transportation, 27
    ground rules, 37–38
    pair programming, 39
    refactoring, 38
    user stories, 39
Andrews, Rick, 46
APIs
    in design process, 108
    security and, 79
Apple Computing, 199
architects
    career stage for, 128
    defining user experience, 111–114
    delegation and, 144
architecture
    organizational structure and, 192–193
    value of, 115–117
architecture team model, 115–116, 144
As Appropriate interviewer, 169
axiomatic design method, 109

B

backlogs, 40–41
backward traceability, 33
Ballmer, Steve, 12, 140, 189, 206
ber-triage, 80
beta releases, 32, 81
BillG. *See* Gates, Bill
black-box testing, 63, 205
Blinn, Jim, 156
bottom-up design, 117
box triage, 80
brainstorming
    in design process, 91–92
    in meetings, 52
branching, process improvement on, 27
breadth-first development, 26, 29
BrianV. *See* Valentine, Brian
buddy builds. *See* buddy drops

buddy drops, 67, 205
buddy systems, 176
bug triage
    by developers, 94
    defined, 206
    out-of-sync data values, 105
    project management and, 8–11
    reviews as, 92–93
    slack time and, 47–48
    software quality and, 85–86
    via integration testing, 90
    via unit testing, 65
bugs
    defined, 47, 205
    external, 205
    root causes, 97
Build Verification Test (BVT), 138, 205
builds
    dogfooding, 96–97
    process improvement on, 27–28
burn-down charts, 3, 40–41
BVT (Build Verification Test), 138, 205

C

capture-recaptures technique, 95
career development
    ambition versus value, 120–122
    excelling in competitive world,
        122–126
    growth paths, 176–177
    personal networking, 129–133
    roles versus aspirations, 126–129
career stage, 127–129, 159
Career Stage Profile (CSP), 126, 205
career status, examining, 50
change process
    for specs, 58
    fuzzies vs. techies, 71–72
checklists, review process and, 93–95
code analysis results, 98
code churn, 98
code complete, 44, 205
code replication, 104–106
code review
    lockdown and, 47
    software quality and, 83, 91–96
CodeBox, 205–206
CodePlex, 205–206
collaboration, 136–138, 153
college hires, 175

commitment
  appreciating employees as, 180
  delegation and, 145
  to customers, 30–32
  to personal networking, 133
  work-life balance and, 139
committee meetings, 45
communication
  architects and designers, 113
  as long-term skill, 135
  between techies and fuzzy logic, 68–69
  customer satisfaction and, 31
  death marches and, 13
  e-mail notification, 27
  goals for specs, 57
  great developers and, 164
  managers and, 181
  risk management and, 4
  suggestions for effective, 152–156
  to new hires, 176
  trust and, 138
  via status reporting, 7
compensation levels
  for lead developers, 128
  for program management/managers, 1
  for software engineering/engineers, 121
competitors, 197–200
completeness in design process, 107–108
compliance police, 54
consensus on bug triage, 9
context switching, 142–144
continuous integration, 38
cost, negotiating, 7
Covey, Stephen R., 157
Crash Watson. *See* Watson
CSP (Career Stage Profile), 126, 205
CTQ (critical-to-quality) measures, 113
curve, 205
customers. *See also* UX (user experience)
  communicating with, 69
  great developers and, 163
  meeting commitments for, 30–32
  tracing requests, 33–34

D

daily stand-up meetings, 40
data replication, 104–106
data validation, 84
DCR (design change request). *See* spec change requests
    (SCRs)
death marches, 11–15
debugging
  bug triage, 8–11
  process improvement for, 27
  zero bug bounce, 46

deception. *See* lying
decision-making
  for bug triage, 9
  in meetings, 52
defects
  process improvement, 30
  reducing, 87–90
delegating work, 142, 144–146
dependencies
  in development schedules, 5–6
  in software design, 112–113
depth-first development, 26, 30
design. *See* software design
design by committee, 92
design change request (DCR). *See* spec change requests
    (SCRs)
design patterns method, 109
DeVaan, Jon, 192
developers. *See* software developers
development schedules
  dependencies in, 5–6
  hard/medium/easy scale, 2
  lying and, 17–18
  milestones and, 2
  motivational tools in, 6–7
  negotiating agreements, 7
  risk management and, 3
differentiated pay, 17
Director. *See* PUM (Product Unit Manager)
discipline specialization, 72–75
diversity in teams, 72–75
documentation
  Agile methods and, 37
  by architecture team, 116
  compliance police, 54
dogfooding, 96–97, 193–196, 205
Don't Shoot the Dog (Pryor), 184

E

e-mail notification
  effective communications, 155
  for status updates, 52
  inefficiencies and, 52
  managing poor performance, 170, 173
  process improvement on, 27
  responsiveness to, 132
  time management and, 143
emergent design, 101
empowerment, 186
Engineering Excellence Handbook, 57
enterprise, turnkey solutions and, 81–82
error handling, 102–103
estimating
  difficulty of, 2
  hard/medium/easy scale, 2

exception handling, 103
expectations, performance, 170, 172
external bugs, 205
eXtreme Programming
    Agile methods and, 26, 36
    applying, 40
    overproduction and, 25
    TDD and, 28
    transportation and, 27

F

Faber, Adele, 182
failure by design, 198
failure information, 85–86
fault injection tests, 85
feature crews
    architecture team and, 116
    choosing features, 125
    co-located, 53–55
    defined, 196, 205
    impact of, 101
    process improvement and, 26
    understanding specs, 53
feature dates
    agreements for, 7
    cautions in using, 6
    milestone dates and, 6
    project dates and, 3
feature level vs. project level, 38
feature list. *See* backlogs
features
    "breadth first" for, 26, 29
    "depth first" for, 26, 30
    Agile methods, 26
    code complete status, 44
    defined, 205
    good enough, 82
    like-to-have, 2
    must-have, 2
    must-ship, 7
    need for specs, 55
    negotiating cost, 7
    negotiating work order, 7
    negotiation method, 7
    overprocessing, 28–29
    prioritizing, 193, 195
    scheduling in milestones, 2
    trapping poorly conceived, 99
    wish, 2
feedback
    Agile methods, 31–32
    during review process, 93
    in interview process, 168
    in Scrum, 41

on poor performance, 173
on specs, 58
Watson, 33
firing employees, 172–173
flow charts in design process, 107, 109
FOCKED acronym, 91
forward traceability, 33
fuzzy logic, 68–72

G

Gates, Bill, 83, 120, 140, 205
Gilbert, Thomas F., 184
Google, 197–200
GPF (ground protection fault), 123
Group Manager. *See* PUM (Product Unit Manager)

H

hallway meetings, 45
hard/medium/easy scale, 2, 6
Harley Davidson motorcycles, 123, 125
Hejlsberg, Anders, 117
honesty vs. integrity, 157, 159
Howard, Michael, 79
Human Competence (Gilbert), 184
Humphrey, Watts S., 107

I

IIS process recycling technology, 85
implementation design, 84
inefficiencies, eliminating
    for meetings, 50–52
    need for specs, 53–55
    poor quality of specs, 56–60
    slack time, 47–50
    spec change requests, 44–46
influencing without authority,
    148–152
information rights management (IRM), 52
inspections, software quality and, 91–96
Instant Messenger, 143
integration testing, 90
integrity
    honesty vs., 157, 159
    managers and, 181
interfaces in software design, 115–116
interns, hiring, 175–176
interoperability, sole authority and, 106
interruptions, time management and,
    142–144
interviewing process, 164–169, 174
inventory (Lean concept), 29
involuntary resignation, 172–173
issue management. *See* bug triage

J

"Joel on Software" column, 163
journey developers, 120–122

K

knowledge warehouse, 176

L

Ladas, Corey, 25, 189
LAME registry setting, 102
Lean Design and Manufacturing
  as spec alternative, 55
  on defects, 30
  on inventory, 29
  on motion, 27–28
  on overprocessing, 28–29
  on overproduction, 25–26
  on reducing wasted effort, 24–25
  on transportation, 27
  on waiting, 28
LeBlanc, David, 79
legacy systems, 203
leverage, time management and, 142, 147–148
liberal arts majors. *See* fuzzy logic
Lincoln, Abraham, 131
lockdown, 47
logging, software quality and, 84
lying
  about development schedules, 17–18
  about reorgs, 18–19
  about software development, 16
  honesty and, 157
  motivation for, 15
  pay for performance and, 17
  process canaries and, 15
  uncovering root cause of, 15–16

M

management. *See also* program management/managers
  challenges of directing, 192–197
  characteristics of, 177–181
  delegation and, 145
  dysfunctional teams and, 181–184
  influencing, 148–152
  managing poor performance, 169–173
  measuring developer productivity, 162–163
  middle, 189–191
  on developer characteristics, 163–164
  recruitment/interviewing, 164–169, 174
  reorgs and, 186–189
  retention/turnover, 173–177
  setting ground rules with, 141
  work-life balance and, 140

Mazlish, Elaine, 182
mean-to-time-failure, 5
measuring work. *See* tracking work
meetings
  agendas for, 50, 155
  committee, 45
  daily stand-up, 40–41
  decision making in, 52
  determining next steps, 52
  hallway, 45
  identifying purpose, 51
  necessary participants, 51–52
  review, 91–96
  switching topics, 51
  time management and, 144
metrics for software quality, 88–89,
    96–99, 206
Microsoft
  death marches and, 12
  employee rating system, 122, 171
  Google competition, 197–200
  growing pains, 200–204
  levels of project management, 1
  strengths, 185–186
Microsoft Competencies, 120
Microsoft Consulting Services (MCS), 48
milestones
  as motivational tool, 6
  defined, 205
  quality as, 192, 195
  scheduling features in, 2
  typical ranges for, 3
motion (Lean concept), 27–28
motivation
  death marches and, 13
  for lying, 15
motivational tools, 6–7
Mundie, Craig, 139

N

Nagappan, Nachiappan, 98
negotiation process
  Agile methods and, 36
  bug triage as, 9
  for development schedules, 7
  influencing without authority and, 150
  suggestions for effective, 136–138
networking, personal, 129–133, 164

O

Office XP, 85, 102
openness vs. transparency, 158–159
operating plans, 190–191
order of work, negotiating, 7

organizational structure
  accountability in, 196
  matching architecture, 192–193
  setting, 194
Outlook Web Access (OWA), 141
overprocessing (Lean concept), 8–9
overproduction (Lean concept), 25–26
OWA (Outlook Web Access), 141

P

pair programming, 39, 176
patent disclosures, 49
pay for performance, 17
PC (politically correct), 120
peer reviews, 92
performance, managing, 169–173
personal networking, 129–133, 164
Personal Software Process (PSP), 88
personas in design process, 107, 109
pigs and chickens, 40
PowerPoint, 104
PREfast tool
  defined, 65, 205
  software quality and, 90, 94
presentations, 150–152, 155
principals, 129
prioritization
  Agile methods and, 26
  process improvement and, 28
  silver bullets and, 10
  suggestions for, 192
  time management and, 142, 146–147
  traceability and, 33
privacy
  involuntary resignation and, 173
  sole authority and, 106
private builds. *See* buddy drops
problem-solving
  death marches and, 14
  Six Sigma methodology, 22–23
process canaries, 15
process improvement
  customer satisfaction, 30–35
  Lean Design and Manufacturing, 24–30
  Six Sigma methodology, 22–23
process recovery, 85
Product Backlog. *See* backlogs
Product Studio, 34
Product Support Services (PSS), 48
Product Unit Manager (PUM), 18, 124, 189–191, 206
productivity, measuring, 162–163
program management/managers
  "Scrum practice", 26
  communicating with, 69
  death marches and, 11–15

defined, 206
  Microsoft levels of, 1
  myths of, 1
  need for, 75
  need for specs, 53–55
  responsibilities of, 2
  view of bugs, 8
project dates vs. feature dates, 3
project level vs. feature level, 38
projects, 206
prototypes, 49
Pryor, Karen, 184
PSP (Personal Software Process), 88
PSQ, 206
public class methods, 29
Pugh Concept Selection, 92
PUM (Product Unit Manager), 18, 124, 189–191, 206

Q

"Quaker" consensus, 9
quality. *See* software quality

R

RAID database, 206
RAMP (Readiness at Microsoft Program), 63
RAS (Remote Access Service), 141
ratings, 205
RDQ, 206
Readiness at Microsoft Program (RAMP), 63
RECH acronym, 102
recruitment, 164–169
refactoring
  architecture and, 115, 117
  defined, 38
  slack time and, 48
  software engineering on, 101
releases
  defined, 206
  managing, 192, 195
Remote Access Service (RAS), 141
Remote Desktop, 141
reorganizations
  defined, 206
  lying about, 18–19
  merit in, 186–189
requirements
  creating architectures, 115–116
  for specs, 58
  tests and, 58
"rest and vest", 121
retention, employee, 173–177
review meetings, 91–96
review system, 205

rework, process improvement and, 30
Richter-scale estimates, 2, 6
risk management
    communication in, 4
    for vulnerabilities, 79
    scheduling and, 3
    shortcuts and, 13
    when delegating, 146
roadblocks, 178–179
role playing, 167

S

sabbaticals, 200
safe environment, 180
scenarios
    creating architectures, 115–116
    defined, 206
    establishing, 192, 194
    in design process, 107
    prioritizing, 195
    user experience based on, 194
schedules. *See* backlogs; development schedules;
        work item lists
Scrum
    applying, 39–41
    as acronym, 37
    design issues at meetings, 51
    project management, 26
    work in progress, 29
Scrum Masters, 40–41
security, software quality and, 78–86
Segall's Law, 104
SEI (Software Engineering Institute), 88
self-directed teams, 6, 41
Send Error Report dialog box, 32
sequence diagrams, 108
service operations, 8–9
Siblings Without Rivalry (Faber and Mazlish), 182
silver bullets, 10
"single piece flow", 143
Six Sigma methodology, 22–23
skill diversity in teams, 72–75
Skinner, B. F., 21
slack time
    death marches and, 13–14
    developers and, 47–48
    suggestions for, 48–50
software design
    brainstorming during, 91–92
    code/data replication, 104–106
    design by committee, 92
    error handling and, 102–103
    for user experiences, 111–114
    impact of, 101

key issues, 83
review meetings, 91–96
suggested practices, 106–110
value of architecture, 114–117
software developers
    characteristics of, 163–164
    measuring productivity, 162–163
    misuses of slack time, 47–48
    need for, 74
    need for specs, 53–54
    relationship with testers, 62–65
    software quality and, 83–84
    testing responsibilities, 66, 84
    uses for slack time, 48–50
    view of bugs, 9
software development
    ambiguity of, 4–5
    lying during, 16
    nature of, 87–90
    pair programming, 39
    unstable code and, 28
Software Engineering Institute (SEI), 88
software engineering/engineers
    avoiding design work, 101
    challenges of directing, 192–197
    compensation levels for, 121
    defined, 206
    nature of, 88–90
    needs of, 179
software quality
    as milestone, 192, 195
    for specs, 59–60
    inefficiencies in specs, 56–60
    metrics for, 88–89, 96–99, 206
    need for, 81–87
    perception of, 111
    reducing defects, 87–90
    review meetings, 91–96
    security and, 78–86
    shortcuts and, 13
    Six Sigma methodology, 22–23
    software design and, 112
    spotting bad software, 97
    testers and, 66–67
    ways to improve, 83
Software Quality Metrics (SQM), 206
sole authority principle, 105–106
source control systems, 27, 206
Source Depot, 27, 206
spec change requests (SCRs), 7, 44–46, 158
specialization in disciplines, 72–75
specifications
    brainstorming process, 92
    defined, 206
    easy to write, 57

eliminating need for, 53–55
improving quality of, 56–60
in design process, 107, 109
late, 44–46
robust, 58
Sprint Backlog. *See* work item lists
sprints, 40–41
SQL, 32
SQL Server, 86
SQM (Software Quality Metrics), 206
stakeholders, 115–116
state diagrams, 107
status reporting, 7, 52
SteveB. *See* Ballmer, Steve
strategic planning, 189–191
stress tests, 85
STRIDE model, 79, 206

T
TDD (Test-Driven Development)
applying, 39–40
defined, 206
depth-first development and, 26
implementation design, 84
in design process, 108, 117
process for, 28–29
Team Software Process. *See* TSP (Team Software
    Process)
teams
diversity in, 72–75
dysfunctional, 181–184
self-directed, 6, 41
skill diversity in, 72–75
techies, fuzzy logic and, 68–72
technical previews, 32
Tesla Roadster, 200, 204
test harness hooks, 84
Test Lead program, 63
test release documents (TRDs), 7
test schedules. *See* development schedules
Test-Driven Development. *See* TDD (Test-Driven
    Development)
testers/testing
black-box, 63, 205
developer responsibilities, 66, 84
fault injection, 85
integration, 90
need for, 75
need for specs, 53–54
relationship with developers, 62–65
role of, 65–68
software quality and, 66–67
stress, 85
unit, 65–68, 84–85

verifying requirements, 58
view of bugs, 8
white-box, 63, 66, 207
zero bug bounce and, 46
Thompson, Bernie, 25, 189
threat and failure modeling, 107–108
T-I-M-E Charting, 46
time management, 142–148
time on task, measuring, 41
Toolbox repository, 17, 205–206
tools
motivational, 6–7
writing, 49
top-down design, 117
traceability of requirements, 33–35
tracking work
dev schedules for, 2–4
status reporting and, 7
via burn-down charts, 3, 41
via work item lists, 3
training during slack time, 49
transparency vs. openness, 158–159
transportation (Lean concept), 27
triage. *See* bug triage
trust
from management, 186
negotiation and, 138
sole authority and, 106
Trustworthy Computing (TwC), 33, 83, 206
TSP (Team Software Process)
formal inspections, 93
process improvement, 27, 30
PSP process, 88
turnkey solutions, 81–82
turnover, employee, 173–177
TwC (Trustworthy Computing), 33, 83, 206

U
UML (Unified Modeling Language), 108
unit testing. *See also* TDD (Test-Driven Development)
role of, 65–68
software quality and, 84–85
unstable code, 28
up-front design
Agile methods and, 37
defining public class methods, 29
software engineers on, 101
use cases in design process, 108
user experience. *See* UX (user experience)
user stories, 39
UX (user experience)
defined, 127, 206
software design and, 111–114
suggestions for, 192–194

V

Valentine, Brian, 80, 205
value(s)
    ambition versus, 120–122
    impact on success, 156–159
    perception of, 111
vulnerabilities, 79, 115

W

waiting (Lean concept), 8
war room, 80
wasted effort, reducing, 24–25, 83
Watson
    bug triage and, 48
    customer feedback, 33
    defined, 32, 206
    failure information, 85
    software quality and, 84
Watson bucket, 207
white papers, 49
white-box testing, 63, 66, 207

Wickline, Pat, 97
Windows Error Reporting. *See* Watson
Windows Vista, 203
Windows XP, 102
Wood, Donald, 46
work in progress
    Lean model on, 29
    measuring, 41
    reviewing, 92
work item lists, 3, 41
work items. *See* bugs
work tracking. *See* tracking work
work-life balance, 12, 139–142
worst case plan, 14
Writing Secure Code (Howard and LeBlanc), 79–80

X

XP. *See* eXtreme Programming

Z

ZBB (zero bug bounce), 46, 207

About the Author

Eric Brechner is the director of development excellence for Microsoft Corporation. His group is responsible for improving the people, processes, and practices of software development across Microsoft through the application of Human Performance Technology. Prior to his current assignment, Eric was director of development training and managed development for a shared feature team in Microsoft Office. Before joining Microsoft in 1995, Eric was a senior principal scientist at The Boeing Company, where he worked in the areas of large-scale visualization, computational geometry, network communications, data-flow languages, and software integration. He was the principal architect of FlyThru, the walkthrough program for the 20 gigabyte, 500+ million polygon model of the Boeing 777 aircraft. Eric has also worked in computer graphics and CAD for Silicon Graphics, GRAFTEK, and the Jet Propulsion Laboratory. He holds eight patents, earned a BS and MS in mathematics and a PhD in applied mathematics from Rensselaer Polytechnic Institute, and is a certified performance technologist. Outside work, Eric is a proud husband and father of two boys. His younger son has autism. Eric works on autism insurance benefits and serves on the University of Washington Autism Center board. In the few remaining minutes of his day, Eric enjoys going to Seattle Mariners games, playing bridge, coaching Math Olympiad and baseball, and umpiring for Little League.

What do you think of this book?

We want to hear from you!

Do you have a few minutes to participate in a brief online survey?

Microsoft is interested in hearing your feedback so we can continually improve our books and learning resources for you.

To participate in our survey, please visit:

www.microsoft.com/learning/booksurvey/

...and enter this book's ISBN-10 number (appears above barcode on back cover*).
As a thank-you to survey participants in the United States and Canada, each month we'll randomly select five respondents to win one of five $100 gift certificates from a leading online merchant. At the conclusion of the survey, you can enter the drawing by providing your e-mail address, which will be used for prize notification only.

Thanks in advance for your input. Your opinion counts!

* Where to find the ISBN-10 on back cover

ISBN-13: 000-0-0000-0000-0
ISBN-10: 0-0000-0000-0

Example only. Each book has unique ISBN.

No purchase necessary. Void where prohibited. Open only to residents of the 50 United States (includes District of Columbia) and Canada (void in Quebec). For official rules and entry dates see:

www.microsoft.com/learning/booksurvey/